Global Financial Crisis: The Ethical Issues

Global Financial Crisis: The Ethical Issues

Edited by

Ned Dobos
Charles Sturt University and the University of Melbourne, Australia

Christian Barry
Australian National University

Thomas Pogge
Australian National University and Yale University, USA

First published 2011 by
PALGRAVE MACMILLAN

Palgrave Macmillan in the UK is an imprint of Macmillan Publishers Limited,
registered in England, company number 785998, of Houndmills,
Basingstoke, Hampshire RG21 6XS.

Palgrave Macmillan in the US is a division of St Martin's Press LLC,
175 Fifth Avenue, New York, NY 10010.

Palgrave Macmillan is the global academic imprint of the above companies
and has companies and representatives throughout the world.

Palgrave® and Macmillan® are registered trademarks in the United States,
the United Kingdom, Europe and other countries.

ISBN 978–0–230–27663–5   hardback
ISBN 978–0–230–29351–9   paperback

This book is printed on paper suitable for recycling and made from fully
managed and sustained forest sources. Logging, pulping and manufacturing
processes are expected to conform to the environmental regulations of the
country of origin.

A catalogue record for this book is available from the British Library.

Library of Congress Cataloging-in-Publication Data

Global financial crisis : the ethical issues / edited by Ned Dobos,
    Christian Barry, Thomas Pogge.
        p. cm.
    Includes index.
    ISBN 978–0–230–29351–9 (pbk.)
        1. Global Financial Crisis, 2008–2009.   2. Financial crises.   I. Dobos,
Ned.   II. Barry, Christian.   III. Pogge, Thomas Winfried Menko.   IV. Title.
    HB3722.G596 2011
        174—dc22   2011001476

10   9   8   7   6   5   4   3   2   1
20   19   18   17   16   15   14   13   12   11

Printed and bound in Great Britain by
CPI Antony Rowe, Chippenham and Eastbourne

Contents

Acknowledgments   vi

List of Contributors   vii

1 Introduction   1
   Ned Dobos

2 Global Financial Institutions, Ethics and Market
   Fundamentalism   24
   Seumas Miller

3 The Legitimacy of the Financial System and State
   Capitalism   52
   Noam Chomsky

4 Neoliberalism – Is This the End?   63
   Ned Dobos

5 Ethical Investing in an Age of Excessive
   Materialistic Self-Interest   82
   John C. Harrington

6 The Achilles' Heel of Competitive/Adversarial Systems   120
   Thomas Pogge

7 Financial Services Providers: Integrity Systems,
   Reputation and the Triangle of Virtue   132
   Seumas Miller

8 Who Must Pay for the Damage of the Global
   Financial Crisis?   158
   Matt Peterson and Christian Barry

Index   185

Acknowledgments

The editors wish to acknowledge the support of an Australian Research Council Linkage grant on Corporate Governance, Regulation and Accountability (industry partner Tiri).

List of Contributors

Christian Barry is Deputy Director of the Centre for Applied Philosophy and Public Ethics (an Australian Research Council Special Research Centre) and Senior Lecturer in Philosophy at the Australian National University. He has served as a consultant and contributing author to three of the UN Development Programme's *Human Development Reports*, was editor of *Ethics & International Affairs* and directed the Carnegie Council's Justice and the World Economy programme. His research focuses on closing the gap between theory and practice in international justice.

Noam Chomsky is Institute Professor of Linguistics at the Massachusetts Institute of Technology and is a world-renowned political theorist and activist. A vocal critic of US foreign policy and the mainstream media, his best-known works include *Profit Over People: Neoliberalism & Global Order* (1998); *Hegemony or Survival: America's Quest for Global Dominance* (2004); *Manufacturing Consent* (2006); *Deterring Democracy* (2006); and *Failed States: The Abuse of Power and the Assault on Democracy* (2007).

Ned Dobos is Research Fellow at the Centre for Applied Philosophy and Public Ethics (an Australian Research Council Special Research Centre), Charles Sturt University and the University of Melbourne. His research interests include political violence, the ethics of war and business ethics. His book *Insurrection and Intervention* is due to published by Cambridge University Press shortly.

John C. Harrington is President and CEO of socially responsible investing and shareholder advocacy firm Harrington Investments Inc. and is a Manager of Community Commercial Ventures, LLC. He is the author of *Investing With Your Conscience: How to Achieve High Returns Using Socially Responsible Investing* (1992) and *The Challenge to Power: Money, Investing and Democracy* (2005).

Seumas Miller is Professor of Philosophy at Charles Sturt University and the Australian National University (joint position) and is Foundation Director of the Centre for Applied Philosophy and Public

Ethics (an Australian Research Council Special Research Centre). He is also a senior research fellow at the 3TU Centre for Ethics and Technology at the Delft University of Technology.

Matt Peterson is a postgraduate fellow in the Global Justice Program at the MacMillan Center for International and Area Studies at Yale University. His work focuses on contributions that global, political and economic structures make to human rights violations. Peterson is an active member of the Health Impact Fund project, which aims to improve access to medicines among the world's poor, and is the producer of Public Ethics Radio, a podcast that engages ethicists in discussion of pressing political dilemmas.

Thomas Pogge is Leitner Professor of Philosophy and International Affairs at Yale University and is Professorial Fellow at the Australian National University division of the Centre for Applied Philosophy and Public Ethics (an Australian Research Council Special Research Centre). He received his PhD in philosophy from Harvard and has published widely on Kant and on moral and political philosophy.

1
Introduction

Ned Dobos

It has been described as 'the Great Crash';[1] 'the Great Recession';[2] 'the Second Great Depression';[3] an 'economic tsunami'; a 'financial Krakatoa';[4] 'the end of Wall Street';[5] 'the end of the age of greed';[6] 'the end of an era';[7] 'an act of God and a sign of the end times';[8] 'the death of a planet [Planet Finance]';[9] and even 'Armageddon'.[10] The global financial crisis is now acknowledged to be the most severe economic downturn since the 1930s, unique not only in its gravity and scope, but also in its underlying causes and wider social, political and economic implications. It continues to generate heated debate amongst economists, historians, pundits, political scientists and the general public. But by and large it has been neglected by philosophers and professional ethicists. *Global Financial Crisis: The Ethical Issues* begins to remedy this neglect. The decisions and actions that ultimately caused the crisis, the institutional and regulatory shortcomings that allowed it to happen, its consequences for both developed and developing countries, and the responses that it has elicited raise myriad moral and philosophical questions, a sample of which will be explored in what follows.

The story so far

In recent years 'sub-prime' borrowers with impaired credit histories and reduced repayment capacity entered the US property market in droves, some with no proof of income, no assets behind them and no down-payment. In 1994 sub-prime mortgages made up only 5 per cent of the market, with a total value of $35 billion. By 2006 it was 20 per cent of the market, with $600 billion worth of sub-prime loans issued in that year alone.[11] Not surprisingly, the rate of homeownership nationwide climbed to an all-time high, with particularly strong growth recorded in low-income and minority neighbourhoods.

The 'securitisation' of these mortgages had become tremendously profitable. Financial institutions were taking individual mortgage loan contracts, pooling them and selling shares in the pools to investors and to one another. These are the now infamous 'mortgage backed securities' (MBSs) and 'collateralised debt obligations' (CDOs). After the mortgages were bundled together, they were chopped up into segments or 'tranches'. Buying shares in the top tranche gave the investor first dibs on the cash flow that the underlying assets generated (from the mortgage repayments and other fees flowing into the pool each month). This investment was considered as safe as government bonds; a cash equivalent; money in the bank. Although it was recognised that some mortgages within the pool would invariably default, the products were set up in such a way that the lowest tranche absorbed all of the losses before the next one up lost anything at all.[12] Thus, only an astronomical spike in the default rate would cause losses capable of reaching the top tier, and the probability of this happening was considered negligible to zero.

The residual higher risk tranches were given commensurably lower credit ratings. Some were snapped up by savvy investors chasing a higher yield. The rest were bundled into new pools with a large volume of other assets (more mortgages, and sometimes credit-card debt and car loans) to create CDOs. These were cut up into new tranches and again the top tier was awarded a triple-A credit rating and sold to investors. But this left behind more residual higher risk tranches. Once again, these were pooled with other assets, producing the 'CDO Squared'. Another round of the same process gave us 'CDO Cubed'.[13] 'In the end', Garnaut explains:

> investors were being offered AAA-rated shares in the top tranche of a pool of residual high risk CDO² that had been cut from a pool of residual high-risk CDO tranches that had been cut from a pool of residual high-risk MBS tranches that were themselves underpinned by America's highest-risk mortgages and other loans![14]

Finally, when there were no more real assets out of which to construct these securities, the *synthetic* CDO was invented. This product does not contain any actual mortgage bonds, but it mirrors one that does. The institution selling the synthetic CDO sells a promise to provide the investor with the same returns that a specified *actual* CDO generates. But if the real world bond loses value or defaults, then so too does the synthetic.[15] 'It was as if Wall Street, in all its mad, Strangelovian genius, had found a way to clone armies of securities from a single strand of mortgage DNA.'[16] Because of these derivatives, explains Lowenstein, 'far more money was wagered on mortgage debt than the total of such debt in existence'.[17] By 2006, half of all CDOs were said to be synthetic.[18] And since the real-world securities carried investment-grade ratings that gave them the appearance of almost perfect safety, so too did their copies.

It may seem curious and even suspicious that reputable rating agencies would award their seal of approval to these instruments. There is no denying that the agencies suffered from a conflict of interest – the institutions whose financial products were being assessed also happened to be the major clients of the assessors. But there is more to the story than this. Before being sold, mortgage securities were often 'insurance wrapped' against default. If a major insurer like American Investment Group (AIG) agrees to absorb any losses, then there is understandably thought to be little or no risk to investors. Moreover, rather than sorting through and assessing the thousands of individual loan files underlying the securities, rating agencies became increasingly reliant on computer-based statistical analysis of the pool at large. Unfortunately, the models used for the purposes of risk-assessment did not take into account the fact that lending practices had changed radically and that the same new products with the same vulnerabilities were now being sold coast to coast. Historically there had been very little correlation between default rates in different parts of the US, but this change made a *nationwide* spike in defaults a real possibility.[19]

Mortgage securities fast became a favourite among even the most conservative investors, as well as banks – both investment and the traditional deposit-taking kind. From 1985 to 2007 the MBS market of government-sponsored mortgage businesses Fannie Mae and Freddie Mac blew out from $367.9 billion to $4.46 trillion, and the mortgage security market of the 'private label' banks grew from $24.7 billion to $2.96 trillion over the same period.[20] The popularity of these instruments meant that demand constantly outstripped supply. A residential mortgage trader at Morgan Stanley described the situation in an award-winning episode of *This American Life*:

> It was unbelievable. We almost couldn't produce enough to keep the appetite of the investors happy. More people wanted bonds than we could actually produce. That was our difficult task, was trying to produce enough. They would call and ask 'Do you have any more fixed rate? What have you got? What's coming?' From our standpoint it's like, there's a guy out there with a lot of money. We gotta find a way to be his sole provider of bonds to fill his appetite. And his appetite's massive.

The insatiable demand accelerated the decline of credit standards and lending practices. The construction of mortgage securities obviously requires a steady supply of mortgages. At first the products were being built out of traditional loans where the borrower made some down-payment and had money in the bank plus a stable income. But soon this well ran dry. Before too long, credit was being made available to the less-than-creditworthy, who could now obtain mortgages without offering any proof of their income and even without revealing its source. Countrywide Financial went so far as to issue mortgages to people who were deemed ineligible for credit cards, to borrowers who were already delinquent on an existing mortgage and even to those who had filed for personal bankruptcy just 24 hours prior![21]

This set off a race to the bottom, as other lenders were forced to lower their own standards in fear of losing market share to the likes of Countrywide.[22] Since the parties originating the mortgages often had no intention of holding them to maturity, the increased risk of default failed to act as a deterrent. Where the loan-maker is also the risk-bearer, due diligence is taken since delinquencies and defaults are likely to hurt the lender financially. Where mortgages are issued with the intention of aggregation and sale, prudence loses its force. Lenders are driven to issue as many loans as possible in order to collect the transaction fees and then simply forward them on to the next link in the chain.

The US government also did its bit to stoke the mania. Successive administrations have endeavoured to extend the opportunity for homeownership to the underprivileged. Mortgage twins Fannie and Freddie were the principal agents of the government's policy of 'credit-democratisation'. In return for certain privileges – access to cheap credit and tax exemptions – the twins were required by Congress to commit a portion of their portfolios to low-income housing. Though neither lent to homeowners directly, their function was to purchase and guarantee the mortgages of other lenders, replenishing their capital, taking risk off their books and thus allowing them to issue more loans. By 1996, 42 per cent of the twins' mortgage financing was required by law to go to borrowers with income below the median in their area. The Department of Housing and Urban Development increased the target to 50 per cent in 2000 and 52 per cent in 2005.[23] Other major lenders signed a government pledge to make 'proactive creative efforts' to extend homeownership to minorities and low-income Americans.[24] Under congressional pressure, mortgage loans with down-payments of less than 5 per cent ballooned from 9 per cent in 1991 to 29 per cent in 2007, and Congress mandated 'innovative and flexible' lending practices which included creative definitions of 'income'.[25]

While competitive pressures and greed no doubt had something to do with the relaxation of credit standards, then, government efforts to promote social ideals by distorting the financial system also seem to have played a role. [26] This unleashed a flurry of criticism. Economist George Reisman later attributed the housing boom to 'the Federal Reserve's policy of credit expansion ... [which] served to give capital to unworthy borrowers who never should have had it in the first place'.[27] In a similar vein, Russell Roberts pointed the finger not at the greedy bankers whose effigies were being burned by protesters across Europe, but at 'a political class greedy to push home-ownership rates to historic highs'.[28]

When inflationary pressures led to an increase in official interest rates and house prices dropped due in part to a surplus of unsold homes, it well and truly spoiled the party. Default rates started to soar shortly thereafter, especially among sub-prime borrowers. Around two-thirds had been enticed into the market with adjustable-rate mortgages characterised by attractive initial terms.[29] The interest rates started out low and would only be reset higher after some predetermined period. But by then there was an expectation – based on recent trends – that the value of the property would have increased enough to afford the borrower the opportunity to refinance on more favourable terms. The problem was that the drop in house prices made refinancing difficult. Many borrowers found themselves unable to escape the higher rates, which they could not afford, forcing them into foreclosure.

To make matters worse, sub-prime loans had been given out to borrowers with credit scores high enough to get a better deal.[30] In light of the profitability of securitisation, there is a simple enough explanation: sub-prime mortgages come with higher interest rates, prepayment penalties and other fees that make them more lucrative for the creditor and accordingly more attractive to investors. This exacerbated the foreclosure problem. A study by the Centre for Community Capital at the University of North Carolina showed that borrowers with nearly identical financial profiles were three to five times more likely to default when they received high-priced sub-prime mortgages.[31]

While some borrowers were genuinely unable to make their repayments, others simply chose not to. In many (though not all) US states mortgage debt is non-recourse, meaning that in the event of default the lender is entitled to seize the property for which the loan was made, but cannot collect other assets or put a lien of future wages if the value of the property is insufficient to cover the outstanding loan balance. The decline in house prices meant that many borrowers – nearly 12 million US homeowners by the end of November 2008 – had either zero or negative equity. Anyone in this situation, locked into a mortgage that was suddenly worth more than the house, had a financial incentive to default 'strategically'. Borrowers that were current on credit card and auto loans curiously started to fall behind on mortgage repayments.[32] This seems to have been one of the key factors in foreclosures in the second half of 2008. Although only 12 per cent of homes had negative equity, they comprised 47 per cent of defaults.[33]

The foreclosures further increased the surplus of unsold homes, which in turn put more downward pressure on house prices, which in turn led to further defaults, and so on in a vicious circle. Overall, foreclosure proceedings were initiated on nearly 1.3 million residential properties in 2007 – 79 per cent more than in 2006. In 2008 2.3 million homes were foreclosed – a further increase of 81 per cent over 2007.[34]

The market for mortgage securities quickly collapsed. As the instruments had been constructed out of a mixture of loans from different risk categories, 'sliced and diced' into tranches, repackaged countless times and passed around from one party to another, it had become nearly impossible to determine how much bad debt any given MBS or CDO was exposed to, and nobody was willing to take the risk. A treasury official reportedly used mad cow disease as a metaphor: the fear that some proportion of every portfolio was contaminated resulted in a situation where 'there is no price at which you buy hamburger'.[35] The products which investors once couldn't get enough of were now virtually unsellable.

The firms that held sub-prime mortgages and mortgage securities on their books were stuck with them, and the value of these assets was plummeting rapidly.[36] On top of this, the entities that the banks had set up to house mortgage securities off their balance sheets – so-called 'Structured Investment Vehicles' (SIVs) – borrowed heavily to finance their investments. But when the markets realised that the SIVs were stuffed with toxic assets, they refused to rollover their debts.[37] This pushed the assets and liabilities of the SIVs back onto the balance sheets of the parent banks. As early as 2007, Citigroup, which was already suffocating under its own CDOs, was forced to re-assume a further $49 billion worth of assets from the SIVs that it had sponsored.[38]

Many banks now found themselves undercapitalised. The Basel Accord requires that banks have a certain amount of capital (consisting mainly of shareholder equity and retained profits) supporting the assets on their balance sheets. This regulation is intended to ensure that a bank can cope with a reasonable amount of loss and still meet its liabilities. Importantly, the assets are 'risk weighted' – the safer an asset, the more a bank is allowed to discount it in its capital adequacy calculation. Thus, there are two ways for the capital ratio of a bank to fall: shareholder equity and profits can be depleted, or the risks on its books can be recalculated upwards. The sub-prime problem presented banks with a 'double whammy': profits were declining and the value of bank shares was in freefall. At the same time, banks were being buried under a growing pile of high-risk assets of which they could not rid themselves.[39]

Falling capital ratios impaired the ability of banks to lend to one another as they desperately held on to what little capital they had left, and even sold assets at fire-sale prices in an effort to recapitalise. Fear compounded the credit crunch as banks grew increasingly sceptical of one another's solvency. They looked at their own port-folios, backed up with toxic assets, and worried that if other banks were similarly situated, they could not be trusted to make good on their commitments. As a result, banks everywhere started to demand huge premiums on business loans and in many cases refused to lend altogether.[40] This put a number of financial institutions in danger of imminent insolvency, unable to sell their assets to replenish their capital and unable to refinance debts whose maturity was fast approaching.

The smaller mortgage originators that were churning out the material for the MBSs and CDOs started to drop like flies.[41] The story of Silver State, an early casualty of the sub-prime collapse, gives us some insight into how the damage spread so far so quickly. The Nevada-based company was in the business of issuing and buying mortgages and then selling them to the large investment banks on Wall Street. Like most such companies, Silver State did not rely solely upon its own capital to fund the operation; it was leveraged by as much as 20 to 1. That is, for every $5 million of its own funds, Silver States borrowed as much as $100 million to buy up mortgage loans. But when the default rate spiked, Silver State's customers on Wall Street abruptly stopped buying its product. The firm had spent millions on assets that it now could not sell. Since Silver State had very little in reserve, it was only a matter of time before the firm defaulted on its own exorbitant loans and closed its doors. Hundreds more mortgage originators would follow. By September 2008 the toll had reached 275.[42]

The contagion was global. Northern Rock, the UK's fifth largest mortgage lender and most aggressive securitising bank, had also taken on extra leverage to amplify its lending capacity. When Northern Rock was unable to rollover its debts, it was forced to seek an urgent government loan, setting off a run by depositors and eventually the bank's nationalisation. In Australia, RAMS Home Loans was unable to refinance more than $6 billion in debt and was taken over by Westpac. In October 2007 UBS in Switzerland was the first major bank to announce massive losses – $3.4 billion – from sub-prime-related investments. Diversified commercial bank Citigroup and investment bank Merrill Lynch soon followed. The stated losses of the former would eventually reach $40 billion, while the latter revealed that it was exposed to $7.9 billion in bad debt.

Bear Stearns, Wall Street's fifth largest investment bank and its number-one dealer in real-estate-based securities, was the first major casualty. In March 2008 concerns were raised about the sub-prime mortgage assets that made up a significant proportion of Bear Stearns' portfolio. The securities continued to decline in value as the foreclosures continued to mount. Bear's stocks fell off a cliff, its trading partners began to desert it and the markets refused to rollover its short-term debt. The firm was forced to start eating into its cash reserves. Soon there was none left, and with stock prices continuing to fall, bankruptcy looked imminent.

Bear Stearns' leverage now became a major concern. The company was indebted to countless others around the US and the world. If it defaulted on its loans, its counterparties would find themselves in quite a bind. The fall of Bear would potentially trigger cascading failures. Fearing the worst, the US government engineered and underwrote a takeover by commercial bank JP Morgan Chase, which, along with Goldman Sachs, had wisely decided to pare back its sub-prime-related investments in 2006 at the first sign of trouble and thus remained in a relatively strong position.[43] Worth $18 billion only a year earlier, Bear Stearns was sold for $240 million and as part of the deal JP Morgan Chase would be held liable only for the first $1 billion in losses, with the remainder being absorbed by the Federal Reserve.[44]

However, there was a much bigger problem unfolding elsewhere. Fannie Mae and Freddie Mac had lost 60 per cent of their stock value within a couple of weeks. The government-sponsored mortgage businesses together owned or guaranteed an estimated $5 *trillion* worth of home loans and yet held as little as half the capital of similarly sized 'private label' banks. Their counterparties were innumerable; almost every institutional investor in the world held their debt. If the collapse of Bear Stearns threatened to disrupt the financial system, the failure of the mortgage giants would have been nothing short of cataclysmic. In a dramatic turn of events the financial authorities seized Fannie and Freddie, nationalising both and firing their management.

In each of these cases Treasury Secretary Hank Paulson warned that the collapse of highly leveraged and interconnected institutions posed a 'systemic risk' threatening to set in train a series of events that would ultimately bring down the entire financial system and have untold consequences for the wider economy. But at the same time Paulson made no secret of his anxiety that the government bailouts would create a situation of 'moral hazard'. Whatever incentive this situation offered other firms in terms of limiting their risk-taking would be diluted by the belief that the government would rescue them too if things went wrong.

Thus, when the next investment bank on Wall Street ran into trouble, posting a $3.9 billion loss for the three months to August 2008, there would be no government rescue and no loans or guarantees to entice a buyer. Lehman Brothers was allowed to fail, and both shareholders and creditors were wiped out – a decision that all concerned would soon regret. Lehman's was the largest bankruptcy in US history. According to *Bloomberg* columnist Roger Lowenstein, its collapse 'opened a trapdoor from which poured forth all the demons and excesses' that had accumulated during the housing boom.[45] The firm left $613 billion in ordinary debts, $155 billion in bond debts, assets worth $639 billion and was counterparty to more than 8,000 firms, among them insurance giant AIG.[46]

AIG had sold billions of dollars worth of credit default swaps (CDSs) with Lehman Brothers as the reference entity. A CDS is essentially an insurance policy that one company takes out on the debt of another company. In its purest form the contract works like this: Company A makes a loan to Company B. If B becomes insolvent and cannot repay the loan, A suffers a loss. To hedge against this risk, A pays a premium to Company C, and in return C agrees to cover A's losses if B goes into default. Here, Company C is the seller of the CDS, Company A is the buyer and Company B is the reference entity. Such contracts can also be used to guarantee the value of a particular security, such as a CDO. If its value falters, the seller must offset the losses of the buyer.[47]

However, risk-management is not the only use of the CDS, which differs from a standard insurance contract in several important respects. One of them is that, while insurance can only be sold to the owner of whatever it is that is being insured, the buyer of a CDS need not own the underlying security or other form of credit exposure. Third parties who would suffer no loss from a default event whatsoever are eligible to buy a CDS covering it. Thus, Company A might buy a CDS to insure itself against loss in the event of B's default, but companies D, E, F and G might also buy CDSs from

C in a gamble to win a payout if B goes bankrupt. In the lead-up to the crash of 2008, large volumes of these products were sold to speculators betting against the solvency of particular debtors. One of those debtors was Lehman Brothers, and AIG was among the chief suppliers of the swaps.[48] Thus, when Lehman Brothers went bust, AIG suddenly faced the prospect of having to pay out billions of dollars worth of claims. Without the cash reserves to make good on these commitments and others like it, AIG went in search of an emergency lender, but the tight credit conditions made this an exercise in futility.

Not only had AIG sold CDS contracts on financial speculation and guaranteed the debts of companies everywhere that were now struggling, it had also been investing in mortgage securities on its own account (so-called 'proprietary trading'), and its own subsidiaries were involved in sub-prime lending. Michael Lewitt warned that the collapse of AIG would be 'as close to an extinction-level event as financial markets have seen since the Great Depression'.[49] So, when AIG executives began pleading for an urgent loan from the Federal Reserve, they got more attention than did Lehman's chief. On 16 September AIG received an $85 billion bailout (with more to come), and in return the US government would help itself to an 80 per cent stake in the company (the full extent of AIG's troubles would only come to light in March 2009, when the firm posted a $61.7 billion quarterly loss for the last three months of 2008 – the largest quarterly loss in US corporate history).

Unfortunately, none of this could prevent a devastating run on the money markets. The money-market fund has long been treated as an alternative to the conventional bank account, with the same low-risk but somewhat higher returns. The investor puts his or her money into the fund and the fund invests it only in the safest AAA-rated securities, such as bonds issued by governments or by blue-chip companies. The funds are restricted to the most secure investments by the SEC's Investment Company Act of 1940.[50] Their attraction is their reputation for '*total* preservation of value'.[51] That is, the value of the capital invested remains constant – pegged at $1 per share – and on top of this the investor profits from the interest rates and dividends. The problem now was that even some of the biggest, most rock-solid companies were in trouble. Consequently, money-market funds, always regarded as the most conservative way of participating in financial markets, started losing money. The response from investors was to flee. Within two days $173 billion – 7 per cent of the total invested in the money markets – was withdrawn. This intensified the credit crunch. In the US and across Europe major banks financed their day-to-day operations largely by selling commercial paper – short-term IOUs – on global money markets. But because the funds were now being inundated with redemptions, they were forced to cancel many of their normal purchases of commercial paper.[52]

The list of casualties continued to grow. Giant mortgage lender Washington Mutual was next in line. On 25 September the bank was closed down by regulators and its assets sold to JP Morgan Chase. A few days later European bank and insurance firm Fortis was part-nationalised to ensure its survival, followed by British mortgage lender Bradford & Bingley. Meanwhile, the Icelandic government was taking control of the country's third largest bank Glitnir – an ominous sign of things to come. On 30 September, Dexia became the largest European bank to be bailed out. Belgium, France and Luxembourg pledged 6.5 billion Euros to keep it afloat. Over the next month the Icelandic government would take control of the country's second largest bank, Landsbanki, the UK government would part-nationalise the Royal Bank of Scotland, Lloyds TSB and HBOS, while across the Atlantic, Wachovia would be taken over by Wells Fargo.[53] In total 37 banks collapsed between September 2008 and March 2009. Thereafter banks continued to fail at a rate of nearly three a week.[54] There had been only four such failures in 2007 and none in 2005 and 2006.[55]

To say that the risk models on which the financial services industry had come to rely failed to anticipate these events would be putting it mildly. A Lehman's risk analyst complained that events which the models predicted would happen only once every 10,000 years occurred every day for three days running. The chief finance officer at Goldman Sachs reported that '-25 Sigma events' were occurring. These are events which, according to the models that had been designed by PhD mathematicians and physicists, should *never* happen, even if the history of the universe repeats itself 14 times over. And these were said to be happening for days in a row.[56] Since the financial institutions using the models had a multitude of uncorrelated investments or positions, it was thought that while a few of them might go wrong at any one time, the probability of all or most of them going wrong simultaneously was almost too small to compute. Unfortunately, 'diversification' proved to be no defence against such a massive, synchronised downturn.[57]

The banking crisis now started to spill over into the real economy. Even non-financial companies that were reliant on short-term credit found themselves paying a lot more for it. Junk-rated corporations were being charged as much as 22 per cent interest.[58] Some found it difficult to borrow from money markets at *any* rate. In addition to the credit problems, there had been a sharp decline in retail sales. Consumer confidence had been hit by falling home equity (house prices had dropped by 32 per cent by early 2009) and low job security (businesses everywhere were closing and downsizing: Citigroup laid off 35,000 workers, Pfizer laid off nearly 20,000, while Starbucks shut 900 stores).[59] Car loans became increasingly difficult to obtain, devastating the auto industry.[60] House construction and the accompanying purchases of household goods, which had been one of the main drivers of the US economy for quite some time, slowed considerably. The 30,000 jobs lost on Wall Street looked insignificant compared to the 8 million that disappeared nationwide.[61] Even non-business sectors were impacted by the credit crunch. In Washington DC a bond offering for an airport expansion was withdrawn due to a lack of buyers, a town in Montana was unable to finance a proposed emergency room, and Maine was unable to raise funds for highway repairs.[62]

The ensuing recession was a global one. Millions more people worldwide lost their jobs, their homes and their savings. Retiree pension funds everywhere were depleted, as half the value of all the publicly traded shares on earth was lost in the space of a year.[63] In China reduced exports to the US triggered a reversal of the largest migration in human history; tens of millions of rural Chinese who migrated to urban centres for work were forced to travel back to poor villages that were often not prepared to handle their return.[64] The plight of the world's poor was exacerbated and many more people were pushed into poverty as remittances to developing countries declined, revenues from tourism fell significantly, credit and trade financing became more difficult to obtain, infant and maternal mortality increased, and the ability of governments to maintain social safety nets and provide other services such as health and education was reduced.[65]

Countries whose exports declined in turn cut back their imports, propelling a cycle of contracting production. Ross Garnaut put the gravity of the economic slowdown in perspective:

> The decline in global production from the September quarter of 2008 until mid 2009 was larger than the world had ever known over a comparably short period. Over this time, both industrial and total output for the world as a whole fell more rapidly than in the corresponding early stage of the Great Depression.[66]

In fact, by March 2009 world trade had fallen proportionately by as much as it did in the first 21 months of contraction through 1929, 1930 and 1931. Banks based in the advanced economies were first to feel the brunt, but this was just the beginning. By the end of it all, relatively few had escaped unscathed.

Along the way, governments and central banks implemented a range of measures in an effort to contain the crisis. They bailed out trouble financial institutions with emergency loans on favourable terms, reduced interest rates to historic lows, guaranteed bank debt, bought up the toxic assets that were clogging the arteries of the financial system, and even injected capital directly into banks and non-financial companies in return for an equity stake. The US government acquired 34 per cent of Citigroup (once the biggest bank), 80 per cent of AIG (the biggest insurer), 60 per cent of General Motors (the biggest car maker) and had mortgage giants Fannie Mae and Freddie Mac under its control. By the end of November 2008, 106 banks in total had received support from the US government through the Troubled Asset Relief Program (TARP).[67] To prevent things from getting any worse in the real economy, governments executed huge stimulus packages to offset the reduction in private sector demand and, in an unprecedented move, the Federal Reserve lent directly to non-financial companies rather than going through the usual intermediaries.

The political focus has since shifted to preventing a relapse or repetition of events. On 20 May 2010 the US Senate passed a bill that, among other things: strengthens capital reserve requirements; allows the Federal Reserve to wind down systemically important institutions; requires companies that originate mortgages to retain at least some of the credit risk; seeks to ensure that troubled companies can be liquidated at no cost to taxpayers; imposes new rules on rating agencies to address sloppy methodology and conflict of interest; and requires that banks spin off their risky derivative trading businesses or else forfeit access to the Federal Reserve's emergency lending window.[68] The bill touches virtually every aspect of the financial services industry. Planet Finance will never be the same again.

Outline of the book

Even this admittedly crude sketch of what transpired opens up a raft of ethical questions. As we have seen, the expansion of the mortgage market to deeper socioeconomic levels played an important role. Should the 'democratisation of credit' therefore no longer be regarded as a legitimate objective of government policy? Angelo Mozilo, CEO of Countrywide Financial, endeavoured to give even the most severely credit-challenged a second chance and to make homeownership a reality for every citizen. Before the crash, his praises were widely sung. But given the risks now known to be associated with it, should the lowering of credit standards still be considered morally praiseworthy? Nobel Prize Laureate Muhammad Yunus has gone so far as to argue that since access to credit is intimately connected to the fulfilment of fundamental human rights, it should itself be accorded the status of a right. Credit, Yunus claims, is directly instrumental to economic development and welfare; it allows the poor to build their own income strength and is the only sustainable path out of poverty.[69] In light of recent events, should we think twice before making this addition to the human rights lexicon?

Many have argued that it is not the expansion of credit markets *per se* that is the problem, but rather the kinds of loans being given out and the predatory lending practices of the mortgage originators.[70] But this raises its own questions: what exactly distinguishes an extortionary or exploitative loan from one whose terms and conditions are a reasonable and legitimate response to the higher default risk of the borrower? Do lenders owe a duty of care to their clients? Is US Senator Phil Gramm right to suggest that borrowing can be just as 'predatory' as lending?

We also need to look beyond proximate causes to deeper socioeconomic circumstances. The real median wage in the US has been stagnant for almost 25 years, and this despite the fact that per capita

GDP has almost doubled. At the same time, income inequality is on the rise; the wealthiest 1 per cent of the population doubled its share of national income from 8 per cent in the 1970s to almost 16 per cent in the early 2000s. Between 1976 and 2006 roughly half of all real income gains were accrued in the richest 5 per cent of households. According to World Bank economist Branko Milanovic, had the wealth been more evenly distributed, the financial services industry might never have created the exotic financial instruments which proved so dangerous, and credit culture might never have emerged among the lower and middle classes.[71] The obscenely rich, even after all the conspicuous consumption they can muster, are invariably left with vast amounts of expendable resources. This pool of capital went in search of profitable investment opportunities. Once the safe options were exhausted, Wall Street invented riskier products to satiate the demand in the form of securitised mortgages, CDSs and various other derivatives. Meanwhile, the only way for low and moderate income earners to augment their purchasing power was through debt. If there are hitherto undetected risks associated with huge income inequalities, what implications does this have for the long-running debate between cosmopolitans and sufficientists?

The effort to contain the banking crisis – the chief cause of which was excessive debt or over-leveraging – was itself financed by national debt. Since the collapse of Lehman Brothers, US debt has risen from $1.9 trillion to almost $12 trillion,[72] which begs the following question: was the crisis *resolved* or merely *transferred* from the private sector to the public? Various European countries are now being suffocated with debt and are imposing wide-ranging austerity measures on their populations. Some are in danger of default. Currency speculator George Soros recently warned that 'the [financial] crisis is far from over ... Indeed we have just entered Act II of the drama', while the Bank of International Settlement has described the European sovereign debt problem as a repeat of the US sub-prime mortgage meltdown. As one would expect, this is bleeding back into the banking system, as European banks are finding it more expensive and difficult to obtain credit. The London Inter-Bank Offered Rate (LIBOR) – the rate at which banks lend money to each other and thus a sign of their mutual trust – has been steadily rising. There is growing concern that Europe's fiscal woes and government measures to curb budget deficits at a time when economic recovery is still weak may push the global economy back into recession. The Euro has plunged to a four-year low against the US dollar, and more than $4 trillion has been wiped off global stock markets this year.[73]

How should the costs of the crisis be allocated, both intranationally and internationally? Who is responsible for protecting the world's poor from, and compensating them for, the impact of the economic downturn? Were the bailouts ethically justified or should the troubled firms have been allowed to suffer the market's justice come what may? Is it morally preferable, or even obligatory, for the state to take an equity share and partly or fully nationalise institutions that it is forced to rescue with taxpayer's money? What would constitute a morally appropriate response in the longer term? Is re-regulation the answer? Has the crisis discredited the moral case for laissez-faire capitalism? Are there deeper institutional shortcomings that traditional forms of regulation will fail to address? Should the crisis perhaps be seen as the materialisation of a defect inherent in our economic system itself or even in cultural factors and societal attitudes more generally?

Though no single volume could hope to adequately address all of the relevant ethical questions, some of the more pressing are taken up in the chapters that follow. In Chapter 2 Seumas Miller argues that the corporate collapses and corruption scandals that marked the crisis should be seen as symptoms of underlying systemic deficiencies in corporate law and regulation, and perhaps of structural deficiencies in the corporate sector itself. The basic normative question that needs to be asked of a business corporation or financial market, according to Miller, is the same as for any other social institution, namely: why does it exist? In the real economy the answer to this question seems obvious: the purpose of a corporation is to provide material goods, and markets exist to coordinate the buyers and sellers of goods. However, in the case of the financial services sector, the prior fundamental ethical question as to its ultimate institutional ends remains unanswered. Herein lies the problem, says Miller. Without an answer to this question, an 'integrity system' for the financial services sector is quite literally without one of its basic purposes: it does not know what ethical ends it is seeking to embed. In light of this, it should come as little surprise that the finance economy is the source of the most severe economic crisis in decades.

In Chapter 3 Noam Chomsky shifts the focus from the causes of the crisis to the US government's response – specifically the taxpayer-funded rescue of troubled financial firms to the tune of hundreds of billions of dollars. This has been widely condemned as a case of socialising losses while privatising profits. Chomsky shares the sentiment, but argues that there is nothing fundamentally new in any of this. The advanced economy is based very extensively on state-organised and directed research and development, subsidy, procurement and bailout. In every developed country one finds a powerful state that intervenes in the market to the benefit of merchants, manufacturers, industrialists and other economic interest groups. This is an inherent feature not of capitalism but of state capitalism, and the recent bailouts simply follow this trajectory.

Along with the public outrage at taxpayer-funded bailouts, there have been intense calls for tighter government control over banks, rating agencies, accounting, insurance and brokerage firms, and the financial services industry more generally, and there is a growing consensus that the alternatives – 'market discipline', civil litigation and voluntary self-regulation by firms and industry associations – cannot be relied upon to deter unethical conduct and to protect us from the adverse consequences that free-market activity sometimes produces. In my contribution to the volume in Chapter 4, I revisit the moral dimensions of government regulation in the context of the current crisis. The standard argument for deregulation has three prongs – one virtue-based, one rights-based and one consequentialist. Considerable pressure has been mounted on all three. It has become apparent that the market does not reliably cultivate honesty, integrity and diligence; the claim that the costs of regulation are excessive has become more difficult to sustain; and as for the rights-based argument, its standard formulation rests on the premise that regulation paternalistically prohibits or constrains the offering and voluntary acceptance of risks. But this seems to have lost its purchase on reality given the now undeniable prevalence of risk *imposition* in financial markets. I argue that the moral presumption has been shifted, and with it the burden of argument, which now falls squarely on neoliberals and other opponents of regulation to show that the risk impositions in question are of the morally innocent kind that do not justify coercive interference by the state.

In Chapter 5 John C. Harrington delves beyond the proximate causes of the crisis to its roots – the deregulation of the financial services industry, the separation of ownership and control, a declining sense of fiduciary responsibility, a growing culture of risk-taking and reliance on 'fast money', deluded faith in the magic of the market and, ultimately, excessive materialistic self-interest. Harrington discusses the various ways in which ethical investing might be employed to address not only traditional social, environmental and corporate governance concerns, but also the growth of global speculation, increased liquidity in secondary markets, leveraged securities and the dangers posed by exotic trading instruments.

The role that corporate lobbying played in creating and sustaining a dangerous regulatory environment should not be overlooked in all of this. In Chapter 6 Thomas Pogge depicts such activities as a case of the classic collective action problem. Both the real economy and financial markets are predicated on an adversarial or competitive system. When properly framed, this has proved to be highly efficient. Proper framing involves designing the rules of the game in such a way as to ensure that the self-interested pursuits of the players are correlated with the creation of social value, and the transparent and impartial administration of these rules. The problem, says Pogge, is that in an adversarial system there are powerful incentives for reward-focused players to manipulate the rules or to interfere with their application. The regulations – and the regulators – charged with constraining and organising the competition can thus become the objects of the competition. This, however, is detrimental to the interests of all involved. Each player is worse off in the long run than they would be if they abandoned their competitive efforts to manipulate the system.

In Chapter 7, his second contribution to the volume, Seumas Miller adds further insights on how self-interest can be mobilised to promote ethical conduct in financial markets. When a high professional reputation is much sought-after by members of an occupational group or organisation, and a low one to be avoided at all costs, there is an opportunity to put this desire to use in the service of promoting ethical standards. Miller argues that a deserved reputation can provide an important nexus between the self-interest of business firms and professional groups on the one hand, and appropriate ethical behaviour towards consumers, clients and the public more generally on the other. Reputation, self-interest and compliance with ethical standards can be made to interlock in what Miller calls a 'virtuous triangle'.

In Chapter 8 Matt Peterson and Christian Barry turn to consider what principles policy makers should adopt in allocating the costs of the financial crisis and subsequent global recession. More specifically who, morally speaking, should bear the costs of trying to alleviate or at least mitigate the severe deprivations that are being suffered by the world's poor? The authors argue that even on a minimally demanding principle of assistance, the costs ought to be shifted significantly from poor and developing countries to the affluent. The obligations of the affluent grow more stringent once we notice that the lion's share of contributory fault is theirs. There is no denying that the regulatory shortcomings of the US and European governments, and the misconduct of the companies that are registered within their territories, are largely to blame for the crisis. In light of this, Peterson and Barry argue that the actual international policy response to the crisis thus far has been grossly morally inadequate.

The reader will hopefully come away not only with a deeper understanding of the recent financial crisis and some of the ethical and philosophical issues that it has raised, but also with insights of more general interest and applicability. As I write this, Europe is facing a sovereign debt crisis, a BP oilrig in the Gulf of Mexico continues to spew millions of litres of oil into the ocean each day, and the SEC is preparing a civil suit against Goldman Sachs for selling securities known to be of poor quality and then betting against them on its own account. Easy credit and overindebtedness, the separation of risk-creation and risk-bearing, the privatisation of profits and socialisation of losses, financial malpractice and institutional and regulatory shortcomings are once again the centre of attention. The chapters in this volume will hopefully shed some light where it is most needed.

Notes

1. Ross Garnaut, *The Great Crash of 2008*, Carlton: Melbourne University Press, 2009.
2. See for instance Nancy Gibbs, 'The Great Recession: America Becomes a Thrift Nation', *Time Magazine*, 15 April 2009; Catherine Rampell, 'Great Recession: A Brief Etymology', *New York Times*, 11 March 2009; Paul Krugman, 'The Great Recession Versus the Great Depression', *New York Times*, 20 March 2009; Justin Lahart, 'The Great Recession: A Downturn Sized Up', *Wall Street Journal*, 20 July 2009.
3. J.S.B. Morse, *Surviving the Second Great Depression*, Seattle: CoDe Publishing, 2009.

4. Paul Mason, *Meltdown: The End of the Age of Greed*, London and New York: Verso, 2009, Chapter 3.
5. Roger Lowenstein, *The End of Wall Street*, Melbourne: Scribe, 2010.
6. Mason, *Meltdown*.
7. George Soros, *The New Paradigm for Financial Markets*, Jackson: PublicAffairs, 2008.
8. Tom Arup, 'Financial Crisis is All God's Work, says MP', *The Age*, 5 December 2008, www.theage.com.au/national/financial-crisis-is-all-gods-work-says-mp-20081204-6rpa.html, date accessed 6 October 2010.
9. Niall Ferguson, 'Wall Street Lays Another Egg', *Vanity Fair*, December 2008, www.vanityfair.com/politics/features/2008/12/banks200812, date accessed 6 October 2010.
10. Brigid Glanville, 'Credit Crisis a "Financial Armageddon": ANZ Boss', ABC Radio National, 23 October 2009, www.abc.net.au/pm/content/2008/s2399635.htm, date accessed 6 October 2010.
11. Ben S. Bernanke, 'Fostering Sustainable Homeownership', Speech at the National Community Reinvestment Coalition Annual Meeting, Washington DC, 14 March 2008, www.federalreserve.gov/newsevents/speech/bernanke20080314a.htm, date accessed 6 October 2010; Garnaut, *The Great Crash*, p. 21.
12. Lowenstein, *The End of Wall Street*, p. 23.
13. Garnaut, *The Great Crash*, pp. 47–8.
14. Ibid., p. 48.
15. Lowenstein, *The End of Wall Street*, p. 56.
16. Ibid.
17. Ibid.
18. Ibid.
19. Ibid., p. 47.
20. Garnaut, *The Great Crash*, pp. 43–4.
21. Mason, *Meltdown*, p. 89; Lowenstein, *The End of Wall Street*, p. 30.
22. Lowenstein, *The End of Wall Street*, pp. 30–1.
23. Russell Roberts, 'How Government Stoked the Mania; Housing Prices Would Never Have Risen So High Without Multiple Washington Mistakes', *Wall Street Journal*, 30 October 2008, A21.
24. David Streitfeld and Gretchen Morgenson, 'The Reckoning, Building Flawed American Dreams', *New York Times*, 19 October 2008, p. A26. Furthermore, the government guaranteed billions of dollars worth of mortgage loans, effectively giving lenders an incentive to issue loans with little regard to the qualifications of the borrower.
25. Edward Pinto, 'Acorn and the Housing Bubble', *Wall Street Journal*, 13 November 2009, A23. In 2003 President George W. Bush added fuel to the fire by signing the American Dream Downpayment Act, which subsidised first-time house purchases in low-income groups with the aim of vastly increasing the number of minority homeowners. Ferguson, 'Wall Street Lays Another Egg'.
26. Peter J. Wallison, 'Barney Frank, Predatory Lender; Almost Two-thirds of All Bad Mortgages in our Financial System Were Bought by Government

Agencies or Required by Government Regulations', *Wall Street Journal*, 16 October 2009.

27. George Reisman, 'The Myth that Laissez Faire Is Responsible for Our Present Crisis', *Mises Daily*, 23 October 2008, http://mises.org/daily/3165, date accessed 6 October 2010.
28. Roberts, 'How Government Stoked the Mania'.
29. Lowenstein, *The End of Wall Street*, p. 37.
30. 'Subprime Debacle Traps Even Very Creditworthy', *Wall Street Journal*, 3 December 2007.
31. Editorial, 'Misplaced Blame', *Wall Street Journal*, 15 October 2008.
32. Lowenstein, *The End of Wall Street*, p. 79.
33. Stan Liebowitz, 'New Evidence on the Foreclosure Crisis', *Wall Street Journal*, 3 July 2009.
34. RealtyTrac, 'Foreclosure Activity Increases 81 Percent in 2008', www.realtytrac.com/ContentManagement/pressrelease.aspx?ChannelID=9& ItemID=5681&accnt=64847, date accessed 6 October 2010.
35. Quoted in Lowenstein, *The End of Wall Street*, p. 104.
36. Those that did eventually manage to find a buyer typically sold for a fraction of what they had paid. Merrill Lynch, for instance, acquired a set of CDOs for $30.6 billion during the boom, which it later sold for $6.7 billion. Lowenstein, *The End of Wall Street*, pp. 147–8.
37. Garnaut, *The Great Crash*, p. 49.
38. Lowenstein, *The End of Wall Street*, p. 106.
39. Mason, *Meltdown*, pp. 42–3.
40. Joseph Stiglitz explains: 'with this complicated intertwining of bets of great magnitude, no one could be sure of the financial position of anyone else – or even of one's own position. Not surprisingly, the credit markets froze'. Joseph Stiglitz, 'Capitalist Fools', *Vanity Fair*, January 2009, www.vanityfair.com/magazine/2009/01/stiglitz200901, date accessed 6 October 2010.
41. By 2004 there were an estimated 53,000 mortgage brokers in the US, employing close to 420,000 people: Garnaut, *The Great Crash*, p. 50.
42. Ibid., p. 101.
43. Lowenstein, *The End of Wall Street*, p. 79.
44. Garnaut, *The Great Crash*, p. 121.
45. Lowenstein, *The End of Wall Street*, p. xxii.
46. Garnaut, *The Great Crash*, p. 102.
47. Lowenstein, *The End of Wall Street*, pp. 54–5.
48. Mason, *Meltdown*, p. 93.
49. Ibid., p. 13.
50. Garnaut, *The Great Crash*, p. 52.
51. Lowenstein, *The End of Wall Street*, p. 204.
52. Mason, *Meltdown*, p. 43; Lowenstein, *The End of Wall Street*, p. 217.
53. Lowenstein, *The End of Wall Street*, p. 240.
54. Ibid. p. 282.
55. Garnaut, *The Great Crash*, p. 104.
56. See J. Danielsson, 'Blame the Models' (2008) *Journal of Financial Stability*, 4, 4, 321–8.

57. Ferguson, 'Wall Street Lays Another Egg'.
58. Lowenstein, *The End of Wall Street*, p. 267.
59. Ibid., p. 274.
60. Ibid., p. 262.
61. Lowenstein, *The End of Wall Street*, p. 283.
62. Lowenstein, *The End of Wall Street*, p. 256.
63. Mason, *Meltdown*, p. 53.
64. Thomas Mucha, 'China: Living in the Shadows', *Global Post*, 14 September 2009, www.globalpost.com/dispatch/commerce/090910/china-economy-migrant-workers-economic-crisis, date accessed 6 October 2010.
65. United Nations, *Draft Outcome Document of the Conference on the World Financial and Economic Crisis and its Impact of Development*, A/CONF.214/3, New York, 24–26 June 2009. See also Kevin Rudd, 'The Global Financial Crisis', *The Monthly*, February 2009, www.themonthly.com.au/monthly-essays-kevin-rudd-global-financial-crisis--1421, date accessed 6 October 2010.
66. Garnaut, *The Great Crash*, p. 114.
67. Ibid., p. 127.
68. An amendment to the bill restricting the freedom of banks to trade on their own accounts rather than on behalf of customers – the so-called Volcker rule – was ultimately withdrawn. See the summary of the Wall Street Reform Bill on the website of the Senate Committee on Banking, Housing and Urban Affairs at http://banking.senate.gov/public/_files/FinancialReformSummaryAsFiled.pdf, date accessed 6 October 2010.
69. See Mark Hudon, 'Should Access to Credit Be a Right?' (2009) *Journal of Business Ethics*, 84, 17–28.
70. Eliot Spitzer is a notable example. See 'Predatory Lenders' Partner in Crime', *The Washington Post*, 14 February 2008, A25. See also 'Misplaced Blame', *Wall Street Journal*, 15 October 2008; Scott James, 'A Foreclosure Crisis Rooted in the Family Says, in Predatory Lending', *New York Times*, 8 January 2010, 19A; Editorial, 'Mortgages and Minorities', *New York Times*, 9 December 2008; Gary A. Dymski, 'Racial Exclusion and the Political Economy of the Subprime Crisis' (2009) *Historical Materialism*, 17, 2, 149–79; Elvin K. Wyly, Mona Atia, Elizabeth Lee and Pablo Mendez, 'Race, Gender, and Statistical Representation: Predatory Mortgage Lending and the US Community Reinvestment Movement' (2009) *Environment and Planning A*, 39, 9, 2139–66.
71. Branko Milanovic, 'Two Views on the Cause of the Global Financial Crisis', *Carnegie Endowment for International Peace*, 4 May 2009, www.carnegieendowment.org/publications/index.cfm?fa=view&id=23053, date accessed 6 October 2010.
72. Lowenstein, *The End of Wall Street*, p. 294.
73. '"Act Two" of Crisis Begins: Soros', *Sydney Morning Herald*, 11 June 2010, www.smh.com.au/business/world-business/act-two-of-crisis-begins-soros-20100611-y188.html, date accessed 6 October 2010.

2
Global Financial Institutions, Ethics and Market Fundamentalism

Seumas Miller

The global financial crisis

The global financial crisis (GFC) sparked by the collapse of the investment bank Lehman Brothers has entered a new phase, namely that of sovereign debt. It is not simply investment banks and other financial institutions that are insolvent or bankrupt and in need of government bailouts, it is now whole economies that are actually or potentially insolvent and in need of bailouts by other governments and/or organisations such as the IMF. Most recently, Greece has made the headlines and there is media speculation and market jitters in relation to Ireland, Portugal and Spain. Moreover, this all comes in the wake of the sovereign debt crises very recently faced by Iceland and Dubai. As with the first phase, the crisis has been revealed to have been due in large part to gross financial over-leveraging, regulatory negligence (e.g., of German banks) and a host of other unethical practices such as, in effect, 'cooking the books' in the case of the Greek government. Moreover, this new phase is related to the first, in that a significant increase in sovereign debt has been incurred as a consequence of bailing out failed or failing financial institutions to the tune of trillions of dollars. This ongoing GFC is evidently the worst since the Great Depression, and the second phase is in some respects more alarming than the first, given that while governments typically can bail out banks, it is unclear whether ultimately they can or are willing to bail out other governments. Arguably, for example, the recent German and French government efforts to assist Greece (including a 110 billion Euro bailout) are a function of the desire to protect their own financial stability and that of the eurozone, as well as German and French banks over-exposed to Greek government bonds, rather than a commitment to Greece *per se*. Governments are institutionally and politically obliged to act to save their own economies and necessary financial institutions, but not foreign economies and institutions. This is so, notwithstanding global economic and financial interdependence, and the consequent rationality of intergovernmental joint action in the service of the collective interest. There is a collective action problem, but at the time of writing no comprehensive solution has been agreed upon, let alone implemented.

Some of the main aspects of the ongoing global financial crisis have been the collapse of investment banks and other financial institutions, frozen credit markets, the sub-prime mortgage crisis, the sovereign debt crisis, slow and inconsistent policy responses, and the threat of a double dip global recession, if not the collapse of whole economies. In its first phase,[1] the crisis involved major corporate investment and mortgage banking collapses and bailouts in the US (Lehman Brothers, Freddie Mac and Fannie Mae), the UK (Northern Rock) and Europe (Fortis, Hypo), and had and continues to have a devastating effect on homeowners who cannot pay their mortgages (foreclosures), retirees whose pension funds have plummeted in value, employees whose jobs have been lost in the resulting recession, and taxpayers whose money was and is being injected into the banking system in vast quantities to rescue it (e.g., trillions of dollars by the US government). In its second phase, there is not only the additional burden being imposed on taxpayers as governments are bailed out, but also the renewed threat of recession, or even depression, as weak recoveries stall, at least in the US, the UK and Europe, in the face of austerity measures, e.g., public sector job cuts, put in place by governments to reduce their spiralling debt.

Unethical – including imprudent, individual and collective – practices and processes have been identified as being among the principal causes of the crisis.[2] These practices and processes include: (i) reckless and predatory lending by banks; (ii) the growth of highly leveraged investment banks; (iii) the selling of toxic financial products, notably non-transparent packaged bundles of mortgages, including sub-prime mortgages; (iv) the failure to avoid or adequately manage structural conflicts of interest, including ratings agencies assessing the non-transparent toxic financial products mentioned above as high quality because the investment banks that packaged them – and who fund the ratings agencies – allegedly had good risk assessment processes; (v) massive frauds, e.g., Bernard Madoff's Ponzi scheme; (vi) excessive executive remuneration that in numerous cases has in effect rewarded management failure, e.g., in the case of the failed investment banks and the giant insurer AIG; (vii) the unconstrained and unwarranted growth of the financial sector ('Wall Street') ultimately to the detriment of, rather than in the service of, the productive business sectors ('Main Street'); (viii) the growth of unsustainable debt by governments and, indeed, whole economies (e.g., the US overseas debt accumulated in 2006 alone was $850 billion); (ix) excessively loose monetary policy by central banks; and (x) the negligence and/or ideologically based complicity of legislators and regulators regarding all of the above.

Moreover, if the GFC has entered a dangerous second phase, it was preceded by a number of preliminary phases, each of which was prescient in various ways. One such phase was marked by the collapse of the US corporation Enron in 2001. This had a devastating effect on shareholders and employees.[3] In its wake came the revelations of a litany of unethical practices, including conflicts of interests, e.g., that of CFO Andrew Fastow, auditing failures, corrupt (if not necessarily unlawful) practices such as the creation of so-called special purpose entities (SPEs) calculated to mislead shareholders in relation to actual performance, etc.[4] Moreover, the Enron collapse was only one of a number of corporate corruption scandals during that period, including WorldCom and the giant accounting firm Arthur Andersen.

The corporate collapses and corruption scandals of the late 1990s and early 2000s in the US, Australia and elsewhere, and now those of 2008 and since, appear to be part of a recurring cycle.[5] Recall the corporate scandals of the 1980s in the US and elsewhere.[6] This period was notable for a stock market crash, a junk bond collapse, the bankruptcy of numerous highly-leveraged clients, the prevalence of the unlawful practice of insider trading, and the fining and imprisonment of the likes of Michael Milken and Ivan Boesky. Milken paid fines in excess of $600 million, Boesky over $100 million.[7] Viewed from the perspective of ethics (or rather lack thereof), arguably the only difference between these earlier periods and the GFC is one of scale – admittedly, an extremely important difference – and the fact that the eye of the storm is the all-important financial sector.

Self-evidently, the GFC, whatever its final outcome, has already been extraordinarily damaging economically and has revealed significant deficiencies in the regulation of global financial markets in particular. However, the problem is surely wider and deeper than this. The fact that the global economy, or large fragments thereof, could have been and might still be brought to its knees by a massive speculative boom/bust is, I suggest, reflective of a set of institutional, including normative, problems in relation to the structure and *raison d'être* of the global financial system itself.

These problems evidently exist at all three fundamental institutional dimensions, namely: (1) *structure*, e.g., the global financial and economic regulatory 'system' (such as it is); (2) *culture*, e.g., predatory and reckless lending, profligate public borrowing and spending, regulatory negligence; and (3) *purpose*, e.g., governmental and regulatory negligence in ensuring that the 'invisible hand' mechanisms of competitive markets actually do their job of serving the greater, long-term *collective interests* of local, national and global communities (rather than the immediate, financial interests of powerful, individual market actors).

The problems can be thought of as existing at two levels. At one level there are problems of regulation or, more broadly, integrity. The system is more or less adequate in its fundamentals, it might be suggested; however, various institutions and actors have been allowed to engage in unethical, incompetent and/or unlawful behaviour and the relevant regulatory and integrity systems need to be revisited and renovated. Unquestionably, the relevant regulatory and integrity systems have been found to be inadequate.

A number of regulatory gaps have been identified, e.g., innovative financial products, the so-called 'shadow banking system' of non-depository banks,[8] the hedge fund industry[9] and private equity firms. In some cases there is arguably under-regulation by virtue of, e.g., inadequate capital-holding requirements for some kinds of banking institutions or the absence of disclosure requirements for various kinds of business and financial institutions. In other cases there is a need to revisit the regulation of specific ethical problems, e.g., conflicts of interest and perverse incentive structures.

Other identified regulatory inadequacies include complexity, inconsistency and a lack of coordination between regulators.

The President of the Federal Reserve Bank of New York has conceded that the US regulatory system 'has evolved into a confusing mix of diffused accountability, regulatory competition, an enormously complex web of rules that create perverse incentives and leave huge opportunities for arbitrage and evasion, and creates the risk of large gaps in our knowledge and authority'.[10] Moreover, the allegedly superior responsive principle-based regulatory regime in the UK has proved to be equally inadequate.[11]

In the case of the global financial sector, regulation and integrity assurance are ultimately in the hands of national governments; this goes for the regulation of financial products and securitisation processes as well as other elements of the sector. However, national governments – and their regulatory authorities – are not simply umpires, they are also players in the financial and, more generally, corporate 'game'. For example, the UK government – and its financial regulator, the Financial Services Authority – cannot be expected to regulate entirely impartially in the interests of ethical ends and principles, given the substantial interest the UK government has in ensuring that the UK corporate and financial sector retains and increases the benefits accruing to it from global financial markets. Thus, there is a need to address the issue of impartiality in the design of the global regulatory system.[12]

So-called integrity systems are arguably the primary institutional vehicle available to reduce ethical misconduct, to combat crime and corruption and to promote institutional virtues. Integrity systems include aspects of legal or regulatory systems, but they are not to be identified with these. Integrity systems include both reactive mechanisms, e.g., police agencies, corporate fraud investigation units, and preventative means, e.g., ethics education and the elimination of perverse incentives. Integrity systems exist at the organisational, professional and industry levels, and also at the national and global levels.

Important as they are, regulatory and integrity systems are, to an extent, derivative. For the design and implementation of regulatory and integrity systems presupposes that the underlying structure and purposes of the institutions in question, be they market institutions or other sorts of institutions, are both well understood and, at least in their fundamentals, more or less as they should be. If this is not the case, then more and/or different regulations and integrity mechanisms are not in themselves going to solve the problems; rather, they must wait on the solution to the underlying problems of institutional structure and purpose.

However, it is precisely this question of the fundamental structure and purpose of the global financial system that is in question. Is, for example, the tail (Wall Street) wagging the dog (Main Street)? What legitimate economic purposes are served by the huge volume of investment in complex financial products, hedge funds, private equity and the like? Has the density of global financial interdependence – and the sheer size of the global economy of which it is an integral part – completely outrun the capacity of current governmental and regulatory authorities to impose the necessary order on it?

Here I note the role of academic disciplines in the provision of economic self-understanding and, therefore, in policy-making in relation to economic and financial markets and their integrity systems. Economics ought not to be the only discipline contributing here; obviously, law and regulation, for example, need to contribute. In addition, normative theorising has, I suggest, an important role to play and, in particular, empirically informed philosophical ethics.

Moreover, classical economics and its favoured rational choice model of decision-making is evidently only a part of the story, even within the narrowly economic dimension. In speculative booms and busts, individual investors can evidently behave rationally as individuals (at least to the extent that they enter at lows and exit at highs) but irrationally as collectives (busts cause great harm and speculative booms inflate monetary values and lead to busts). The individualistic, rationalist choice model of standard economics is not well suited to model this kind of collective behaviour and thus to assist in the design of counter-cyclical and other measures to curb it. Behavioural macroeconomics seeks to refine our understanding of the discipline by accounting for relevant features of human behaviour that are absent in the standard economics framework; the basis for analysis are empirically well-documented psychological and psychosociological factors such as cognitive bias, herding and social status. Notice that these factors have an implicit or explicit normative or ethical aspect and in some cases constitute so-called epistemic vices (e.g., cognitive bias) and virtues (e.g., informed decision-making, behaviourally evidenced in the avoidance of opaque financial instruments). The research and policy challenge is to design and implement elements of a triangular, mutually-reinforcing nexus between the counter-cyclical economic policies, the incentivisation of epistemic virtues in investors and the actual (or probable) economic performance of firms.

At any rate, in this chapter I explore the fundamental underlying normative dimension of the global financial system – its philosophical roots, if you will.

In the next section I sketch a normative theoretical account of social institutions, and in the third and final section, in light of my accounts of social institutions, I identify and interpret some of the ethical problems confronting the corporate sector in general and the financial services sector in particular from this theoretical perspective.

Market institutions: a teleological normative account

In this section I argue that the basic normative question that needs to be asked of a business corporation or financial market is the same as for any other social institution, namely for what collective good(s) does it exist to provide? I further argue that, normatively speaking, social institutions, including business corporations and markets, exist for ultimate – and not merely proximate – purposes or ends, namely to provide collective goods, e.g., material goods and the coordination of buyers and sellers of material goods.[13] Here Adam Smith's invisible hand mechanism is salient. The outcome of the workings of the invisible hand is the ultimate purpose of this institutional mechanism; the pursuit of financial gain, the proximate end.

But we are getting ahead of ourselves. Our first task is the provision of a viable account of social institutions. In fact, the term 'social institution' is somewhat unclear both in ordinary language and in the philosophical literature. However, contemporary sociology is rather more consistent in its use of the term. Typically, contemporary sociologists use the term to refer to complex social forms that reproduce themselves, such as governments, universities, hospitals, business corporations, markets and legal systems. A typical definition is that proffered by Jonathan Turner: 'a complex of positions, roles, norms and values lodged in particular types of social structures and organising relatively stable patterns of human activity with respect to fundamental problems in producing life-sustaining viable societal structures within a given environment'.[14]

Social institutions need to be distinguished from less complex social forms such as conventions, social norms, roles and rituals. The latter are among the constitutive elements of institutions.[15]

Social institutions also need to be distinguished from more complex and more complete social entities, such as societies, polities or cultures, of which any given institution is typically a constitutive element. A society or polity, for example, is more complete than an institution since a society – at least as traditionally understood – is more or less self-sufficient in terms of human resources, whereas an institution is not.

Social institutions are often organisations. Moreover, many institutions are *systems* of organisations. For example, capitalism is a particular kind of economic institution, and in modern times capitalism consists in large part of specific organisational forms – including multinational corporations – organised into a system. Further, some institutions are *meta-institutions*; they are institutions (organisations) that organise other institutions (including systems of organisations). For example, governments are meta-institutions. The institutional end or function of a government consists in large part of organising other institutions (both individually and collectively); thus, governments regulate and coordinate economic systems largely by way of (enforceable) legislation. Note that in the modern world many global social institutions transcend in various respects the boundaries and jurisdictional and/or enforcement reach of the meta-institutions (e.g., governments) that regulate and coordinate their activities. Consider here the recently re-emerged jurisdictional problems associated with holding Union Carbide to account in respect of the Bhopal Gas Disaster of 1984 in which thousands of nearby slum dwellers lost their lives and over 100,000 suffered permanent, severe ill health as a consequence of inadequate safety measures at Union Carbide's plant.[16]

Having informally marked off social institutions from other social forms, let us turn to a consideration of some general properties of social institutions. Here there are four salient properties, namely, structure, function, culture and sanctions.

Roughly speaking, an institution that is an organisation or system of organisations consists of an embodied (occupied by human persons) structure of differentiated roles. These roles are defined in terms of tasks and rules regulating the performance of those tasks.

Importantly, these roles are related to one another in part by virtue of their contribution to (respectively) the *end*(s) or *function(s)* of the institution, and the realisation of these ends or functions normally involves interaction between the institutional actors in question and external actors. These ends or functions are diverse. An overarching end of the criminal justice system, for example, is the administration of justice, and a particular end of the professional role of an auditor is the provision of true and fair financial records.[17]

The constitutive roles of an institution and their relations to one another can be referred to as the *structure* of the institution.

Aside from the formal and usually explicitly stated, or defined, tasks and rules, there is an important implicit and informal dimension of an institution roughly describable as institutional *culture*. This notion comprises the informal attitudes, values, norms and the ethos or 'spirit' which pervades an institution. Culture in this sense determines much of the activity of the members of that institution, or at least the manner in which that activity is undertaken. So, while the explicitly determined rules and tasks might say nothing about bending or breaking the rules – or even forbid such activity – or about being driven by the need to generate favourable quarterly reports, these attitudes and practices might in fact be pervasive; they might be part of the culture (as appears in fact to have been the case at Enron, for example).

In addition to structure, function and culture, social institutions necessarily involve sanctions of various kinds. Social institutions involve *informal* sanctions, such as moral disapproval following on non-conformity to institutional norms. However, formal sanctions, such as punishment, are also a feature of institutions.[18]

The normative character of social institutions includes the collective goods that they produce, the moral constraints on their activities and a variety of *institutional* moral rights and duties (as opposed to moral rights and duties that are logically prior to institutions, i.e., natural rights and duties). Such institutional moral rights and duties include ones that are derived from institutionally produced collective goods and, indeed, that are constitutive of specific institutional roles, e.g., the rights and duties of a fire officer or a banker. They also include more broad-based institutional (moral) rights and duties that are dependent on community-wide institutional arrangements, e.g., the duty to obey the law in the jurisdiction in which one resides, the duty to assist the national defence effort of one's country in time of war, the right of access to paid employment in an economy in which one participates, the right to own land in some territory, and the right to freely buy and sell goods in an economy in which one participates.

These moral rights and duties are institutionally relative in the following sense. Even if they are in part based on an institutionally prior human right (e.g., a basic human need, the right to freedom), their precise content, strength, context of application (e.g., jurisdiction, national territory, particular economy) and so on can only be determined by reference to the institutional arrangements in which they exist and, specifically, in the light of their contribution to the collective good(s) provided by those institutional arrangements.

On my teleological account of social institutions, collective ends are collective goods by virtue of their possession of the following three properties: (1) they are produced, maintained or renewed by means of the *joint activity* of members of organisations, e.g., schools, hospitals, welfare organisations, agribusinesses, electricity providers and police services (i.e., by institutional role occupants); (2) they are *available to the whole community*, e.g., clean drinking water, a clean environment, basic foodstuffs, electricity, banking services, education, health, safety and security, and; (3) they *ought* to be produced (or maintained or renewed) and made available to the whole community since they are desirable (as opposed to merely desired) and such that the members of the community have an *(institutional) joint moral right* to them.

Note that my notion of a collective good, as defined, is different from standard notions of so-called public goods deployed by economists and others. Economists typically define public goods as being non-rival and non-excludable. If a good is non-rival, then my enjoyment of it does not prevent or diminish the possibility of your enjoyment of it, e.g., a street sign is non-rival since my using it to find my way has no effect on you likewise using it. Again, a good is non-excludable if it is such that if anyone is enjoying the good, then no one can be prevented from enjoying it, e.g., national defence. However, my notion of a collective good is defined not in terms of non-rivalness or non-excludability, but in terms of its being jointly produced and having an explicitly normative character as the object of a joint moral right.

An important underlying assumption here is that *contra* much economic theory, human beings are not always and everywhere motivated by self-interest, albeit that self-interest is a powerful and pervasive driver; moral beliefs and, specifically, doing one's moral duty for its own sake – as the German philosopher Immanuel Kant stressed – are an important additional motivation for action, and one not reducible to self-interest (no matter how self-interest is conceived, e.g., self-centeredness and the pursuit of one's own goals, whatever they might be, at the expense of the goals of others).[19] So, institutional design needs to proceed on the assumption that both self-interest and morality are important motivations for human action, neither of which necessarily dominates the other when they come into conflict, as they often do.

On my teleological, normative account (roughly speaking) the university has as its fundamental collective end the acquisition, transmission and dissemination of knowledge, whereas police organisations have as their fundamental collective end the protection of the human and other moral rights (including institutional moral rights) of the members of the community. Again, the traditional professions have a range of specific collective ends, e.g., the administration of justice (lawyers). The collective end of each of these institutions is a collective good: a jointly produced good that is, and ought to be, produced and made available to the whole community since it is a desirable good and one to which the members of the community have a joint moral right.

By contrast with these social institutions, business corporations and markets in general do not have ethico-normative purposes (collective goods in the above sense) that are *internal* to them. Rather, they should be understood in instrumentalist terms, e.g., as an institutional means for the production of desired (but not necessarily desirable) goods. Accordingly, a business organisation in a competitive market is not deficient *qua* institution merely because it produces candy rather than basic foodstuffs; obviously, many business organisations operating in competitive markets produce material goods and services that are desired but are not needed or otherwise desirable – and they should continue to do so. Nevertheless, there are moral and other value-driven purposes that should give direction to the design and operation of at least some markets and business organisations. Specifically, there are collective goods, e.g., aggregated needs-based rights to basic foodstuffs, clean water, clean air, clothing, housing, medicines, etc., that markets and business organisations ought to produce as a matter of priority.

In addition, business organisations operating in competitive markets – including organisations that only produce desired (as opposed to desirable) goods – provide jobs; in doing so they fulfil a moral right, namely the right to paid work. In contemporary societies there is a (derived) moral right (and a corresponding moral obligation) to work for a wage, i.e., a right to a job (some job or other), since (other things being equal) without a job one cannot provide for one's basic needs and one cannot contribute to the production, maintenance and renewal of collective goods, e.g., via taxes. In short, while business organisations in competitive markets *per se* do not serve inherently valuable collective ends that are internal to them, they do have enormous instrumental value. Accordingly, they are available to serve value-driven purposes, including moral, purposes, and should be made to do so by way of regulation, incentive structures, etc., as required.

In the case of market-based organisations, we need to note the existence of a distinctive kind of collective end, namely profit maximisation (or at least the making of a profit in the financial sense). The existence of profit maximisation adds a complication in the case of market-based organisations that is not present in the case of other social institutions. In the case of market-based organisations, but not necessarily other social institutions, there are *three* collective ends, namely: the constitutive collective end, e.g., the production of cars; the collective good, e.g., transport; and, thirdly, profit maximisation. Moreover, while this third collective end is not a collective good, it is undoubtedly desired, namely by the owners; indeed, it is in the collective self-interest of owners to maximise profit. So, profit maximisation is a collective end to which the constitutive collective end is a means, e.g., cars are produced and sold for profit.

Accordingly, there are now two potentially competing collective ends, namely collective goods and profit maximisation. However, as is well known, a solution of sorts has been offered to this problem, namely the so-called invisible hand. The claim is that the single-minded and self-interested pursuit of profit will, as a matter of contingent fact, maximise collective benefits (on some construal of collective benefits, e.g., utilitarianism). Relativised to my account of social institutions, the claim is that the pursuit of the collective end of profit maximisation as an end will, as a matter of contingent fact, realise the collective good definitive of the social institution in question.

Unfortunately, the empirical claim upon which the efficacy of the invisible hand is predicated is contestable and, in some cases, evidently false. At any rate, the normative principle which my account of social institutions compels me to advance is that profit maximisation is, or ought to be regarded, simply as a *means* to the realisation of collective goods; so, profit maximisation is only a proximate end, while the realisation of collective goods is an ultimate end.

More generally, business organisations operating in competitive markets *per se* ought to be viewed instrumentally, i.e., as the means to realise collective goods. Note that in many cases these collective goods are indirectly produced; in particular, the aggregated right to work for pay is a collective good that is indirectly produced by market-based businesses (as indeed it is by public sector institutions).

The fact that business institutions have the self-interested pursuit of profit maximisation as an end is both an opportunity and a potential source of problems. On the one hand, it enables business institutions to be used instrumentally in relation to a wide range of ends, and not only desired ends but also desirable ends, e.g., private schools and universities, private hospitals and private security firms. Here we will need to distinguish between the proximate end of the business and its ultimate end. Thus, the proximate end of a private hospital might be the profit it earns for its owners. However, the ultimate end would be the provision of health services to the needy.

On the other hand, being mere institutional instruments, market-based organisations *per se* can easily be used to serve harmful purposes, e.g., corporations that produce and distribute tobacco or armaments.

It is also important to stress that business organisations operating in competitive markets cannot necessarily be expected to adequately achieve the larger (indirect) purpose that justifies their existence, i.e., the production of a collective good, by simply being left alone; there is a need for incentivisation, regulation, accountability and, where appropriate, institutional redesign in order to ensure that Adam

Smith's famous invisible hand actually delivers on its promises. If the current global financial crisis has demonstrated nothing else about free markets, it has surely demonstrated this.

The teleological account of social institutions, including market-based organisations and systems of organisations, emphasises collective goods. But what of moral rights and duties?

As already noted, here we need to focus on institutional moral rights as opposed to natural rights. There are at least two species of institutional (moral) rights. There are *individual* institutional (moral) rights and there are *joint* (institutional) moral rights. Joint moral rights are moral rights that attach to individual persons, but do so jointly. For example, in the context of the social institution of property rights, the joint owners of a piece of land might have a joint right to exclude would-be trespassers, and one single owner of a piece of land might have a right to exclude would-be trespassers, but only on condition that another single owner of a second piece of land likewise had such a right of exclusion.

Joint rights need to be distinguished from universal individual human or natural rights (as opposed to individual *institutional* rights). The right to life is an example of a universal individual human right. Each human being has an individual human right to life. However, since one's possession of the right to life is wholly dependent on properties one possesses as an individual, it is not the case that one's possession of the right to life is dependent on someone else's possession of that right.

As we have seen, sometimes the end realised in joint action is not merely a collective end, it is also a collective *good* (by *collective good* I simply mean that the good is collectively or jointly produced; I don't mean to imply that it is collectively or jointly consumed – it might be, and often is, individually consumed). If so, then a joint right may well be generated. What is the relationship between joint moral rights and collective goods? The good is a realised collective end, and the participants in realising that collective end, i.e., the contributors to the production of that good, possess a joint right to this collective good.

It is easy to see why these persons, and not some other persons, would have a right to such a good; they are the ones responsible for its existence or continued existence. In this connection consider the shareholders, members of the board of directors, managers and workers (shareholders, officers and employees) in a factory that produces cars that are sold for profit. Board members, managers, shareholders and workers in the factory have a joint right to be remunerated from the sales of the cars that they have jointly produced. It is also clear that if one participating agent has a right to the good, then – all other things being equal – so do the others. That is, there is an interdependence of rights with respect to the good.

Now notice that the board members, managers, shareholders and workers – and indeed the car company itself – depend for their skills, knowledge, security and transport on other social institutions, including educational and policing institutions, legal and political institutions, transport and communication infrastructure, etc. Accordingly, the moral rights to the collective goods produced by the car company include rights that attach to members of the wider society; this moral fact is reflected in tax regimes, including corporate tax, albeit often inadequately. Evidently, many corporations often pay less tax than is fair or reasonable by virtue of 'creative accounting' and/or their ability to exploit offshore tax havens, e.g., in poor countries desperate to attract investment.

Notice further that these joint moral rights are not equivalent to, or reducible to, moral rights based on legal contracts. A contract might or might not reflect a person's contribution to the production of a collective good, depending on a host of contingencies (notably relationships of power). Consider in this connection the extraordinarily generous executive compensation packages on offer in some corporations.

As argued above, social institutions are in part defined in terms of their collective ends. Moreover, as we have just seen, when such collective ends are also collective goods, this gives rise to joint moral rights to those goods. That is, 'functional' properties (collective ends) give rise to deontic properties (joint rights) under certain conditions – especially the condition that the collective end in question is also a good.

Let us now give more detailed attention to the moral duties or obligations that attach to institutional roles and the sources of such institutional obligations. Obligations, like rights, are deontic properties. In our above example of a factory, workers and managers obviously have duties, including moral duties that go hand in hand with their rights, e.g., a worker's moral duty to do a reasonable day's work or a manager's (director's) fiduciary duties to shareholders to not recklessly to put their money at risk. But shareholders also have duties and responsibilities, and not simply rights. For example, they have responsibilities not to invest their money in corporations that are generating profits not by virtue of a superior economic performance, but by bribing public officials to gain lucrative contracts.

Just as is the case with rights, the obligations attached to institutional roles flow in part from the purposes or ends of the institution. Moreover, the purposes or ends of the institution themselves derive – ultimately – from social needs (and not simply aggregated individual desires).

Consider the individual human and society-wide needs for adequate food, clothing, shelter, health, etc. No single member of a social group could provide for any of these needs, but if they act jointly, they can do so. However, needs, as opposed to desires, generate moral obligations, so the various needs of social groups that can only be adequately met by the joint action of members of the same or other groups generate collective responsibilities on the part of these groups to jointly so act. Moreover, where such collective responsibilities can most effectively be discharged by establishing institutions and institutional roles whose institutional duties consist of providing for these needs, e.g., the agricultural, clothing, building and pharmaceutical industries (and associated institutional roles), then members of the social group who have the collective responsibility have a derivative responsibility to establish such institutions and to see to it that they realise their institutional purposes, e.g., governments have a responsibility (where required) to establish such institutions and to regulate such institutions (once they are established) to ensure that they are realising their institutional purposes.

When institutions and their constitutive roles have been established on some adequate moral basis, such as, say, the social need for adequate housing or (derivatively) the need for housing loans, those who undertake these roles necessarily put themselves under obligations of various kinds – obligations that attach to, and are in part constitutive of, those roles.

Let us now turn briefly to some competing accounts of business corporations and markets and, in particular, to the so-called shareholder view (associated with Milton Friedman)[20] and the influential stakeholder view.

According to the shareholder view, by virtue of a contractual agreement, managers stand in a principal-agent relationship to owners (the shareholders) and their primary responsibility is to their shareholders, which is the responsibility to maximise profit. The only other relevant obligations are the so-called minimal moral requirements,[21] the most important of which are those enshrined in the law (e.g., the obligation not to commit assault). Here there are three moral notions at work: (1) the right to private property (of the owners); (2) contractual obligations of the managers to function as the agents of the owners in a principal-agent relationship (the manager as the instrument of the owner); and (3) minimal moral requirements.

The first thing to notice about this theory is the stringency it accords to the right to private property. Specifically, the moral right to property in this theory is such that it overrides aggregated needs-based rights and other collective goods. However, property rights are, I suggest, based in part on needs-based rights; property regimes are established in large part to ensure that material needs are met. To this extent needs-based rights are available to override property rights and, specifically, the transfer rights of property owners whose own needs are well catered for. Moreover, transfer rights – the right that the owner of property has to transfer the right to use, exclude and in turn transfer the good in question to others – are a very weak link in the argumentative chain. From the fact that I might have certain use and exclusion rights to something because I produced it – or otherwise 'mixed my labour with it' (to use John Locke's famous phrase) – it simply does not follow that I have the right to transfer all those rights to someone else or that, if I do, the transferred rights have the same strength as they had when they attached to me as the producer of the good in question.

The second thing to notice is the stringency it accords to the manager's moral responsibility to shareholders deriving from the contract-based principal-agency relationship between owners and managers. However, managers have a range of moral responsibilities that potentially conflict with and override their responsibilities to shareholders. They have moral responsibilities to their workers (e.g., duties of care) and to the wider community (e.g., not to pollute the environment). These responsibilities are not necessarily reflected in the law and, even if they are, they may well be prior to any such legal obligations. The massive – and, at the time of writing, ongoing – oil spill in the Gulf of Mexico dramatically exemplifies a failure on the part of BP to adequately discharge its responsibilities to each of these groups: workers (who died on the rig), shareholders (who have seen the value of their BP shares collapse) and the communities whose environs and livelihoods have been destroyed.

Moreover, it is far from obvious that all or most of these moral responsibilities can be regarded as minimal in the required sense. If minimal moral obligations are limited to so-called negative rights – as many libertarians believe they should be – then problems arise from the fact that many of the obligations of managers in question evidently derive from positive rights, e.g., a manager's duty of care to one of his or her workers under severe stress. On the other hand, if minimal moral obligations are not limited by some such principle, then we lose purchase on the sense in which they are minimal.[22]

The third point to be made is that the naïve version of the shareholder theory (call it market fundamentalism)[23] fails to address what I take to be the fundamental normative questions at issue here, namely should the institution in question (the modern limited liability business corporation) exist and, if so, what should its nature and purpose be? Obviously, individual shareholders, managers, workers, suppliers, customers and others individually freely (let us assume) participate in their various ways in business corporations. However, their free participation in an existing institutional arrangement is only one part of the normative story. For the corporation is a legally established entity with a certain structure (and presumably purpose) and its activities are governed by an array of regulations. This raises a number of fundamental normative questions at the institutional level. Should corporations be subject to the current specific set of regulations rather than some other competing set? Should the limited liability corporation have its current structure rather than some alternative structure? Should the limited liability corporation continue to exist in any shape or form?

These normative questions are not adequately answered by pointing out that various participants have individually freely entered into contracts with one another *within* the institutional and legally binding framework that is the corporation or system of corporations. For one thing, this framework rather than some alternative one is an enforced framework established by a non-consensual collective decision-making process. For another thing, even if not enforced but rather consensually chosen, consent is not the only yardstick to determine the moral legitimacy of institutional arrangements and is by no means necessarily the overriding one.

A response to this might be that the shareholder theory is committed to the invisible hand mechanism and that therefore the claim is that when managers act only to maximise profit, they thereby optimise overall economic and associated social benefits – the latter being the moral purpose of business organisations and markets. This version of the shareholder theory does offer a normative institutional theory of sorts and one that is similar in certain respects to the teleological normative theory. However, it differs in that, in place of relatively specific collective ends that are also collective goods, it posits the relatively vague and indeterminate notion of economically and socially beneficial consequences. Here I simply want to stress that this version of the shareholder theory is inconsistent with market fundamentalism, for in this version – at least in principle – markets should be heavily regulated or even jettisoned in their entirety if they are failing to deliver the economic and social benefits in question.

Let us now consider the so-called stakeholder view.[24] The so-called 'stakeholder theory' is not really a theory in the required sense; rather, first, it identifies an indeterminate set of groups with financial (and other?) interests in, or who might otherwise be affected by, corporations, e.g., shareholders, employees, customers, etc., and, second, it assumes that such 'stakeholders' ought to some extent or in some respects have their interests taken into account in decision-making by, or in relation to, the corporation. That is, stakeholder 'theory' gestures at an indeterminate set of moral claims that an unspecified list of 'stakeholders' might make in relation to corporations. However, such an indeterminate list and associated vague moral claims do not qualify as a theory; at best they constitute raw data that itself stands in need of normative theorising. Certainly, as we saw with the shareholder theory (in its naïve market fundamentalist version), the 'stakeholder theory' is no substitute for a normative theory of the nature and point of the corporation.

Global financial institutions and the GFC

Armed with the teleological normative account of social institutions elaborated in the section above, I now return to the ethical problems confronting global financial institutions identified in the first section of the chapter with a view to framing and interpreting them in the light of the teleological account.[25]

According to the teleological normative account, financial institutions are no different from any other social institution in respect of their collective ends; there is a need to identify a collective good that is the *raison d'être* for their existence. However, evidently in the case of the financial services sector in particular, the prior fundamental ethical question as to the ultimate institutional ends of this sector remains unanswered. Yet, without an answer to this question, governments, regulators and policy-makers cannot give rational direction to the financial services sector. They cannot, for example, determine whether or not the financial services sector is doing its job or whether it has become bloated and economically dysfunctional (as many commentators now claim). Moreover, an integrity system for the financial services sector – and a regulatory system insofar as it is concerned with institutional (ethical) integrity, as it surely must be – is also without direction; it does not know what ethical ends it is seeking to embed in its target institution, i.e., in the financial services sector.

In the light of the teleological normative account of social institutions, let us posit a purpose for corporate financial service providers in capital markets. Let us accept what is agreed on all sides to be the case, namely that they have as a purpose to maximise shareholder value. In accordance with the teleological normative account, let us assume that this is merely a proximate end or purpose and that these financial service providers have some further, indeed ultimate, purpose to which this proximate purpose is merely a means. Let us posit that this ultimate end is to make capital available at reduced costs to productive firms.[26] *Qua* ultimate institutional purpose, the provision of capital to productive firms at reduced costs gives direction to governments, regulators and policy-makers in their various roles, albeit that it can only usefully do so if it is further elaborated.

As noted above, market actors do not have an ethical purpose as their proximate end; rather, they have some commercial end, such as profit maximisation. The ultimate end is one provided for by the invisible hand. Market actors pursue (individual and collective) self-interest and – by virtue of the workings of the invisible hand – the material well-being of society is provided for. In this respect market actors are unlike, say, doctors or hospitals. The latter can reasonably be required to have the promotion of life and health at the forefront of their concerns, i.e., as their proximate as well as ultimate (professional and institutional) ends.

Economic self-interest, especially when linked to social status and power, is a powerful driver, and establishing markets in previously non-market economies and deregulating previously heavily regulated market economies have unleashed a great deal of hitherto dormant human energy. Moreover, the modern corporation as an institution and the development of global financial markets have enabled the mobilisation of vast capital sums in the service of this human energy (they have, of course, in turn relied heavily on scientific and technological developments). One only has to visit Shanghai today and remember what it was like 20 years ago to appreciate the power of market forces (especially government-assisted market forces).

However, from an ethical point of view, the *institutionally structured* self-interested orientation of market actors – including corporations – may well give rise to an immediate problem. How is this institutionally structured impetus and habit of pursuing economic self-interest to be contained within reasonable limits and channelled in appropriate directions? Presumably, this is in part to be achieved by means of some mix of self-regulation and external regulation. However, it is also predicated on the guiding ethico-conceptual frameworks (as opposed to prevailing ideologies) and related self-understandings of these market actors. At any rate, this brings us to a second set of problems.

It is one of the principal tasks of those who design and oversee the market system, including governments and – under the direction of governments – regulators, to ensure that the ultimate purposes of markets (and therefore market actors) are in fact achieved, i.e., to contain and channel the pursuit of economic self-interest. Perhaps there is a lack of clarity in the collective minds of governments and regulators in relation to their role in this regard. Some politicians, and many market actors, are market fundamentalists and, as such, talk as if the market was an intrinsic good, i.e., good in itself and independently of its outcomes in terms of human material well-being. But on the view elaborated above, markets need to be conceived in purely instrumentalist terms; they are simply a means to an (ultimate) end, even if this is not the end to be pursued by the market actors themselves.

Moreover, if one looks, for example, at the objectives of many regulators, one typically finds only limited aims (e.g., to reduce crime and protect consumers) and procedural concerns (e.g., to promote competition and efficiency).[27] There is little or no reference to what I have been referring to as the ultimate ends of markets, i.e., the outcome the invisible hand is supposed to bring about. Rather, the image of regulation is one in which regulators are umpires whose sole job is to impartially enforce the rules of the game. But in games, the pleasure of playing aside, there is only one end, namely winning, and this is an end pursued by the players not the umpires. But here the analogy between markets and games breaks down; markets, unlike games, have an end beyond 'winning'; they have ultimate, as opposed to proximate, ends. In the case of markets, 'winning', e.g., making a profit, is only a proximate end and, as such, a means to a further and larger purpose, namely the material well-being of society (both national and, in the case of international financial markets, global).

Further, there is the problem mentioned above of the ambiguous role of national governments and regulators when it comes to global markets, including global financial markets. National governments and their regulators are to some extent partisan and (understandably) seek to look after the economic interests of their own industries and businesses, including their financial service providers. Moreover, in the absence of a uniform set of global regulations and a single global regulator with real authority, regulators operating at a national level can be played off against one another by multinational corporations, i.e., there is regulatory arbitrage.

In the case of the global financial sector, regulation and integrity assurance are ultimately in the hands of national governments. However, as noted in the first section of this chapter, national governments – and their regulatory authorities – are not simply umpires, they are also players in the financial – and, more generally, corporate – 'game'.

As also noted in the first section of this chapter, another set of ethical problems pertains to the professions. Lawyers and accountants have important roles to play in the integrity systems of corporations, including financial service providers. However, the ethico-professional standing of many of these groups operating in the finance sector has been damaged. Thus, the status of auditors as independent professional adjudicators of, for example, financial health has been significantly compromised.[28] To this extent, an important element in the integrity system for corporations has been weakened.

There are various additional unethical practices, such as insider trading and conflicts of interest that derive in part from the decoupling of ultimate ethical purposes from the self-understanding of market actors, and also from the regulation of market actors by governments and their regulatory agencies. The unethical practices in question are not *mala in se*; they are not bad in themselves.

Consider insider trading. Insider trading is not bad in itself as, for example, murder is bad in itself. Rather, insider trading is only morally problematic in a particular institutional context. Now assume that one holds the view, putting it crudely, that markets exist only to further the self-interest of market actors, e.g., to maximise profit or return to shareholders. Why not, then, engage in some insider trading, given that it is in one's self-interest, i.e., it is financially very rewarding and it is not easily detected? A response to this might be that one should not do so because one is breaking the rules, indeed the law. But, unlike murder, insider trading is not morally wrong in itself. Compliance with the law is reinforced by strong moral sentiment, but equally compliance is reduced in the absence of strong moral sentiment, and so if the practice is not bad in itself, the following attitude may take hold – if one can get away with it, why not do it?

Perhaps fair competition is the ethical issue here. But competition in the corporate sector is inevitably unfair; appeals to fairness may (reasonably enough) carry little moral weight. Rather, the substantive moral objection to insider trading is presumably that if enough people practice it in the long run, then it undercuts the ultimate, not simply the proximate, ends of the corporate sector.[29] Without compliance with a set of rules or laws that promote competition, the market will not deliver the outcomes promised by the invisible hand. However, this ultimate purpose of markets is not at the forefront of the minds of market actors, preoccupied as they are and as they need to be with the proximate ends of generating profit or maximising shareholder value.[30] This is perhaps especially the case in the financial services sector. For this sector is arguably at a double remove from the ultimate purposes of the market as a whole; in accordance with the invisible hand, it seeks to provide finance to firms that in turn – and again in accordance with the invisible hand – generate the products actually required for the material well-being of the wider society. But if this ultimate purpose is lost sight of – in the self-understanding of market actors and in the policy-making of and regulation by governments and regulators – then perhaps insider trading is bound to be viewed by market actors as much less serious an ethical (as opposed to legal) offence than in reality it is.

Perverse incentives are a further feature of financial and other institutions that have not been designed to ensure that they are fit for purpose but have rather been allowed to evolve in accordance with the ideology of market fundamentalism. Competition, including competitive markets, can and does provide discipline to market actors. However, this is not necessarily or always the case. Consider the so-called tragedy of the commons in which everyone pursuing their self-interest destroys the environment. Again consider bribery. It might be the case that for most corporations in some sector, bribing officials is necessary in order to be competitive, given that even a small number of other corporations will engage in this practice. Compliance with a legally enforced ethical principle might be in a market actor's self-interest, but only if the enforcement mechanisms are such that everyone (or nearly everyone) complies. Similarly, there might be competitive pressure to invest in unethical corporations, given the highly lucrative returns and given that one's competitors are doing so. Again, when liability does not appropriately track ethical responsibility, this can lead to perverse incentives. For example, an incentive structure in which market actors are allowed, indeed encouraged, to take great financial risks with other people's money in order to achieve enormous financial benefits for themselves (and not simply for the investors and shareholders), yet can do so without commensurate legal and financial liability attaching to themselves in the event that things go wrong, is surely tailor-made for corruption. Accordingly, there is a need for institutional redesign of a kind that either decreases the potential financial benefits to such market actors, increases their liability or introduces some mixture of both.

More generally, the collective responsibilities of industries to realise their institutional purposes, including the collective responsibilities of financial service providers in capital markets, typically consist of highly dispersed individual responsibilities that attach to individual persons within firms, individual firms within the industry, institutions without the industry, and so on and so forth. For example, the collective responsibility to lower the cost of capital is not one that can be discharged by any one market actor or even a small group of market actors within a given capital market. Given the diffuse character of such collective responsibilities – and its attendant incentive structure – many industries, financial service providers included, will not discharge these collective responsibilities and, as a consequence, will not adequately realise their institutional purposes, hence the need (and resultant responsibility) on the part of governments in particular to intervene to adjust these incentive structures and, if necessary, to design-in appropriate institutions or sub-elements thereof.

Perverse incentive structures can be addressed by recourse to interventions that reconfigure the incentive structures.[31] Such interventions can take the form of solving jurisdictional problems in global settings and increasing enforcement options and/or the intensity of enforcement. Thus Joseph Stiglitz suggests that: 'Any country in which the corporation (or the substantial owners of the corporation) has assets should provide a venue in which suits can be brought or in which enforcement actions to ensure payment of liabilities can be undertaken. The corporation may incorporate where it wants, but this should not make it any less accountable for its actions in other jurisdictions.'[32] In addition, he suggests a global widening of the possibility of class action in relation to corporate price-fixing. While obviously of great importance, these jurisdictional and enforcement methods are not always sufficient. Other options are themselves market based, e.g., reducing supply of a product or service by factoring in real costs (and requiring that they be paid) or reducing demand for a product by high sales tax or limiting availability. Some of these options involve ambitious innovations to the market system itself, including the global financial system. For example, Stiglitz has proposed a radical extension of the concept of Special Drawing Rights to create a new global reserve currency that would help stabilise financial markets and also make reserves available for wealth-creation projects in impoverished countries, increasing literacy, reducing poverty-related diseases, addressing global warming and other 'ultimate' market ends.[33] Still other options are based on the importance of reputation to the self-interest of market actors, e.g., ethics reputational indices might be established to seek to draw attention to their unethical practices or orientations. Here, as elsewhere, it might be useful to recall the possible utility of the above-described triangle of virtue with its strategy of mobilising a set of interlocking ethical and self-interested motivations.

Let me conclude this chapter by briefly mentioning a set of ethical problems pertaining to education, ethos and ideology. If the prevailing ethos or culture of an organisation, and perhaps even the ideology of central elements of a sector, downplays ethical considerations in favour of self-interest, then it should hardly be a surprise when self-interest overrides compliance with ethical principles, even ones enshrined in the law. This is no doubt especially the case in the context of high temptation and opportunity on the one hand, and low risk of detection and conviction on the other hand, e.g., insider trading in some corporate settings. The point here is not that the majority of individuals themselves engage in corrupt or unethical practices, but rather that in certain cultural or ideological contexts they may well refrain from reporting or otherwise preventing a minority from doing so. Many key elements of integrity systems such as ethics codes, codes of practice, education programmes, etc. do not exist for the most part directly to prevent or deter the few people who are wrongdoers from doing wrong, but rather to ensure that the many are intolerant of the wrongdoing of the few. In this context it is perhaps worth pointing out that most fraudsters are detected and convicted as a consequence of the disclosures of their colleagues.

Notes

1. An earlier version of some of the material in this section appeared in Seumas Miller, 'Financial Service Providers, Reputation and the Virtuous Triangle', in I. MacNeil and J. O'Brien (eds), *The Future of Financial Regulation*, Oxford: Hart, 2010, pp. 387–400.
2. Paul Krugman, *The Return of Depression Economics and the Crisis of 2008*, New York: Norton & Co., 2009; Justin O'Brien, *Redesigning Financial Regulation*, Chichester: Wiley, 2007; and *Engineering a Financial Bloodbath*, London: Imperial College Press, 2009.
3. Peter C. Fusaro and Ross M. Miller, *What Went Wrong at Enron*, New York: John Wiley & Sons, 2002.
4. See Seumas Miller, 'Corruption', *Stanford Encyclopedia of Philosophy*, Winter 2005 for an account of corruption and its divergence (at times) from illegality.
5. Frank Clarke, Graeme Dean and Kyle Oliver argue as much in *Corporate Collapse: Accounting, Regulatory and Ethical Failure*, Cambridge University Press, 2003 (revised edition).
6. See, e.g., Trevor Sykes, *The Bold Riders*, Sydney: Allen & Unwin, 1984.

7. James B. Stewart, *Den of Thieves*, New York: Simon & Schuster, 1992, p. 20.

8. Krugman, *The Return of Depression Economics*, p. 160.

9. IOSCO, Report on Hedge Funds, 19/3/2009, www.iosco.org.

10. Timothy Geitner, 'The Current Financial Challenges: Policy and Regulatory Implications', Speech delivered at the Council on Foreign Relations Corporate Conference, New York, 6 March 2008.

11. A. Turner, 'A Regulatory Response to the Global Banking Crisis', London: Financial Service Authority, 2009, www.fsa.gov.uk.

12. Seumas Miller, 'Institutions, Integrity Systems and Market Actors', in J. O'Brien (ed.), *Private Equity, Corporate Governance and the Dynamics of Capital Market Regulation*, London: Imperial College of London Press, 2007.

13. For the developed version of the material in this section, see Seumas Miller, *The Moral Foundations of Social Institutions: A Philosophical Study*, New York: Cambridge University Press, 2010. Some of the material in this section is drawn from that volume.

14. Jonathan Turner, *The Institutional Order*, New York: Longman, 1997, p. 6.

15. The following teleological model of social institutions is elaborated in more detail in Seumas Miller, *Social Action: A Teleological Account*, Cambridge University Press, 2010. See also his 'Social Institutions', *Stanford Encylopedia of Philosophy*, Winter 2006.

16. Amnesty International, *Clouds of Injustice: Bhopal Disaster 20 Years On*, London: Amnesty International, 2004. While Bhopal was a case of negligence rather than intent to do harm, in terms of actual loss of life and damage to health, this was a much worse disaster than, e.g., 9/11, where 3,000 died in the attack on the Twin Towers. However, the response to the Bhopal disaster on the part of the US authorities was far from adequate and in June 2010 (25 years after the disaster) the India Supreme Court finally delivered its verdict convicting a handful of local managers of criminal negligence and handing out two-year jail sentences. The Chairman of Union Carbide at the time, Warren Anderson, who had been arrested by Indian police back in 1984 but had then somehow managed to leave India, was convicted of absconding but has evaded extradition and has otherwise escaped sanction.

17. This claim might be regarded as controversial. However, normatively speaking, it is difficult to see what the end of auditing could be if not to provide a true and fair record (see, e.g., Tom Campbell, 'True and Fair to Whom: A Philosophical Approach to Auditing', in Tom Campbell and Keith Houghton (eds), *Ethics and Auditing*, Canberra: ANU Press, 2005, Chapter 5). At any rate, if this is rejected as the normatively appropriate end or purpose of auditing, then let some other preferred purpose be substituted. Either way, my point in relation to institutional and occupational ends, purposes or functions will be unaffected.

18. Jon Elster, *Cement of Society*, Cambridge University Press, 1989, Chapter XV.

19. Amarty Sen, *Rationality and Freedom*, Cambridge, MA: Harvard University Press, 2002.
20. See, e.g., Milton Friedman, 'The Social Responsibility of Business to Increase its Profits', *New York Times Magazine*, 13 September 1970.
21. See, e.g., David Rodin, 'The Ownership Model of Business Ethics' (2005) *Metaphilosophy*, 36, 1–2, 163–81.
22. For further discussion of these issues, see ibid.
23. The term is used by George Soros in *The New Paradigm for Financial Markets: The Credit Crisis of 2008 and What it Means*, New York: Perseus Books, 2008.
24. Kenneth E. Goodpaster, 'Business Ethics and Stakeholder Analysis' (1991) *Business Ethics Quarterly*, 1, 53–71.
25. An earlier version of some of the material in this section appeared in Miller, 'Institutions, Integrity Systems and Market Actors'.
26. John Coffee suggests as much in a paper entitled 'Law and the Market: The Role of Enforcement', presented to a symposium held at the Australian National University in 2007.
27. The Australian Consumer and Competition Commission, for example, is concerned among other things with the traditional professions, but appears to place little or no focus on the distinctive ethical ends of the traditional professions, such as legal practitioners, as compared with other occupational groups. See Andrew Alexandra and Seumas Miller, *Professionalisation, Ethics and Integrity Systems: The Promotion of Professional Ethical Standards, and the Protection of Clients and Consumers*, Report for the Professional Standards Council of Australia, December 2006. Incidentally, I am not here necessarily blaming regulators; they can only carry out the tasks governments give them.
28. Clarke, Dean and Oliver, *Corporate Collapse*, p. 319.
29. In fact, some have argued that insider trading should not be a legal offence, since if it were allowed, it would not have harmful consequences.
30. On the other hand, I do not accept the proposition that market actors need not have any understanding or pay any heed to the larger ultimate purposes of markets. The latter attitudes on the part of market actors can lead to an attitude of, for example, breaking the law if one can get away with it.
31. See Susan Rose-Ackerman, *Corruption and Government: Causes, Consequences and Reform*, Cambridge University Press, 1999, for a variety of types of prescription, including adjusting incentive structures, in relation to corruption.
32. Joseph Stiglitz, *Making Globalization Work: The Next Steps to Global Justice*, London: Penguin, 2006, pp. 206–8. Stiglitz has other suggestions in this regard.
33. Ibid., Chapter 9.

3
The Legitimacy of the Financial System and State Capitalism

Noam Chomsky

The global financial crisis (GFC) is but one of several interlocking crises facing the world today. The direst in the short term is the food crisis, which has left a billion people facing severe malnourishment and even starvation. The United Nations World Food Program announced recently that it would slash food aid operations in places like Rwanda and Ethiopia because of the fiscal crisis, which has cut back the pledges of donor countries by an estimated 20–25 per cent. And this is at a time when food prices and unemployment are once again on the rise and remittances are declining. For years food crises have been seriously exacerbated by financial speculation, increasingly with the rapid growth of the financial sector and its shenanigans in recent times. The more severe crisis in the long term is environmental, which is also closely related to the financial crisis. A group of researchers at MIT recently released what has been described as the most comprehensive modelling of the environmental crisis to date. Their conclusions are shattering, suggesting that the situation is probably twice as dire as was predicted by the Stern Report, which is widely seen as the gold standard. These latest findings indicate that, unless immediate action is taken to address climate change, there won't be another crisis to talk about. We are caught in a predicament which cannot be dealt with simply through 'cap and trade', and while technological innovations are certainly critical, significant social changes are also required.

Unfortunately, institutional imperatives pose significant barriers to dealing with these crises. One is a well-known inefficiency of market systems: in a transaction, the participants consider their own interests, but not the effects on others: such 'externalities' are put to the side in competitive systems. A CEO who doesn't understand this is swiftly replaced by someone who does. In the case of financial institutions, one result is underpricing of risk: 'systemic risk' – the risk that a failed transaction will have harmful effects on the whole financial system – is ignored, insofar as market principles function unimpeded by regulation. After the current financial crisis erupted, a consensus developed among economists that it is foolhardy to ignore systemic risk. This is not a novel insight – there had been occasional warnings within the profession, among them an important book by John Eatwell and Lance Taylor, *Global Finance at Risk*, a decade ago. This market deficiency alone makes a financial crash a highly likely contingency, and the risk is amplified by the perverse incentives that follow from the influence of private power over the political system, among them the 'too big to fail' government insurance policy, but others as well. Much the same logic holds for the environmental crisis: in this case the fate of the species is an externality that corporate executives must dismiss in their necessary quest to maximise short-term gain, insofar as market systems prevail. Given the enormous power of concentrated capital in the political and doctrinal systems, overcoming such institutional barriers will be no easy matter.

The socialisation of losses: so what's new?

These interweaving crises are a function of what might be called the state-capitalist economic model. The fact that the advanced economy relies very heavily on the state sector is often overlooked. Throughout economic history, developed countries have always been characterised by a powerful state intervening dramatically in the market to the benefit of merchants, manufacturers, industrialists, agribusiness, etc. During the rapid growth period in the nineteenth century, for example, the US had far and away the highest tariffs in the world. This remained the case until the mid-twentieth century, when the US was so much in advance of every other country that it was willing to tolerate market exchanges. But even this came to an end. When US manufacturing started to fall behind that of Japan, Ronald Reagan practically doubled protectionist barriers, one of many examples of state intervention in the economy during the terms of the President crowned as the apostle of free markets by worshipful propaganda.

Protectionism is only the tip of the iceberg, of course – the part often studied by economists. But the modern economy is based very extensively on state-organised and -directed research and development, subsidy, procurement and bailout. The information technology revolution is an example – computers and the Internet, as well as biotechnology, do have and always have had a substantial state component. Computers were being developed in the lab where I worked back in the 1950s under Pentagon contracts. At the time they were far too big and clumsy to be marketable. In the early 1960s, IBM – which had been learning at public expense how to shift from punched cards to electronic computers – was able to manufacture a computer, but one that was too expensive to be introduced into the market. The government bought the product. It wasn't until around 1980 that computers became profitable. The same can be said for the Internet, which had been in the public sector for some 30 years before it was privatised. In earlier years the role of the state was far more extreme. Take cotton for example: the 'oil' of the early industrial revolution. The US became the leading producer thanks to the elimination of the indigenous population, slavery and conquest (including half of Mexico), rather serious market interventions. Throughout, the US radically violated the prescriptions addressed to the colonies by Adam Smith, essentially those of the contemporary Washington consensus. And the US benefited enormously by violating the rules, just as England had done before it, and others would do later.

One amusing example is the World Trade Organization's hosting of constant legal battles between the US and Europe over civilian aircraft production. The two major civilian aircraft producers in the world – Boeing and Airbus – fight it out over who gets the bigger government subsidy. One is subsidised directly, while the other receives its share via the airforce and aerospace programmes. Both receive so much public funding that they can properly be described as offshoots of the state sector. A decade ago I read a speech by Alan Greenspan to newspaper publishers extolling the magnificence of our free-enterprise system. He did something that most free-market enthusiasts do not do: he gave examples. Every one of these examples crucially involved research and development and procurement inside the state sector, often over a long period of time. What most of us take to be a capitalist system of entrepreneurial initiative and consumer choice is far from it.

It is interesting, then, that there is so much outrage today over the US government's recent interventions to rescue the financial industry when, in fact, the government has been intervening on the side of business all along and the public has always played the role of cash cow. The public pays the cost and takes the risk, and eventually – sometimes after many decades – profit is privatised. This is nothing fundamentally new and runs right through the economy (of course, there are no objections from the business world; only intervention for the benefit of the *public* causes a stir, whether it be in the form of interference with managerial prerogatives or the imposition of minimum wages and working conditions). The state's intervention on behalf of corporations remains largely concealed from the public. If it were exposed, it would undercut the argument against intervention in the public interest.

While the government bailout of sinking banks aroused much public anger, the government rescue of the banks involved many devices beyond direct bailout. Take Goldman Sachs, perhaps the leading beneficiary of public largesse. It had bet against the highly risky securities it created with credit default swaps issued by the insurance giant AIG. When AIG was facing bankruptcy, 'Goldman even got the government to pick up the bankrupt AIG's debts', economist Dean Baker observes, and thanks to government intervention, 'Goldman got paid every penny on its bets with AIG', amounting to $13 billion. The friendly Fed and Treasury also arranged for Goldman to borrow at very low rates to pay off creditors and invest handsomely. And there were other devices to ensure that the big banks would come out of the crisis they largely created even richer and more powerful than before, and handing out huge bonuses to those who know how to play the state capitalist game at the expense of the public.

Over the last 30 years the system which has governed financial institutions has come close to approximating a free market, and has crashed repeatedly, unlike the earlier decades of government regulation. But even after the shift to more of a market system, the government is and always has intervened crucially. Take the 'too big to fail' policy, essentially a government insurance policy, which creates a raft of perverse incentives. These encourage Citigroup and others to take huge risks without too much concern for the consequences. If they get into trouble, they can rest assured that the public will bail them out. It's not 'irrational exuberance', as Alan Greenspan once muttered during the tech boom of the 1990s; rather, it's quite rational, as long as the nanny state is firmly under control.

In this connection, it is important to bear in mind that bailing out a financial institution is not the only alternative to allowing its failure. A third alternative would involve the government simply buying these institutions. To buy Citigroup would have cost a fraction of what it costs to bail it out. But the decision on how best to respond to the crisis was made by a political system which is extensively dominated by the financial sector, and this third alternative would have interfered with managerial prerogatives. It is little surprise, then, that Wall Street is so exultant. The whole system is being reconstituted with almost no modifications.

In July 2010 the Dodd-Frank Wall Street Reform and Consumer Protection Act was passed into law. As the financial reform bills were working their way through Congress, the business press summarised their results: 'The bottom line: The financial reform bill imposes a raft of new rules, but critics say it does not go to the heart of the problems that created the crisis' (Christine Harper and Bradley Keoun, *Bloomberg Businessweek*, 1 July 2010). They quote Dean Baker, co-director of the Center for Economic & Policy Research in Washington and one of the very few professional economists who, early on, warned that the $8 trillion housing bubble was unsustainable and would cause a severe crash. He observes that the congressional legislation is 'largely a fig leaf': 'Given where we were when this got started, I'd have to imagine the Wall Street firms are pretty happy.' One illustration is the fate of the Volcker rule, named for former Fed chair Paul A. Volcker. 'Originally the rule would have prevented any systemically important bank holding company from engaging in proprietary trading, or betting with its own money, as well as investing its own capital in hedge funds or private equity funds', Harper and Keoun write. But it was so diluted in the conference proceedings, presumably under lobbyist pressure, that, according to William T. Winters, former co-chief executive officer of JP Morgan's investment bank, 'I don't think it will have any impact at all on most banks'. These seem fair assessments throughout.

Adam Smith – who we are expected to worship but not read – had the right comment about this. In *The Wealth of Nations*, Smith recognises that the 'principal architects' of policy in England – merchants and manufacturers – ensure that their own interests are attended to, however 'grievous' the impact on others, including the people of England. He had in mind the mercantilist system of his day, but the observation generalises. This is perfectly natural and to be expected. Today the principal architects of policy are no longer merchants and manufacturers, but multinational corporations and financial institutions. The latter account for about one-third of corporate profits, thanks to the financialisation of the economy since the 1970s. They also make massive campaign contributions at election time and expect to be paid back – and typically are. The first period following the Second World War was governed by the so-called Bretton Woods system, designed by John Maynard Keynes and Harry Dexter White. This system was based largely on the regulation of capital. Governments were given the power to control capital exports, currencies were more or less regulated, etc. Keynes and White anticipated that this would lead to rapid growth. And it did – rapid and quite egalitarian growth. They also recognised that this would leave an opening for governments to carry out social democratic programmes. But the financialisation of the economy and the corresponding hollowing out of the productive economy as production is shipped abroad, along with the removal of constraints on capital flight and speculation against currencies, created what some economists have called a dual constituency for governments. There is the voting public on the one hand and representatives of the international financial sector on the other. The way that the latter vote is simple: if the government introduces a policy which is not to their liking, they threaten the economy – by capital flight, by attacks on currencies, etc. This happens often: France under Mitterand in the early 1980s is one well-known case in a wealthy country, and there have been many others. To take a more recent example, when Hugo Chávez was inaugurated as President of Venezuela, capital flight escalated to the point where capital held abroad by wealthy Venezuelans equalled one-fifth of Venezuela's GDP, according to OECD economist Javier Santiso, who adds that after the US-backed military coup in 2002 that overthrew the elected government, 'the response of the markets approached euphoria' and the Caracas Exchange registered huge gains, collapsing when the government was restored by popular protests. That not only impeded social spending but also served as a warning to President Lula da Silva in Brazil to satisfy financial markets before seeking to carry out badly-needed social programmes. In a competition between these two sets of constituents, the financial institutions will quite commonly win.

State capitalism and democracy

The principal architects of policy can only be held accountable by an organised, active public. But in our modern democratic system, the public has been essentially atomised and marginalised. Again, none of this is by accident. It is quite purposeful. Opinion polls recently conducted in the US showed that 80 per cent of the public felt that the government was being run by 'a few big interests looking out for themselves', not for the public. The two major political parties are more or less the same – different factions of the business party. Elections are essentially bought and the public is disorganised. This is a serious democratic deficit, and a global one, but people everywhere are unfortunately convinced that nothing can be done.

However, there are some interesting exceptions. What I would regard as the most democratic country in the Western hemisphere – and possibly the world – is the poorest country in South America, namely Bolivia. In Bolivia the majority of the population, which is the most repressed population in the hemisphere, namely indigenous people, became active and organised, took control of resources, eventually entered the political arena and elected someone from within their own ranks. And they elected him on the basis of serious issues, such as cultural rights, justice and control over resources, rather than his body language, image or soaring rhetoric. This is a model of what democracy ought to be.

Admittedly, the difficulties associated with affecting change are reinforced by the fact that in every society, there are rewards for conformity and punishments for dissidence. This creates and fosters a natural tendency to conform – to take the easiest route. Academia is no exception. If I wanted to write an article about Iranian support for terror, I wouldn't even need a footnote or a reference. I could do it right now, without research, and everybody would cheer. But suppose I wanted to write an article about US support for terror. I would need documentation that meets the standards of physics, and even then I'd be bitterly denounced. When a young academic or reporter is faced with a choice, there's a strong tendency to take the former path.

The production of information and knowledge is therefore responsive to the demands of power. This is true of every society throughout history. In classical Greece the man forced to drink the hemlock was not the one supporting power, but the one who was charged with corrupting the youth of Athens and encouraging the worship of false gods. Take as another example the Hebrew Bible or Old Testament. There we find a category of people who we would call intellectuals, criticising the king and engaging in geopolitical analysis, calling for mercy towards widows and orphans. They are referred to as prophets – a bad translation of an obscure word. Were they treated nicely? No, they were imprisoned or driven into the desert. There was another category of people who centuries later were referred to as false prophets. They were the flatterers of the court and they did quite well.

This brings me to my next point about the role of the media in contemporary democracy. If one gains the impression that media treatments of economic affairs do not provide clarity and understanding as they should, this is entirely predictable. It must be remembered that the media are run by huge corporations, parts of even larger conglomerates. They rely for their income on advertising revenue from other businesses and they are also very closely linked to the power of the state.

The way forward

Despite all this, there is I think reason for optimism given recent developments which have put power in the service of the people rather than interest groups. The US, in many ways the freest country in the world, was founded on the principle – quoting James Madison, the main framer – that power should be in the hands of the *wealth* of the nation, the most responsible set of men who have sympathy for property owners and their rights. That is why the Senate was established as the most powerful component of the state system. It is comprised of those least accountable to the public – wealthy men – and the most powerful. Madison explicitly states that one major goal of the government is to protect the minority of the opulent from the majority. But over the centuries power has devolved, at least to some extent. In the 1920s women were allowed to vote. Technically, blacks were allowed to vote in the 1860s. But it was 100 years until it was formally allowed. Such progress was not given as a gift from above – it was achieved through struggle. That is why today the American system is no longer constructed exclusively on the Madisonian model.

Further progress is possible through coordination. The case of Latin America is instructive here. Ever since the Spanish and Portuguese conquests, Latin American countries have been split from one another and also split internally, with a very wealthy dominant sector and a huge mass of poverty. But this has been changing over the past couple of decades. The countries are beginning to integrate with the Union of South American Republics, the Bank of the South, etc. This kind of integration is a prerequisite for independence, acting as a safeguard against foreign conquest.

It is striking that Latin America failed to develop in the same way that East Asia did, even though it had many more natural advantages. But the economy was not controlled. Those who profited sent their capital off to London or Zurich. In East Asia, by contrast, there were controls. In South Korea, for example, capital export was banned and punishable by death during the country's development. The East Asian tigers imported capital goods. The wealthy, mostly Europeanised Latin American elites imported luxury goods. And there have been other distinctions tending in the same direction. Constraining the predatory character of state capitalism takes public pressure, which is precisely what created the New Deal. Many of the reforms were a government response to organisation and activism, sometimes reaching levels that led the business press to warn of the 'hazard facing industrialists in rising power of the masses'. Sit-down strikes were a particularly ominous threat – one step short of taking over production – but the same was true of much else.

At the international level, progress towards authentic independence and social reform in Latin America requires integration among countries. As would be expected, the traditional elites of Bolivia have been hostile towards the country's democratisation, launching an autonomy movement which became violent in September 2008. There was a meeting of the Union of South American Nations held in Santiago, Chile, which dealt with the internal crisis and issued its support for President Morales. Morales expressed his gratitude and noted that this was the first time since the European conquest that South America had taken its fate into its own hands without the interference of foreign powers. This is a model of how the United Nations ought to function.

In this connection there is no magic key. It takes education and organisation. I think that the World Social Forum is on the right track here. Every January there are two major economic meetings – the World Economic Forum in Davos, Switzerland, and the World Social Forum in Porto Alegre, Brazil, or some other country of the South. The first meeting is called 'Pro-Globalisation', while the latter is called 'Anti-Globalisation'. Here we have a telling example of how power controls terminology. The World Social Forum is very much pro-globalisation. Indeed, it is itself a model of globalisation, bringing together people from all over the world, from all walks of life: rights activists, professionals, workers, farmers, etc. What is opposed is globalisation which does not serve the interests of the people – unlike the meeting in Davos, where the concern is economic integration in the interests of powerful sectors, investors, etc. Our goal should be to take structures like the World Social Forum and its many offshoots, and the UN, and to make them work in the interests of people, not dominant sectors of power. There is nothing wrong with globalisation of this sort – as long as it serves, rather than damages, the interests of the majority of the population.

This will no doubt be a constant battle, involving regression and progress. Over time, however, I am optimistic that the tendency is towards progress: slow, difficult progress. Take the last US election as a prime example. Personally I did not like any of the candidates. However, it is quite striking that the Democrats had a black man and a woman contesting the primaries. Forty years ago this would have been absolutely unthinkable. In fact, 20 years ago it would have been unthinkable. Why is it happening? This, I believe, was a long-term effect of the activism of the 1960s, especially among young people. The activism was and still is bitterly denigrated, but it had a civilising effect on the country – and perhaps this is why it is denounced! It broke down barriers to women's rights and civil rights, raised awareness of environmental issues and mobilised opposition to aggression and war.

In 20 years' time, further developments are conceivable. The US government is today effectively dismantling the auto industry. At the same time, it has a stimulus package with funds set aside for alleviating the environmental crisis – such as building high-speed rail. The *Wall Street Journal* recently reported that the US Transportation Secretary was in Spain looking for a manufacturer of high-speed rail infrastructure. Yet the US government is dismantling its own industrial structure which can do exactly the same thing. In the financialised economy, the welfare of the population is not a relevant concern. What matters is how much profit can Wall Street make? One day the so-called stakeholders – the workforce and the community – might take over the industries and all this would change. As of right now, this is not on the radar. But it may not be far off.

4
Neoliberalism – Is This the End?

Ned Dobos

Introduction

The debate between laissez-faire free-marketeers and advocates of regulated or 'leashed' capitalism reached something of an intellectual stalemate in recent decades. In the public consciousness at least, this stalemate was broken by the recent global financial crisis. There have been intense calls for tighter government control over banks, mortgage originators, rating agencies, accounting, insurance and brokerage firms, and the financial services industry more generally. And there is a growing consensus that the alternatives to government regulation – 'market discipline', civil litigation, voluntary self-regulation by firms and industry associations – cannot be relied upon to deter unethical conduct and to protect us from the adverse consequences that free-market activity sometimes produces. Commenting on the crisis in September 2008, French President Nicolas Sarkozy announced that 'self-regulation as a way of solving all problems is finished. Laissez-faire is finished. The all-powerful market that always knows best is finished'.[1] In a similar vein, German Finance Minister Peer Steinbrück pointed the finger at neoliberal ideology, describing it as 'simplistic' and 'dangerous'.[2] Martin Wolf, chief economics writer at the *Financial Times* in London, declared that 'another ideological god has failed. The assumptions that ruled policy and politics over three decades suddenly look as outdated as revolutionary socialism'.[3] In the introduction to *Meltdown: The End of the Age of Greed*, Paul Mason gives us his upshot of the situation: 'Basically, neoliberalism is over; as an ideology, as an economic model. Get used to it and move on.'[4] Even

Francis Fukuyama, who not so long ago proclaimed *The End of History* with the triumph of free-market liberal democracy, has admitted that the crisis represents the end of Reaganism in the financial sector.[5]

Former Australian Prime Minister Kevin Rudd recently joined the chorus: 'The time has come, off the back of the current crisis, to proclaim that the great neo-liberal experiment of the past 30 years has failed, that the emperor has no clothes.'[6] Two unassailable truths have been vindicated by the crisis according to Rudd:

> that financial markets are not always self-correcting or self-regulating, and that government (nationally and internationally) can never abdicate responsibility for maintaining economic stability. These two truths in themselves destroy neo-liberalism's claim to any continuing ideological legitimacy, because they remove the foundations on which the entire neo-liberal system is constructed.[7]

But it is a mistake to think that neoliberalism stands or falls with free-market infallibility and the self-correcting hypothesis. The ideology is ultimately based on the judgment that government regulation of business is *morally objectionable*. Importantly, the argument which supports this position draws upon the resources of all three major theories of normative ethics and does not depend for its cogency on the premise that the 'hidden hand' consistently prevents all market failures and economic calamities. Whether neoliberalism has been stripped of its ideological legitimacy will hinge on whether the financial crisis has done enough to discredit the premises underpinning this moral argument.

What's wrong with regulation?

The idea that government regulation is immoral – and not simply a threat to economic efficiency and political integrity – is a central tenet of neoliberal ideology.[8] In this section I revisit the standard argument for why deregulation should be regarded as a moral imperative. As we shall see, the argument is pluralistic rather than monistic, invoking all three major theories of normative ethics. For some, regulation is objectionable because it stunts the growth of virtue or because its costs are excessive relative to its benefits. For others, the wrongness of regulation is independent of such contingencies; it unjustly infringes the rights and liberties of market actors, specifically their property rights, commercial autonomy and freedom of association.

Let us begin with the consequentialist prong, whose fundamental premise is that, all things considered, regulation does considerably more harm than good. As a cure for market failure, state intervention is said to be worse than the disease.[9] The point is perhaps best illustrated by way of examples. Consider mandatory safety tests for pharmaceuticals. We tend to focus on the intended beneficiaries of such restrictions – those spared the suffering associated with taking defective drugs. But what about those who suffer needlessly while waiting (sometimes many years) for a safe and effective drug to be approved by a government agency, even though there is not so much as prima facie evidence of dangerous side-effects?[10] What about those who die in the meantime? Or take minimum wage laws. The beneficiaries are easily identified; they are the ones taking home a fatter pay cheque. Those who fail to gain employment or lose their jobs – either because the minimum wage has made it unprofitable for anyone to hire them, or because the minimum wage has encouraged businesses to adjust their production techniques so as to become more reliant on technology and less on labour, or because the minimum wage has forced marginally profitable firms out of business – remain anonymous.

The same might be said for tariffs and other such government interventions in the economy. Import restrictions on steel are estimated to have saved nearly 17,000 jobs in the American steel industry, but the resulting higher steel prices led to a loss of 52,400 jobs in American steel-*using* industries as companies were forced to downsize in order to offset the increased production costs – a net loss of 35,400 jobs.[11] The consumer also suffers. To use a famous example, Ronald Reagan's efforts to protect jobs in the US auto industry with import restrictions increased the average price of Japanese cars imported to the US by $900 and increased the price of American cars by $350. Consumers consequently spent $4.3 million more on automobiles than they otherwise would have. Walter Williams does the maths:

> That comes to a cost of $160,000 per year for each job saved in Detroit ... From a national wealth point of view, we would have

benefited immensely simply by striking a deal with Detroit auto workers whereby we gave the workers, who would have been laid off in conditions of free trade, $60,000 a year so they could buy vacation residence in Miami. That way, collectively, we would have been better off to the tune of $100,000 per job saved.[12]

Finally there is the taxpayer – not the least of the invisible victims. Across the developed world, hundreds of regulatory agencies employ hundreds of thousands of workers at a cost of hundreds of billions in public funds.[13] These various costs are said to dwarf whatever social or economic harms regulation is supposed to prevent or remedy. Productivity declines, innovation stalls and the costs of compliance are distributed in a way that allows companies to continue to operate without loss of profit – prices are increased, workers are laid off, wages are frozen, fewer new jobs are created, etc.[14] Some customers are priced out of the market and some companies – particular smaller companies – are forced to close their doors. To add insult to injury, the taxpayer foots the bill. The only winners, according to free-market ideologue Milton Friedman:

> are the do-gooders responsible for this type of legislation and for these effects. They have the high-minded satisfaction of promoting a noble cause. The good intention is emblazoned forth for all to see. The harm is far less visible, much more indirect, much harder to connect with the good-hearted action.[15]

To make matters worse, there are said to be viable alternatives to regulation which achieve its objectives – the protection of consumers, investors, employees and the public – without the costs and constraints. A coercive regulatory regime might therefore be ruled out simply by virtue of being unnecessary. These alternatives come in the form of civil litigation, self-regulation, government certification and of course 'market discipline'.

Instead of forcing businesses to comply under the threat of punishment, the state might instead award its seal of approval to those that comply with its standards voluntarily. The compliant business can then put the certificate on display as a way of attracting customers. If subsequently found to be breaching the standards and conditions for which the certificate was awarded, the state's endorsement can accordingly be revoked, potentially hurting the company financially.[16] Alternatively, those caused harm can seek damages in court. The prospect of civil litigation can prove just as reliable a deterrent to misconduct as punishment for regulatory breach, which seldom takes the form of incarceration and is typically limited to a small fine.[17] This has several ethical advantages. First, those harmed receive compensation. Second, only those determined to have wrongfully caused harm through due process of law are punished, in contrast to regulation, which coerces and imposes burdens upon a whole class of people on the basis of the harms that they *might* cause (more on this later).

Furthermore, the market has its own ways of promoting responsible behaviour. A fast-food restaurant that allows customers to use the drive-thru on foot is tempting a collision between motorist and pedestrian. A restaurant that has a strict policy against serving pedestrians at the drive-thru window is for this reason likely to be offered more favourable insurance rates than its competitors. In this way the market can reward businesses that act responsibly and prudently, and punish those that do not.[18] Moreover, with ethical and responsible conduct eventually comes a reputation for it, which confers its own competitive advantage. Alan Greenspan, former chairman of the US Federal Reserve, made the point forcefully:

> Reputation, in an unregulated economy, is a major competitive tool. It requires years of consistently excellent performance to acquire a reputation and to establish it as a financial asset ... Thus the incentive to scrupulous performance operates on all levels. It is a built-in safeguard of the free-enterprise system.[19]

At this point one might interject that certification, civil law and market discipline may very well contribute to regulatory objectives, but this does not in itself give us any reason to oppose the government's efforts to coerce compliance with ethical and prudential standards. One might say that everything possible should be done to protect the public from harm, and that regulation should therefore be used in conjunction with the aforementioned methods to give consumers, investors and other stakeholders the greatest possible protection. Since market discipline does not always work like it should, and deserving litigants sometimes lose their cases or are under-compensated, why not introduce regulations to supplement the courts and market forces?

However, according to advocates of the laissez-faire model, using regulation to make up for the deficiencies of market discipline, civil litigation and the like is wrongheaded since regulation is among the chief causes of these shortcomings. In other words, the effectiveness of regulation's alternatives is said to be undermined by regulation. Greenspan is worth quoting again in this connection:

> Government regulation is not an alternative means of protecting the consumer. It does not build quality into goods, or accuracy into information. Its sole 'contribution' is to substitute force and fear for incentive as the 'protector' of the consumer ... What are the results? To paraphrase Gresham's Law: bad 'protection' drives out good. The attempt to protect the consumer by force undercuts the protection he gets from incentive. First, it undercuts the value of reputation by placing the reputable company on the same basis as the unknown, the newcomer, or the fly-by-nighter. It declares, in effect, that all are equally suspect.[20]

On this line of argument the incentive to build a reputation for excellence grows weaker as the state becomes more intrusive. In addition to this, regulations can potentially subvert the efforts of those seeking compensation through the courts. If a company facing a lawsuit can show that it has complied with the letter of the relevant regulation, the case is more likely to be dismissed or damages reduced. Through minimalistic and ritualistic compliance, then, a company can achieve some measure of insulation from liability, making compensation more difficult to attain for the injured party.[21]

This leads us to the virtue-based prong of the argument. It is only a matter of time before a company that defrauds its investors and neglects its customers goes out of business. Reliability, punctuality, integrity, trustworthiness, honesty, fairness and diligence all confer a competitive advantage. The greater the degree to which a business exhibits these traits, the more attractive it is to customers and investors. Thus, there is an incentive to outperform one's competitors *ethically* – to be *more* diligent, *more* trustworthy, *more* reliable. An unregulated market, so the argument goes, provides fertile ground for the cultivation of virtue, and introducing regulation deposits salt into the soil.

In a heavily regulated economy, businessmen and businesswomen become obsessed with 'compliance'. In a speech to the European Business Ethics Network, Howard Davies, the former head of Britain's Financial Services Authority, acknowledged that 'the existence of a regulator and a rulebook leads in some cases to the laundering of conscience'.[22] Conformity with the rules becomes mechanical or ritualistic, and the ends to which the rules are geared are lost sight of. There is little incentive to go beyond the bare minimum. In fact, this comes to be seen as dangerous. Andrew West, economics editor for Capitalism Magazine, explains: 'When standards are seen as government-authorized, there is little reward but great risk in deviating from or going beyond those standards.'[23] Regulation is thus said to feed the dual, mutually supporting vices of ritualism and ethical minimalism in the marketplace.[24]

As for the Keynesian notion that unregulated capitalism fosters a callous attitude towards the suffering of those who fail in the economic struggle, producing a society that is devoid of valuable human sentiments, neoliberals routinely point to the evidence that suggests that the free market does not snuff out compassion and benevolence as thoroughly as this lets on.[25] For instance, in 2006, Americans – the inhabitants of what is widely perceived as the country most closely approximating the laissez-faire model – gave nearly $300 billion dollars to charitable causes. And it is not only the Warren Buffets of capitalist economies that are making the donations. It is estimated that as much as 65 per cent of US households with a combined income of less that $100,000 regularly give to charity.[26]

Finally, we can turn to the rights-based prong of the argument. For some neoliberals regulation is wrong in principle, independently of the contingencies discussed thus far, on the grounds that it unjustly infringes the rights and liberties of market actors.[27]

The promulgation and enforcement of law requires moral justification insofar as it restricts individual liberty. In the case of criminal laws that prohibit murder, theft, assault, etc., the justification is that the restrictions are necessary to protect people from harm or to defend their rights. Attempts to justify the regulation of business typically take on a similar form – the state may compel a pharmaceutical firm to put a new drug through rigorous safety tests, for instance, in order to protect consumers from harmful side-effects. But opponents of regulation are right to point out that there are important differences between the two cases. Assault by its very nature causes harm. Selling a drug without the state's seal of approval does not. In the latter case, harm to the consumer is not certain and in most cases is not even probable; it is merely *possible*. This complicates matters a great deal, since restricting the liberties of some citizens and imposing significant burdens upon them in order to protect others from harms that are merely possible looks a lot like preventive punishment. Since this is clearly unacceptable, except perhaps in special circumstances, then so too is regulation. Edward Soule explains:

> Statutory regulation seems to jump the gun in terms of meting out punishment. Many statutory regulations are cumbersome, intrusive, and expensive to comply with. The question is whether, in advance of any harm to any individual, there is any basis in morality for forcing compliance. Reducing evil, even violent crime does not warrant pre-emptive punishment.[28]

But although releasing a new drug without meticulous testing may turn out to have no harmful consequences, it nevertheless puts consumer safety at *risk*. Is this not enough to justify regulation? For the committed neoliberal, as long as there is no coercion or deception involved – that is, as long as we are talking about a genuinely free and informed market exchange – the answer is an emphatic 'no'.

If a pharmaceutical company releases a drug with a warning label which reads 'Not thoroughly tested: Can cause serious illness or death', a risk is merely being *offered*. Should you decide to take the drug despite the warning, the risk of harm is not foisted upon you; you *accept* it. Or take a company that decides to issue shares of stock to the public in order to raise capital for its operations. The company in question, for whatever reason, does not wish to make public the nature of its business model or to reveal any other details that are generally of interest to investors. Despite this, I decide to purchase the company's securities. I happen to trust the management and just have a good gut feeling. Again, a risk is merely being offered, not imposed.

In light of this, for a government to deny market entry to untested pharmaceuticals or to compel periodic disclosure statements seems paternalistic.[29] It involves prohibiting and punishing free and voluntary exchanges between competent adults, where no party has coerced, defrauded or attempted to mislead the other. If we agree that paternalism transgresses against the rights and liberties of its objects, then regulation indeed starts to look deeply problematic.[30]

Imposing risks

There is no denying that the global financial crisis has mounted considerable pressure on all three prongs of the moral argument for deregulation. It has become radically apparent that the market does not reliably cultivate honesty, integrity and diligence. Executives often have a personal incentive for prioritising short-term over long-term performance. This neutralises the desire for reputation, which might otherwise foster virtue. Moreover, the claim that the costs of regulation are excessive has become more difficult to sustain in light of the severity and scope of the damage. The harms that regulation aims to prevent can no longer sensibly be described as trivial relative to the costs of a regulatory regime.[31] As for the rights-based argument, its standard formulation rests on the premise that regulation interferes with consensual transactions between competent adults. More specifically, it prohibits or constrains the offering and voluntary acceptance of risks. But if the meltdown and ensuing recession have made anything abundantly clear, it is that a series of voluntary exchanges can also impose significant risks upon unsuspecting third parties.

While some of the people affected by the crisis were neck-deep in exotic financial instruments, others had steered well clear of them and did nothing that could plausibly be interpreted as consent to the risks that catastrophically materialised in 2008.[32] Investment banks and other financial institutions that were trading heavily in mortgages and derivatives were the first to feel the brunt of the subprime collapse, but this was just the beginning. Within a year, millions of people worldwide had lost their jobs, their homes and their savings. Retiree pension funds lost much of their value. Taxpayers were forced to bail out troubled financial institutions to the tune of hundreds of billions of dollars. The plight of many of the world's poor was exacerbated and many more were pushed into poverty.[33] The standard anti-paternalist position has no purchase here. It is hopelessly ill-equipped to deal with the now undeniable prevalence of risk imposition in financial markets.[34]

This, however, still does not settle matters. Might the neoliberal not rejoin that, just as the state has no business interfering with the offering and acceptance of risk, it also has no business interfering with the imposition of risk – or at least not with the kinds of risk impositions under consideration? There are two ways of making this argument. On the stronger formulation there is simply no right against risk imposition, and insofar as the only justification for the restriction of individual liberty is the defence of rights – a conviction widely shared beyond neoliberal circles – coercive regulation cannot be justified on the grounds that it is necessary to protect people against involuntary exposure to risk.[35] On the weaker version, although there is some such right, once it is properly circumscribed or its content is properly specified, we see that the risk impositions under consideration do not infringe it. Let us consider each in turn.

If we agree that rights protect interests, then wherever a right is infringed, the rights-bearer must accordingly suffer some setback to those interests – that is, he or she must suffer some harm. But is this true of the 'victims' of risk imposition in advance of the materialisation of any harm? As John Oberdiek observes, 'nothing at all changes in the lives of those who are risked. And if one's goals or other interests are not actually thwarted or otherwise adversely affected, one suffers no setback. One's well-being remains unassailed and intact'.[36] To be sure, imposing a risk on an individual might very well lead to a setback of his or her interests. If I become aware of the risk, I might take a detrimental course of action that I would not have otherwise taken, or I might experience some level of distress and anxiety. But here it is the awareness of risk, rather than risk in and of itself, that is at issue.

Heidi Hurd drives the point home:

> If one never knows of a risk to which one has been exposed (so as to be free from any psychological trauma), and if the risk never materialises, can one meaningfully say that one has been harmed? Is one worse off than another who was never exposed to such a risk … If the safe does not fall, and if one never gains knowledge that one has stood under it, can one say that one's life has gone worse, or that one has been a victim of more harm than one would otherwise have been if one had never stood under the unknown suspended safe? It would seem that to be hit with an unknown risk is not to be hit at all![37]

If the imposition of risk cannot be said to set back anybody's interests, so the argument goes, it cannot be said to violate anybody's rights. To this Judith Jarvis Thomson adds that wherever a right is infringed, even justifiably, we tend to feel that the rights-infringer owes something to the infringee by way of compensation; we feel that *damages* are owed. But Thomson denies that this obtains in even those cases of risk imposition thought to be most objectionable:

> If I play Russian roulette on you, and there is no bullet under the firing pin when I fire, do I owe you damages? No doubt I ought not to have done what I did; but do I owe you anything for doing it? I am inclined to think I do not.[38]

For Thomson, the absence of a moral right is confirmed by the absence of moral residue.

A further reason for scepticism is that risk is essentially an epistemic construct rather than a feature of objective reality. Stephen Perry illustrates by way of example:[39] A exposes B to a toxic substance, S, without her consent. Ten percent of all people exposed to S contract a disease, D. We might be inclined to say that a risk has been imposed on B in this scenario; she now has a 10 per cent chance of contracting D. But this will not do. Presumably there are certain factors that will determine which of the people exposed to S will in fact be afflicted with D. Let's say that anyone who possesses physical attributes X, Y and Z will contract D when exposed to S, while those who do not possess these attributes will remain disease-free. Thus, we can identify two narrower reference classes within the broader 'all people' reference class. One consists of members of the general population who possess X, Y and Z, while the other consists of members of the general population who do not possess these attributes.

It might not be possible for us to tell which reference class B belongs to given our epistemic limitations, but she does in fact belong to one or the other. Now, if B does possess attributes X, Y, and Z, then it is certain that she will contract D. She has not been risked or endangered by A's action – she has been plainly harmed. On the other hand, if B does not possess any of these physical attributes, she has a zero per cent chance of contracting D. 'Either way', Perry explains, 'there is no basis for saying that risk is a form of harm in itself.'[40] We might talk of B having a 10 per cent chance of contracting D, but this is merely a symptom of our imperfect knowledge. In truth, the probability of harm befalling her is either zero per cent or 100 per cent. And the same can be said for each and every act that we unreflectively take to be a risk imposition. In reality, there is only harm or its absence.

But even though the imposition of risk may not 'impact life' in the same way that the infliction of harm does, there is still, I think, some sense in which it can be said to set back interests. Autonomy has a number of preconditions. Freedom from coercive pressure is one of them and possession of the basic mental capacities necessary to form and execute intentions is arguably another.[41] It is also necessary to have a range of choices or options available – and a range of acceptable or adequate options at that. 'To lead one's own life and to be autonomous, one must chart one's own course, but in order truly to chart one's own course, there must be a variety of worthwhile courses from which to choose.'[42]

Now consider a simple case of risk imposition: someone carelessly fires a gun in your direction. The bullet narrowly misses, whizzing past the left side of your head. Even though the harm did not materialise (therefore proving that you belonged to a reference class where the probability of actually being shot was zero per cent), by firing the gun, the shooter foreclosed one of your acceptable options – the option of moving to your left for whatever reason. This option now involves death or serious injury, rendering it unsafe and therefore un-choiceworthy. Herein lies the harm of risk imposition: it involves the foreclosure of acceptable options by the narrowing of safe options, which is a diminution of autonomy. In this respect the imposition of a risk can be likened to the laying of a trap.[43] And insofar as we agree that an individual's interest in autonomy is important enough to put others under moral duties, we can say that risk imposition, by virtue of diminishing autonomy, involves the infringement of a right.

The fact that defending oneself against risk imposition is clearly permissible, at least under certain circumstances, would seem to confirm this. Consider again the Russian roulette case. It may be true that nothing changes in the target's life if there is no bullet under the firing pin. Still, no reasonable person would deny that the target is entitled to prevent the gun-wielder from pulling the trigger, even with deadly force if necessary. But how do we account for this if not by invoking the rights of the person put at risk? What is more, if the victim has a right to defend himself or herself, then surely he or she may enlist the freely-given aid of some third party or empower an agent to act on his or her behalf. Where self-defence is justified, so too is other defence, other things being equal. This is but a specific application of what James Rachels has identified as a 'basic principle of moral reasoning':[44] if A is permitted to bring about X, then, all other things being equal, A is permitted to enlist the freely-given aid of B. B, accordingly, is permitted to assist A in bringing about X or to bring about X on A's behalf. On this point the philosophical consensus is unanimous and it would seem to justify the state's use of coercion to prevent the imposition of risk in at least those cases where self-defence against risk imposition is acknowledged to be legitimate.

So, the claim that there is no right against risk imposition and that its defence cannot therefore be invoked to justify government coercion is implausible. It seems the neoliberal must rely on the weaker argument, which says that although there is a prima facie right against risk imposition, it is circumscribed in such a way as to not be infringed by the activities of bankers and financiers, and that the prohibition or regulation of these risk impositions is therefore illegitimate.[45]

To admit that there is a right to X is not to say that any and every denial of X constitutes an infringement of that right. When the state prohibits one person from making a religious sacrifice of his or her neighbour, we do not say that his or her right of religious expression has been infringed. Rather, we say that the right simply does not extend that far; there is only one right 'in play' here and that is the neighbour's right not to be set alight. The same goes for the right against risk imposition. Even sensible driving within the speed limit invariably involves imposing risks on pedestrians and other motorists, since accidents happen. Using a gas cooker involves imposing risks on one's neighbours, since gas leaks and explosions are always a remote possibility. Yet we do not feel that either of these activities is even prima facie impermissible. The fact of the matter is that many of the things we do from day to day carry risks for people that do not consent to them. A moral code which posits a boundless, absolute right against risk imposition is simply paralysing. Like all rights, this one needs to be carefully circumscribed.

But how is the scope of this right to be determined? Scanlon's contractualism might be usefully deployed here:[46] an acceptable risk is one that conforms to a principle which cannot be 'reasonably rejected' from the point of view of anyone whose interests are at stake. If all concerned would endorse the principle, given the opportunity to do so with access to the relevant information and unimpaired reasoning, then the risk imposition permitted by the principle cannot be said to infringe anybody's rights; it can be justified to each and every person affected.

This can account for our intuition that driving and using a gas cooker are perfectly legitimate activities. A principle that prohibits me from imposing a negligible risk of harm on my neighbours in the preparation of my meals must also, as a matter of consistency, prohibit everyone else from imposing risks with relevantly similar features (comparable probability and seriousness of injury, equal importance of the end being sought, etc.). Clearly this would severely limit the scope of freely-chosen individual activity, almost to the point of making life not worthwhile. The same risks and benefits that attend my cookery are also components of an infinitely wide range of other activities. Thus, from the point of view of all concerned, a world governed by a principle that allows me to impose this risk is preferable to a world governed by a principle that denies me this freedom.

Now if all risky financial activities live up to this standard, then all such risk impositions are of the morally innocent kind and do not justify coercive prohibition or regulation. But this premise is rather difficult to swallow. Take but one example: the selling of credit default swaps (CDSs) to speculators. The first thing to note is that the potential harms are significant: unemployment, pension fund depletion and financial ruin. The reader will recall from the introduction to this book that excessive speculative CDS trading is what multiplied and spread the losses caused by the sub-prime collapse. Second, the financial heavyweights imposing the risks were not tending to their basic needs but amassing vast fortunes. AIG CEO Joe Cassano earned $280 million orchestrating the creation of $80 billion-worth of CDS contracts over a five-year period. Other executives from AIG's Financial Products Unit also pocketed 30 per cent of the profits from the operation, which steered the firm to an $11.5 billion quarterly loss in March 2008, a $61.7 billion quarterly loss a year later – the largest in US corporate history – and a 95 per cent drop in the share price, from $70 to just $1.25.[47] Finally, the majority of those exposed to the risk did not stand to benefit from it.[48]

Rejecting a principle that allows risk impositions with this combination of features seems to me to be perfectly reasonable. The state of affairs that would obtain if all risks with similar properties were prohibited or restricted would be acceptable and indeed preferable from the point of view of some, if not most ordinary people.

Conclusion

While there are conceivable circumstances under which the mere offering of a risk is objectionable, the presumption admittedly must be that any voluntary transaction between competent adults is morally permissible. On the other hand, in relation to the *imposition* of risk, the presumption is always against. By exposing the prevalence of risk imposition in financial markets, then, the global financial crisis has shifted the burden of argument. It now falls squarely on the neoliberal to make the case that the risk impositions under consideration are of the morally innocent kind that do not warrant coercive interference by the state. I have not gone so far as to suggest that the case cannot be made, but if we insist that every risk must be justified to the individual or group upon whom it is imposed, the prognosis does not look good for much of what routinely transpires on 'planet finance'.

Notes

1. Phillip Corey, 'Rudd Calls for Greater Financial Transparency', *Sydney Morning Herald*, 26 September 2008.
2. Michael Woodhead, 'Angela Merkel: The Woman Who Saw the Crisis Coming', *Sunday Times*, 12 October 2008.
3. Martin Wolf, 'Seeds of its Own Destruction', *Financial Times*, 8 March 2009, www.ft.com/indepth/capitalism-future, date accessed 6 October 2010.
4. Paul Mason, *Meltdown: The End of the Age of Greed*, London and New York: Verson, p. x.
5. Francis Fukuyama, 'The Fall of America Inc.', *Newsweek*, 4 October 2008.
6. Kevin Rudd, 'The Global Financial Crisis', *The Monthly*, February 2009, available at www.themonthly.com.au/monthly-essays-kevin-rudd-global-financial-crisis--1421, date accessed 6 October 2010.

7. Ibid.
8. The claim that regulation threatens political integrity was made most recently by former Australian treasurer Peter Costello. See 'Staying Out of the Economy Stops Cronyism', *The Age*, 12 August 2009, available at www.theage.com.au/opinion/staying-out-of-the-economy-stops-cronyism-20090811-egwo.html, date accessed 6 October 2010. See also Charles Wheelan, *Naked Economics: Undressing the Dismal Science*, London and New York: WW Norton & Co., 2002, Chapter 4.
9. Mason, Meltdown, p. 124.
10. J.C. Smith, 'The Process of Adjudication and Regulation: A Comparison', in Tibor Machan and M. Bruce Johnson (eds), *Rights and Regulation: Ethical, Political, and Economic Issues*, Cambridge, MA: Ballinger Pub. Co., 1983, p. 80.
11. Walter Williams, 'The Argument for Free Markets: Morality vs. Efficiency', in Dennis O'Keeffe (ed.), *Economy and Virtue: Essays on the Theme of Markets and Morality*, London: Institute of Economic Affairs, 2004, pp. 44–5.
12. Ibid., p. 45.
13. Tibor Machan and M. Bruce Johnson, 'Introduction' and Smith, 'The Process of Adjudication and Regulation', in Machan and Johnson (eds), *Rights and Regulation*, pp. 5 and 72–3 respectively.
14. Tibor Machan, 'The Petty Tyranny of Government Regulation', in ibid., p. 274.
15. Milton Friedman, *An Economist's Protest*, 2nd edn, Glen Ridge: Thomas Horton and Daughters, 1975, p. 223.
16. Manuel Lora, 'Replacing Government Regulation with Superior Market Alternatives', www.lewrockwell.com/lora/m.lora11.html, date accessed 6 October 2010.
17. Smith, 'The Process of Adjudication and Regulation', pp. 79–80.
18. Tibor Machan, 'Should Business be Regulated?', in Tom Regan (ed.), *Just Business*, New York: Random House, 1983, p. 226.
19. Alan Greenspan, 'The Assault on Integrity', in Ayn Rand, Nathanial Branden, Alan Greenspan and Robert Hessen, *Capitalism: The Unknown Ideal*, New York: Signet, 1986.
20. Ibid.
21. Lora, 'Replacing Government Regulation'.
22. Howard Davies, 'Ethics in Regulation' (2001) *Business Ethics: A European Review*, 10, 4, 284.
23. Andrew West, 'Less Government Regulation and More Laissez-faire Required to Prevent Further "Enron" Scandals', *Capitalism Magazine*, 7 March 2002, www.capmag.com/article.asp?ID=1473, date accessed 6 October 2010.
24. And it is not only the character of the professional businessperson that is adversely affected. The virtues of prudence and cautiousness among consumers and investors are also listed among the casualties. The existence of a regulatory regime gives off the false impression that all companies,

insofar as they continue to be tolerated by the regulator, are safe and trustworthy. This did not escape Greenspan's attention: '[Regulation] grants an automatic guarantee of safety to the products of any company that complies with its arbitrarily set minimum standards ... The minimum standards, which are the basis of regulation, gradually tend to become the maximums as well ... A fly by night securities operator can quickly meet all the S.E.C. requirements, gain the inference of respectability, and proceed to fleece the public. In an unregulated economy, the operator would have had to earn a position of trust.' Greenspan, 'The Assault on Integrity'.

25. Most famously, John Maynard Keynes insisted that on the ideal of laissez-faire, 'there must be no mercy or protection for those who embark their capital or their labour in the wrong direction. It is a method of bringing the most successful profit-makers to the top by a ruthless struggle for survival, which selects the most efficient by the bankruptcy of the less efficient. It does not count the cost of the struggle, but looks only to the benefits of the final result which are assumed to be permanent. The object of life being to crop the leaves off the branches up to the greatest possible height, the likeliest way of achieving this end is to leave the giraffes with the longest necks to starve out those whose necks are shorter'. Quoted in Machan, 'Should Business be Regulated?', p. 214.

26. Giving USA Foundation, 'U.S. charitable giving reaches $295.02 billion in 2006', 25 June 2007, www.charitynavigator.org/index.cfm/bay/content. view/cpid/619.htm, date accessed 6 October 2010.

27. See for instance Machan, 'The Petty Tyranny', p. 260: 'regulation is wrong in principle because any bona fide instance of it – as distinct from instances that really amount to judicial processes or managerial functions of government – infringes upon human liberty, something to which everyone has a natural right, including members of the business and professional community, who are most thoroughly regulated.'

28. Edward Soule, *Morality and Markets: The Ethics of Government Regulation*, Oxford: Rowman & Littlefield, 2003, p. 83.

29. Firms are usually required to file an initial registration statement with the relevant regulatory authority, and often periodic statements thereafter, which provide detailed information about the issuing company's prospects and business model, the potential risks for investors, etc.

30. Judith Jarvis Thomson comments that 'increasing the penalty for actually causing harm does not trouble most opponents of government regulation. What they *really* find irksome is, rather, adopting (new) penalties for imposing risks of harms'. Judith Jarvis Thomson, 'Some Questions about Government Regulation of Behaviour', in Machan and Johnson (eds), *Rights and Regulation*, p. 146. More accurately, what opponents of regulation find irksome is the imposition of penalties for the *offering* of risks.

31. See for instance Nicholas Rescher, 'On the Rationale of Government Regulation', in ibid., p. 255: 'A program of statutory regulation often

makes a leap in the dark – creating a monster that dwarfs the evils it is designed to remedy.'

32. Niall Ferguson, 'Wall Street Lays Another Egg', *Vanity Fair*, December 2008, www.vanityfair.com/politics/features/2008/12/banks200812, date accessed 6 October 2010.

33. Kevin Rudd, 'The Global Financial Crisis'.

34. I will be focusing exclusively on the rights-based prong of the argument, since for the staunch neoliberal who insists that regulation is wrong *in principle*, consequentialist and virtue-based considerations are neither here nor there. From his or her perspective, the financial crisis can be said to have stripped neoliberalism of its ideological legitimacy if and only if it has discredited the claim that regulation constitutes an unjust infringement against the rights and liberties of market actors.

35. Tibor Machan seems to have some such claim in mind when he denies that people have 'rights to innumerable deeds and services ... [including] protection from risks involved in contemporary life' – a position that he attributes to Kelman and Claybrook. Machan, 'Should Business be Regulated?', p. 227.

36. John Oberdiek, 'The Morality of Risking: On the Normative Foundations of Risk Regulation', PhD dissertation (unpublished), University of Pennsylvania, 2003, p. 31.

37. Heidi M. Hurd, 'Nonreciprocal Risk Imposition, Unjust Enrichment, and the Foundations of Tort Law: A Critical Celebration of George Fletcher's Theory of Tort Law' (2002–3) *Notre Dame Law Review*, 78, 725.

38. Jarvis Thomson, 'Some Questions about Government Regulation of Behaviour', p. 149.

39. Stephen Perry, 'Risk, Harm, Interests, and Rights', in Tim Lewens (ed.), *Risk: Philosophical Perspectives*, Abingdon: Routledge, 2007, pp. 190–209.

40. Ibid., pp. 196–7.

41. John Oberdiek, 'Towards a Right Against Risking' (2009) *Law and Philosophy*, 28, 4, 379.

42. Ibid., p. 373.

43. Ibid., p. 374.

44. See James Rachels, *The End of Life: Euthanasia and Morality*, Oxford University Press, 1986, p. 86.

45. Ferguson, 'Wall Street Lays Another Egg'.

46. Thomas Scanlon, *What We Owe to Each Other*, Cambridge, MA: Harvard University Press, 1998.

47. Ibid., p. 82.

48. In the words of distinguished economist Ross Garnaut, 'beyond the generation of extraordinary incomes for those who manufactured and sold [speculative credit-default swaps] ... the magnitude and youth of these products leads to the unsettling answer that nobody knows [what purpose they serve]'. Ross Garnaut, *The Great Crash of 2008*, Carlton: Melbourne University Press, 2009, p. 64. The same could probably be said for many of the products that financiers regularly trade in. Of synthetic CDOs, also

discussed in the introduction, Roger Lowenstein writes: 'Synthetic CDOs did not add to the country's economic output any more than did a bet on the track or, for that matter, a wager on the direction of the stock market. To paraphrase the financial journalist Michael Lewis, synthetic CDOs had as much to do with real estate as fantasy football had to do with the NFL. They built no houses and painted no walls; they simply multiplied the Street's gamble.' Roger Lowenstein, *The End of Wall Street*, Melbourne: Scribe, 2010, p. 56.

5
Ethical Investing in an Age of Excessive Materialistic Self-Interest

John C. Harrington

Since the 1970s a number of institutional investors have been developing responsible investing guidelines to address ethical issues surrounding share ownership of publicly-traded corporations. Initially a response to social and environmental issues raised at annual shareholder meetings, the guidelines were designed to establish a methodology of self-regulation requiring these institutions to limit corporate injury, and generally to encourage engagement with management and shareholder advocacy to ameliorate defined socially injurious practices consistent with traditional fiduciary responsibility.

Socially responsible investing (SRI) in the US has since grown into a $5 trillion industry. Yet corporate social and environmental injury is as pervasive as ever, for while socially responsible investing has gained momentum, materialistic self-interest has, at the same time, become the dominant global secular philosophy. This self-interest has become excessive, leading to increased risk-taking, leverage and a belief in the 'magic of the markets'. Particularly acute among investment bankers, it is what led to the creation of speculative exotic and highly leveraged trading instruments (primarily derivatives) which produced a global financial crisis that has significantly depleted institutional portfolio valuations.

This chapter begins by tracking the growth of SRI in the US. I evaluate current SRI guidelines and corporate voluntary codes of conduct, and ask why such guidelines and codes have failed not only to prevent corporate injury, but also to protect investors from speculative excesses and significant portfolio devaluation. I then turn to discuss a range of recent developments in the world of business and finance which, when combined with materialistic self-interest, produced the financial crisis from which we are still reeling. I begin with the deregulation of the financial services industry, which allowed so many of the practices that proved so dangerous, before moving on to discuss the growing reliance on fast money, the widening gap between ownership and control, and finally the regrettable decline of fiduciary responsibility. I conclude with some remarks about how ethical investing, despite its failure to prevent the recent crisis, could be the key to preventing a relapse or the onset of a more serious and sustained global financial meltdown in the years ahead.

Ethical investing

There are three commonly recognised means by which individuals currently participate in global economic activity: spending or consuming, donating goods or services to charity (philanthropy) and investing. All generate economic activity either directly or indirectly, but only one, philanthropy, has traditionally been associated with moral conduct or ethical behaviour. However, in the twentieth century, many public and private institutions as well as government agencies refused to purchase products and services of corporations operating in South Africa, including the termination of financial relationships with banks that made loans to the South African government. In addition, for many investors, ethics have become embedded in a form of individual and institutional investment behaviour. This chapter will specially discuss ethical investing or SRI.

Historically, pursuant to Jewish law, Jews were enjoined from selling or producing non-kosher food or engaging in business activities that may help others violate moral or religious codes, as well as prohibiting Jews from owning businesses that destroyed natural resources, were involved in usury, selling offensive weapons or engaged in deceitful or misleading practices. As early as the thirteenth century, the Catholic Church declared a usurer a pariah of society and threatened to excommunicate anyone who rented a house to such a person, and in the eighteenth century, Quakers refused to do business with firms involved in the slave trade.[1] In the US, many church organisations declared tobacco and alcohol morally repugnant and prohibited church funds from being invested in such businesses, but it was not until 1928 that a US mutual fund was created that specifically excluded companies from the portfolio whose primary activities involved alcohol, tobacco or gambling.[2]

In the mid-1960s, leading churchmen and seminary students called for a positive approach to church investing by advocating for church institutional investments in integrated and public housing, as well as excluding investments in weapons manufacturers producing for the Vietnam War and investments supporting the apartheid regime controlling the Republic of South Africa. These actions provided an impetus for community, church and public interest groups taking controversies into annual corporate shareholder meetings at: (1) Eastman Kodak and the Teachers Insurance and Annuity Association/College Retirement Equities Fund (TIAA/CREF) regarding minority employment; (2) Honeywell Corporation relating to the production of antipersonnel weapons used in Vietnam; and (3) General Motors Corporation ('Campaign GM') in an effort to have shareholders adopt three resolutions on corporate governance, the environment and minority employment.

In the case of Kodak, a predominately African-American community organisation, FIGHT, in Rochester, New York, purchased ten shares of company stock in an effort to persuade management to resume negotiations relating to job training and hiring practices in the city. By holding demonstrations and writing hundreds of letters to individual and institutional shareholders, FIGHT was successful in reaching an agreement with management on job training soon after the meeting.[3]

In 1970, while 'Campaign GM' was unsuccessful in obtaining enough shareholder votes for the adoption of its resolutions, it caused GM management to nominate and shareholders to elect Rev. Leon Sullivan, an African-American minister experienced in minority economic development and critical of GM in South Africa, to the board of directors. He was subsequently successful in getting the board of directors to create a committee to oversee GM's public policy impacts and to create a committee of conservationists to monitor the effects of GM's operations on the environment.[4] He was also later successful in initially lining up 30 large corporations operating in South Africa to sign a voluntary code of conduct agreeing to move towards 'equal pay for equal work' and agreeing to work within South Africa to eliminate apartheid. At the height of Sullivan's work, over 350 US corporations had signed the code, but after ten years of no change in the fundamental structure of apartheid, Sullivan abandoned his voluntary principles and called for economic sanctions and US corporate disengagement.

Corporate shareholder controversy reached college campuses at the same time that the Vietnam War and South African apartheid generated political dialogue among faculty, students, administration and alumni groups. Ivy League schools such as Harvard, Princeton, Yale, Cornell, Dartmouth and many others responded by holding conferences, seminars and studies on corporate responsibility, seeking an appropriate response by the university community, specifically the governing trustees of the universities' portfolios.

Following Yale University's decision to 'abstain' from voting its shares in the Campaign GM controversy, three Yale University professors, John G. Simon, Charles W. Powers and Jon P. Gunnemann wrote a groundbreaking book in 1972 entitled *The Ethical Investor*, which established guidelines for investors to avoid or correct 'social injury' based upon a 'moral minimum' utilising the criteria of 'need', 'proximity', 'capability' and 'last resort'. While these guidelines were recommended primarily for educational institutions, the authors suggested that all charitable organisations could reasonably implement such guidelines as self-regulation, and that non-charitable institutional investors, including pension and mutual funds, insurance companies and other financial institutions, could utilise modified guidelines specific to the organisational mission.

Simon, Powers and Gunnemann defined 'social injury' as:

> activities which violate, or frustrate the enforcement of rules of domestic or international law intended to protect individuals against deprivation of health, safety or basic freedoms.[5]

According to them, once a social injury is recognised, the criterion of need is met. The second and third criteria of 'proximity' and 'capability' are met by the fact that the investor holds common stock which is legally 'ownership' in the corporation. The fourth and final criterion, 'last resort', is met once management has ignored the investor's expression of concern over an issue or has refused to respond to shareholder communication.

The moral minimum concept was an attempt to make a distinction between negative injunction and affirmative duties in the assertion that all men have a minimum moral obligation to avoid social injury, as well as to take a position favouring moral effectiveness as opposed to moral purity.[6] The catalyst for developing this approach to address a moral obligation through investment guidelines or policy was based upon what became known as the Kew Gardens Principle, which is part of the criminal code in the state of Vermont and which has been recognised by many European civil codes. Essentially, this is a law that requires citizens to respond to a cry for help when they are capable and nearby. The Kew Gardens section of New York City was the site of the brutal death by stabbing of Kitty Genovese, where 38 people watched or heard and did nothing. The failure to act by 38 bystanders was an act of apathy, or indifference, or an act of omission that turned into an act of commission.

Shortly after the publication of *The Ethical Investor*, state legislation was introduced in the California legislature defining social injury, identical to that described above, but adding 'environmentally injurious' operations[7] in 'The Social Responsibility Act of 1973', which also would have created the Commission on Social and Environmental Responsibility. While the legislation was defeated in the State Assembly Policy Committee, the Edmund G. Brown Jr. administration staff successfully worked with the boards and staffs of the two large state pension funds, CALPERS and CALSTRS, which adopted a proxy voting policy as an adaptation of *The Ethical Investor* guidelines. In 1974, for the first time since it was authorised by California voters to invest state retirement funds in corporate stocks, CALPERS did not vote in accordance with management's recommendations on eight social and political issues before the annual shareholder meetings of Goodyear Tire & Rubber, Exxon Corporation and Phillips Petroleum.[8]

By the mid-1970s, several state legislatures held hearings on state pension fund investing and proxy voting policies, and the California legislature adopted several proposals that were enacted into law that continued to streamline and standardise proxy voting for state and local government agencies. Numerous state and local government public employee retirement funds, college and university endowments, foundations, environmental and social justice organisations also developed proxy voting guidelines and policies on voting shares at annual corporate shareholder meetings.[9]

In 1971, two Methodist ministers, Dr Luther Tyson and Jack Corbett, opened the Pax World Fund, a mutual fund created as an alternative to traditional funds that supported the production of military hardware and armaments. Pax World's social criteria avoided US Department of Defense (DOD) prime contractors, as well as companies involved in alcohol, tobacco and gambling. This fund was followed by the creation of the Dreyfus Third Century Fund which opened in 1972. Its founder, Howard Stein, was a major fundraiser for Eugene McCarthy's 1968 Presidential Campaign. Unlike Pax World's exclusionary criteria, the Dreyfus Third Century Fund advertised itself as investing in companies that enhanced the quality of life in America, by evaluating a company's record in areas of 'protection and improvement of the environment and the proper use of our natural resources, occupational health and safety, consumer protection and product purity, and equal employment opportunity'.[10]

However, it was not until the early 1980s that an avalanche of new mutual funds were opened for individual and institutional investors, allowing such investors to access multiple investment management styles and investment objectives, as well as introducing an abundance of funds with various social and environmental criteria. These early SRI funds utilised both exclusionary and inclusionary criteria, generally excluding tobacco, gambling, alcohol, nuclear power, weapons and armaments, while purchasing companies with positive social and/or environmental records.[11]

According to the Social Investment Forum (SIF), a non-profit tax-exempt organisation comprised of SRI adherents and professionals, the industry currently represents over 260 mutual funds and almost $5 trillion in assets. Professionals in the SRI field include private individuals, academics, registered investment advisors, financial planners, mutual funds, broker-dealers, private and public pension funds, financial institutions, consultants, foundations, colleges and universities, trusts and others applying some form of SRI or utilising investment guidelines based on some aspect of responsible investing criteria in addition to traditional financial criteria.

SRI assets grew steadily in the twentieth century and have continued to grow throughout the first decade of the twenty-first century. According to a recent paper published by Robeco Investment Management and Booz & Company, global responsible investing assets under management will reach between 15 and 20 per cent of total global assets or around $26.5 trillion and will become 'mainstream' by 2015. The report indicated that SRI assets have been growing at a rate of about 22 per cent annually since 2003 and, with increased investor emphasis on environmental, social and corporate governance (ESG) issues, could grow up to 30 per cent per year.[12] Most of the growth in SRI assets has been institutional, including mutual funds, private asset management companies, personal retirement accounts, trusts and foundations, and public employee pension funds. What is considered SRI is most commonly associated with passive exclusionary screening, that is, avoiding portfolio purchasing of stocks in companies primarily engaged in the production of tobacco products, alcohol and/or gambling, as well as weapons, armaments and nuclear power. Many institutional investors have adopted exclusionary screens, as well as inclusionary investment guidelines, developed specifically to align the organisation's mission statement objectives with its investment objectives. For example, 'mission-based' investing guidelines of civil rights organisations normally prohibit investments in debt instruments funding prison construction, in companies employing prisoners and/or in private prison employee-contracting firms, while encouraging investments in companies protecting consumer and employee privacy.

Many environmental organisations develop mission-based investment criteria that support investing in the alternative energy and green technology sectors, while avoiding major polluters, such as petroleum, chemical and coal companies. Social justice organisations and family foundations and trusts often encourage investments in companies that engage in community charitable activities and are the corporate leaders in donations to community-based projects. Emphasis is also placed on prioritising investment in Community Development Financial Institutions (CDFIs),[13] community credit unions and local banks, and other financial institutions that have specialised lending programmes in their respective communities, neighbourhoods or regions supporting low-income housing construction and rehabilitation.

Many investors have also expanded inclusionary social and environmental criteria by focusing on investment opportunities that fund green technology, alternative energy and microcredit enterprises, and invest in private and non-profit corporate investment vehicles that expand employment opportunities for the rural poor, especially businesses that produce organic and sustainable agricultural products. Many of these investments are made by CDFIs, as well as through short-term debt instruments issued and funded by the Calvert Foundation.[14]

Some foundations, but mainly private asset managers, mutual funds and public employee pension funds, also engage in shareholder advocacy, which may include communicating and meeting with corporate management on specific issues of concern and engaging in more serious dialogue about an issue or several related topics. Frequently, dialogue may be followed by active shareholder advocacy in the form of introducing or co-sponsoring a shareholder resolution, or requesting information on a specific action taken by corporate management. Normally, such resolutions are precatory or are written in the form of an advisory resolution which, if adopted by a majority of shareholders, would not be binding upon management.

Literally hundreds of precatory resolutions are introduced by investors every year. For example, the Interfaith Center for Corporate Responsibility (ICCR), a coalition of 275 faith-based institutional investors started in the 1970s, have introduced over 200 resolutions annually. According to its website www.iccr.org, in 2009 ICCR members filed 391 shareholder proposals.

Recently, shareholders have begun to write resolutions that are bylaw amendments which, if adopted, would amend corporate bylaws. However, these resolutions are most often challenged by corporate legal counsel pursuant to Securities and Exchange Commission (SEC) Rule 14a-8(i), which sets forth 13 substantive bases under which a company may exclude a shareholder proposal. Corporate general counsel normally seeks 'no action' approval by the SEC, allowing the corporation to exclude a resolution from the proxy statement. Management requests that the SEC takes no regulatory action against the company if the company excludes the proposal from the shareholder ballot at the annual general meeting of shareholders.

Early shareholder resolutions concentrated primarily on social and political issues, but beginning in the early 1990s they began to focus on ESG issues. In the first decade of the twenty-first century, SRI proponents and shareholder advocates have concentrated their attention more on climate change, environmental sustainability and corporate governance. The economic crisis of 2008 resulted in increased attention on US economic security, corporate executive compensation, majority voting for directors and other corporate governance issues.

In 2008, investors filed 54 shareholder resolutions on global warming, primarily seeking greater disclosure on corporate efforts to combat the emission of greenhouse gases, as well as requesting information on the financial risk posed by climate change to corporate earnings. Most of the resolutions were filed by members of the Investor Network on Climate Risk (INCR), an alliance of 60 institutional investors with assets totaling more than $5 trillion. According to its website (www.environmentalleader.com), INCR introduced 68 global warming resolutions in 2009.

Corporate CEO compensation has also been a major concern following the latest economic crisis. Since 1980, CEO pay in the US has increased by 442 per cent, adjusted for inflation,[15] as top executives earn about 364 times the average employee salary.[16] In the midst of the worst US financial crisis since the Great Depression, in an AFL-CIO report posted on its website (www.aflcio.org), entitled '100 Highest Paid CEOs', which collected data on CEO pay in 2008 and 2009, the highest-paid CEO received over $133 million and the lowest-paid on the list received almost $18 million. Since 1999, the non-profit United for a Fair Economy (www.unitedforafaireconomy. org) has been filing shareholder resolutions on executive compensation, most recently filing resolutions with six large publicly-traded corporations, requesting that the companies allow shareholders to vote in annual advisory elections at annual meetings on directors and officers' compensation policy of the corporation ('Say on Pay').

At the end of the 2007 proxy season, 656 investor proposals appeared on corporate ballots, up from 581 in 2006. Executive compensation and board-related issues continued to dominate the proposals, including 'pay-for-performance' proposals, which increased in number by nearly 60 per cent from 2006.[17]

According to a 2009 study by the *Wall Street Journal,* a record was set for the total amount of money set aside by banks and securities firms in the US to compensate executives, traders, investment bankers, money managers and others at the 38 top financial companies. The *Journal* expects these individuals to earn nearly 18 per cent more than they did in 2008 and slightly more than the record year of 2007 (about $145 billion).[18] These were the very firms that were 'bailed out' by the US government to the tune of $700 billion in funds from the Troubled Asset Relief Program (TARP) administered by the US Treasury Department. Never before have so many paid so much to so few for so much damage.

Excessive materialistic self-interest[19]

The English philosophers Thomas Hobbes (1588–1679) and John Locke (1632–1704) and the Scottish philosophers David Hume (1711–76) and Francis Hutcheson (1694–1746) as well as Bernard de Mandeville (1670–1733), among others, all wrote extensively about man's natural self-interest. However, the Scottish moral philosopher Adam Smith (1723–90) uniquely juxtaposed the often conflicting personal morality of benevolence with the impersonal morality of materialistic self-interest.

In *The Theory of Moral Sentiments*, Smith described man as naturally compassionate, benevolent and sympathetic, but in writing *The Wealth of Nations* 17 years later, he described man, in dealing with impersonal economic relationships, as primarily concerned with advancing personal materialistic self-interest, while often ignoring, overriding or harming the public interest.[20] Smith also recognised that individual, impersonal, materialistic self-interest could unintentionally benefit the community by providing economic growth, employment and the creation of private wealth. He also understood that those engaged in self-interested economic transactions may intentionally or unintentionally harm the public interest because individual self-interest is 'never exactly the same as that of the public, who have generally an interest to deceive and even to oppress the public, and who accordingly have, upon many occasions, both deceived and oppressed it'.[21]

Smith wrote extensively in *The Wealth of Nations* about British law and the old English East India Company, understanding that it had been created as a joint stock company with an exclusive charter (a monopoly) to serve its own corporate interests, but also those of the state and civil society. The British Parliament regularly reviewed charter proposals, which were enacted into law. Unlike Britain, in the US, private companies were granted a charter by individual states. By the mid-nineteenth century, however, the structure of business began to change in both the US and Britain. To raise larger amounts of capital in Britain, companies were given temporary limited liability and granted a monopoly in exchange for ventures deemed to be in the public interest. As companies grew in number and needed to rapidly raise capital, the government acceded to companies' requests for expedited licensing or chartering and it quickly became simply an administrative process.

In the US, as the need for rapid corporate capitalisation also grew, state legislatures liberalised incorporation statutes, and by the 1870s all state corporate chartering restrictions had disappeared.[22] Not unlike Britain, chartering became a state administrative process, with states competing with other states to enact the most favourable ('liberal') incorporation laws to financially benefit corporations. According to William G. Roy, when the right to incorporate became 'generalised', some privileges were discontinued, such as legal monopolisation, the right of eminent domain and free land, and other important ones were continued – owners were not liable for the company's debts, companies were given the right to own stock in other companies, and managers could operate corporations without direct accountability to their owners.[23]

In the late-nineteenth and early-twentieth centuries, the US economy experienced a wave of corporate consolidation. Between 1897 and 1904, 4,227 companies were consolidated into 257 giant trusts; Standard Oil controlled 70 per cent of the world's kerosene market and International Harvester sold 85 per cent of all US farm equipment.[24] These large business combinations were controlled by a small group of wealthy men and families who had consolidated economic power, which President Theodore Roosevelt described as a 'riot of individualistic materialism'.[25]

While President Roosevelt's 'trust busting' activities slowed down economic consolidation by wealthy industrialists, it did little to break up their power and influence over the US economy. Not long after Roosevelt's warning of excessive individual materialistic self-interest, in 1926 British economist John Maynard Keynes (1883–1946) raised concerns over individualistic 'decadent' capitalism and the unquestioned faith of laissez-faire capitalism.[26] More importantly, however, he warned of the growing power of professional corporate managers and the consequences of the evolving separation of corporate ownership and control.[27] This warning was repeated in 1932 by two corporate attorneys, Adolph A. Berle and Gardiner C. Means in *The Modern Corporation and Private Property*, who declared that economic power had become concentrated in the hands of a small class of professional managers, inspired by the rise of corporations. These corporate executives were insulated not only from legal owners but also from civil society and, if unchecked, could have very negative consequences for democratic institutions and the economy. They feared that these individuals had the 'power to build and destroy communities, to generate great productivity and wealth, but also to control the distribution of that wealth, without regard for those who elected them (the stockholders) or those who depended on them (the larger public)'.[28]

More importantly, for the future of the American economy and markets, Berle and Means described how private property defined by Adam Smith as 'a unity of possession' had been radically altered or broken into 'passive' property in the form of stock and 'active' property, or the physical enterprise itself being controlled by individuals who had only minor, if any, ownership interests in it.[29] Similarly, 'wealth' as thought of by Smith in the physical sense now consisted of a liquid and impersonal 'bundle of expectations which have a market value and which, if held may bring him income and, if sold in the market, may give him power to obtain some other form of wealth'.[30] They essentially pinpointed the separation between passive stockholders as owners who had given up control for liquidity, being able to sell their stock at a moment's notice, and a board of directors, excessively materialistically self-interested, who had absolute control of the corporation but did not own a majority of stock.

As we have experienced in the twenty-first century, ownership has become even more 'passive', diffused and diverse, the speed of stocks changing hands has evolved, thanks to the rapid advancement of technology, from 'a moment's notice' to milliseconds and in volume from hundreds of millions of shares to billions of shares, while the new class of managers and traders have enriched themselves beyond anyone's wildest expectations. All the while these managers have further consolidated the economy into fewer wealthy hands and have created esoteric and exotic trading instruments to gain increasing amounts of wealth. In what follows I discuss some regrettable developments in the world of business and finance which, in combination with excessive materialistic self-interest and the instruments that it spawned, endangered the global economy with a meltdown of a scale not seen since the Great Depression. I conclude with some remarks about how ethical investing, despite the shortcomings discussed above, could help us meet today's unique challenges and might be the key to preventing a relapse of the most recent crisis and the onset of the next one.

Deregulation of financial services

In the midst of the Great Depression, the enactment of the Glass-Steagall Act of 1933 was an attempt to limit excessive risk-taking and conflicts of interest by financial institutions involved in both banking and securities underwriting.[31] Coupled with the Depository Institution Deregulation and Monetary Control Act of 1980, which increased federal deposit insurance and required all banks to maintain reports and hold reserves at the Federal Reserve, the regulations were effective in minimising bank failures throughout most of the twentieth century.

As early as the 1960s, banks lobbied Congress to weaken Glass-Steagall, but it was not until 1987, after Alan Greenspan had been appointed as Chairman, that the Federal Reserve 'reinterpreted' Glass-Steagall and effectively rendered the Act obsolete.[32] The reality of the demise of Glass-Steagall occurred in 1998 when Citigroup, the largest New York bank, carried out a $72 billion merger with Travelers Group, Inc., creating the largest financial services conglomerate at that time which included banking, insurance and brokerage.

The demise of Glass-Steagall and the expansion of economic power exerted by the financial sector did not happen overnight, nor did it occur happenstance. The tradition of corporate lobbying and pumping millions of dollars into election campaigns in the US is as American as apple pie. Annually, corporations' political action committees (PACs) spend billions of dollars expressing their version of 'free speech' pursuant to the First Amendment of the US Constitution at all levels of government. This not only includes lobbying expenses and asking career politicians to 'educate' their professional associations while paying them enormous sums for speaking junkets, but includes money contributed directly to political campaigns. In the 2004 election, the race for Congress and the White House raised about $3.9 billion.[33] Of this amount, finance, insurance and real estate interests contributed a total of about $50 million to federal candidates, while in 2008 their PACs donated about $63 million.[34]

Earlier, in 1997 and 1998, banking, insurance and brokerage industry lobbyists spent over $300 million on Congress: $58 million directly to candidates, $87 million to the Republican and Democratic Parties and $163 million on the direct lobbying of elected officials. The Chair of the Senate Banking Committee at that time, Phil Gramm, collected more than $1.5 million from the three industries,[35] prior to his sponsorship of the Financial Modernization Act of 1999, also known as the Gramm-Leach-Bliley Act.

The Gramm-Leach-Bliley Act repealed all Glass-Steagall Act restrictions and allowed financial institutions – banks, credit card companies, insurance firms and broker-dealers – to take personal customer information and sell it to other corporations under joint marketing agreements.[36] This legislation was followed by the Commodity Futures Modernization Act of 2000, which passed without debate or review as a rider to an 11,000 page appropriations bill, which exempted derivatives[37] from regulation or oversight and made a special exemption for energy derivative trading that gained notoriety as the 'Enron loophole'.[38]

Senator Gramm was also one of the driving forces behind the Commodity Futures Modernization Act and, upon retirement in 2002, was hired by Swiss-based UBS Warburg (which owned Paine Webber brokerage) and which in the same year acquired Enron's energy trading company. Gramm's wife Wendy served on Enron's board of directors from 1993 to mid-2002, receiving between $915,000 and $1.8 million in salary, director fees and Enron stock.[39]

The result of the Commodity Futures Modernization Act was to allow credit default swaps (CDSs), a form of derivative, to rapidly expand trading in unregulated markets primarily between financial institutions, hedge funds and other speculators or those entities wishing to hedge risk. CDSs are considered to be insurance where an issuer promises to pay for a loss in the event that a corporate or government bond or loan defaults. Unlike regulated and transparent stock, bond and options trading, securities that trade on an exchange, there is no clearing house for CDS trades and no transparency, and, unlike insurance contracts, there are no capital requirements. In 2001, the total outstanding nominal value of CDSs was $106 trillion, increasing to $531 trillion in 2008.[40] The market value of CDS securities at the end of 2009 was $31 trillion.[41]

In addition to a rapidly increasing and unregulated derivatives market, the Alternative Mortgage Transactions Parity Act of 1982 allowed financial institutions to create exotic adjustable-rate (after which rates would be reset at much higher rates) and interest-only mortgages that were 'securitised' so that, along with other mortgages, they could be pooled together, repackaged into securities and sold to investors, including pension and hedge funds, financial and securities firms, mutual funds and other primarily large institutional investors. According to Mathew Sherman: 'Other financial obligations mixed aspects of options and futures and insurance contracts, and they allowed financial firms to bet on or hedge against all sorts of possible outcomes.'[42]

Mortgages, as well as other forms of public and private debt, were also pooled and collateralised by the underlying assets, and became known as collateralised mortgage obligations (CMOs) and collateralised debt obligations (CDOs), which were securitised and also traded in public markets, primarily by large institutional investors, including financial services firms. Much of this debt received high ratings by bond rating agencies and as real estate values in the US increased, so too did additional mortgage lending, packaging and securitisation of loans, trading and speculation. The first securitised mortgage loans were packaged as mortgage-backed securities (MBSs) as early as 1983. In 1970 the Government National Mortgage Association (GNMA or Ginnie Mae) was created, which was comprised of loans securitised by Veterans Administration (VA) and Federal Housing Administration (FHA) mortgage loans. The Federal Home Loan Corporation (FDHMLN or Freddie Mac) and the Federal National Mortgage Association (FNMA or Fannie Mae) were also created as government-sponsored agencies to create liquidity in a rapidly growing secondary mortgage securities market.

Individual homeowners, excited over the increase in real estate values of their properties and already over-extended as consumers utilising increasingly liberal consumer credit, took advantage of low second mortgage rates and borrowed against their primary residences.[43] This led to higher consumer debt levels, fuelled by increased consumption, as well as higher mortgage debt.[44] Inevitably, as housing prices started to decline and adjustable-rate mortgages reset to higher levels, many homeowners began to default on their mortgages. Consequently, mortgage-backed securities linked to residential real estate valuations lost value, resulting in a widespread decline in security valuations as institutional failures mounted.

The fallout from the mortgage and real estate fiasco caused the US Treasury from 2008 to spend $112 billion to shore up Fannie and Freddie, and the Federal Reserve to spend over $1 trillion to purchase mortgage-backed securities since the start of 2009.[45]

By the end of 2008, the stock market, as represented by the Standard and Poors 500 Index, declined about 37 per cent and the SEC temporarily banned the short-selling of all financial stocks.[46] Bear Sterns, a major investment banking firm, was liquidated and sold quickly to JP Morgan Chase, while Lehman Brothers, another major financial institution, declared bankruptcy. Merrill Lynch was sold to the Bank of America in a firesale, and Congress passed the Emergency Economic Stabilization Act of 2008, providing $700 billion to purchase troubled assets and inject capital into an endangered banking system. The $330 billion auction-rate securities market also collapsed as credit tightened and auctions failed, owing to insufficient bidders.[47] Hundreds of companies still have billions of dollars trapped in auction-rate securities, even after several state attorney generals reached negotiated settlements with some banks and brokerage firms which agreed to provide liquidity to some smaller, individual investors.[48]

Personal bankruptcy filings in the US during 2009 hit 1.41 billion, up 32 per cent from 2008 according to the National Bankruptcy Research Center.[49] Distressed debt sales of companies resulting in seized ownership of troubled companies totalled $84.4 billion, dwarfing the $20 billion figure for 2008, encompassing an array of transactions including bankruptcies, restructurings, recapitalisations or liquidations, with corporate default rates at about 10 per cent.[50]

While the global and US economies were undergoing cataclysmic challenges, financial interests went on the offensive. Corporate interests spent $251.1 million lobbying Congress in 2009 and, of this amount, the US Chamber of Commerce alone contributed $65 million. The Chamber and their allies, Business Roundtable, an organisation comprised of the chief executives of over 160 major corporations, spent $656 million on lobbying from 1998 to 2009. Other corporate interests, including the Securities Industry and Financial Marketing Association, contributed another $95 million. Never before had so few spent so much to lobby so few to protect so few who have so much.

The failure of deregulation and the success of fast money

The US Congress, the Obama Administration and federal regulators in 2009 all expressed a strong public commitment to reform Wall Street and create a framework to re-regulate the banking and securities industry. A financial overhaul bill passed the US House of Representatives on 11 December 2009, which was amended to eliminate much in the original bill which would have required all derivatives, including CDSs, to trade on public exchanges where their prices would be disclosed and margin requirements imposed to ensure that securities transactions could be financially covered. However, the bill exempted 'nearly half of the $600 trillion in outstanding derivatives transactions from clearing requirements, following a congressional educational process by dealers and customers'.[51] The bill also exempted non-financial companies seeking to hedge positions, which will give enormous openings to hedge funds to take big risks. A similar bill was adopted by the US Senate on 20 May 2010 and will need to be reconciled with the House bill.

It has been suggested that many in the Congress elected in 2008 are tied to the financial services industry by more than a recognition of the needs of securities dealers and their customers. For example, since the start of the 2008 election cycle, the financial industry has donated $24.9 million to members of the 'New Democrats', some 14 per cent of the total funds the law-makers have collected.[52] These 'New Democrats' are conservative, pro-business members who fill 15 of the party's 42 seats on the House Financial Services Committee.[53]

According to www.campaignmoney.org, in July 2009 it was reported that House Financial Services Committee members received a total of $62.9 million in campaign donations from the financial, insurance and real estate sector in 2009. In addition, according to the Sunlight Foundation (http://blog.sunlightfoundation.com), in 2009, 27 committee members received over one-quarter of their contributions and 12 members received over 35 per cent of their contributions from this sector. The derivatives lobby, an influential group within the finance, insurance and real estate sector, is headed by JP Morgan Chase, Goldman Sachs and Credit Suisse.

Thanks to their successful lobby efforts and targeted 'free speech' at the Congressional level, derivative dealers will be able to continue to use alternatives to public exchanges so that they can retain high trading profits with no public price disclosure. For CDSs, information about trades and prices has long been controlled by a handful of large banks that handle trades and earn large profits from every transaction they facilitate away from public scrutiny. According to the *Wall Street Journal*, a typical pricing gap between a bid and offer price is about 0.1 of a percentage point, translating in a $40,000 margin for every $10 million in debt insured for five years. Greater price transparency would narrow the gap, lowering costs to buyers and sellers but substantially reducing fees for banks.[54]

Commercial banks in the US have had very large liabilities against CDSs that they hold and trade. The International Monetary Fund (IMF) calculated that Goldman Sachs had the largest adjusted liability at $91 billion at the end of March 2009, followed by JP Morgan Chase at $86 billion and Citigroup at $81 billion.[55] Ironically, the US Justice Department anti-trust division is investigating the company Markit Group Holding Ltd., which controls a large amount of the pricing information on which dealers and traders depend and which is owned by some of the very commercial banks that dominate the trading of CDSs. These include JP Morgan Chase, Goldman Sachs, Citigroup, Deutsche Bank AG, the Bank of America and others.[56]

Wall Street traders, dealers and banks, and bank-holding companies have made much of their money not only by creating exotic trading securities, such as CDSs, but also by developing trading platforms, trading strategies and high-frequency trading algorithms to manufacture money from money. For example, Goldman Sachs, a recipient of TARP funding and a convert from an investment bank to a bank-holding company (primarily to gain federal bank funding, guarantees and discounted – inexpensive – money from the Federal Reserve), in one quarter generated over $100 million in trading profit on each of 34 trading days in the first quarter and, in the second quarter of 2009, had 46 $100 million trading days.[57] This is the result of high-speed or high-frequency trading which five years ago was responsible for about 30 per cent and now represents about 70 per cent of the trading volume in the US equity market.[58]

Algorithm-based trading strategies are not new, only much, much faster. The October 1987 stock market crash was caused in part by what was called a dynamic portfolio insurance strategy based on algorithms. The sheer number of people following the same algorithm brought about a wave of selling and, by the end of the day, 19 October 1987 ('Black Friday'), the S&P 500 Index lost over 20 per cent.[59] Every day about 61 per cent of the 10 billion shares traded daily are traded at 'high frequency' across numerous exchanges in the US, with the heaviest activity in the last hour of trading. Trading is a 'virtual art' with silent server farms run by exchanges and broker-dealers across the country, with the New York Stock Exchange (NYSE), which in 2005 handled 80 per cent of trading volume, now comprising only about 40 per cent of all trades. Profits on high-frequency trades in the first nine weeks of 2009 totalled $8 billion or more.[60]

Algorithmic trading executes about 1,000 orders a second for hedge funds and other traders, which could, if trading the wrong way, create billions of dollars in unintended trades. In a letter to the SEC, John Jacobs, the Chief Operations Officer of Lime Brokerage, said that such a mistake had 'the potential for trading-induced multiple domino bankruptcies', cautioning that 'unrestrained computer-generated trading has the potential to create catastrophic economic damage to the US national market system'.[61]

While the SEC has recently adopted a rule to eliminate 'flash trading',[62] little has been done to restrict high-frequency trading among hundreds of hedge funds, pension funds, mutual funds, brokers and banks, using their own money in this huge casino, making money out of money by trading hundreds of millions of shares electronically literally in seconds. Paul Wilmott, founder of *Wilmott*, a journal on quantitative finance, has said that by allowing so many institutional investors, including hedge funds, to use algorithmic formulae in high-frequency trading, the entire market could be destabilised:

> High frequency trading is the latest bandwagon, and everyone is jumping on board. Wall Street always piles onto the next thing, and it always blows up.[63]

In early March 2010 shares of the biotech company Dendreon plunged more than 69 per cent in 70 seconds, caused by a combination of short-sellers and high-frequency trading programmes, and on 6 May 2010, the Dow Jones Industrial Average (DJIA) dropped 1,000 points in 20 minutes, caused by heavy selling in Standard & Poor's 500 futures contracts by a trader at Waddell & Reed Financial, Inc., a brokerage and mutual fund firm. The Chairman of the Commodity

Futures Trading Corporation testified before a Senate Subcommittee that high volume created a misleading indication of liquidity, causing the trader to exclusively enter sell orders through a preprogrammed algorithm.[64]

Another major concern is that many traders and brokers engaged in high-frequency trading have not been 'validated' as having enough capital or credit margin to determine if they actually have enough capital to back up their multiple, rapid-fire and large volume trades. Ironically, excessive leverage continues to be used to engage in high-frequency trading and derivatives, derivatives of which are often leveraged bets against excessive leveraging or debt. Another issue of concern recently expressed by the SEC is 'naked access', which is the increasing practice of high-frequency traders having access to broker-dealers through numbered accounts, which are totally unidentified. The SEC fears that large rapid-fire traders trading anonymously could trigger destabilising losses and threaten market stability if trading mistakes are made. According to Aite Group, a Boston-based research group that tracks electronic trading, naked access accounts have increased from 9 per cent of market volume in 2005 to 38 per cent today.[65] The SEC has proposed new rules requiring large traders to have identifiers requiring them to report next-day transaction data when requested by regulators. This would allow the SEC to track high-speed automated trading to monitor the trading impact.[66] Unfortunately, it would put no controls on such rapid-fire 'naked' algorithm trading.

Little has changed, but much has been said about the need to re-regulate the financial services industry, especially banks, bank-holding companies, investment mortgage bankers, realtors, brokers, security dealers and traders. In a congressionally created Financial Crisis Inquiry Commission (FCIC) hearing, every key regulator that testified expressed dissatisfaction in the regulatory oversight of the industry and the need for additional regulation. Sheila Bair, chair of the Federal Deposit Insurance Corporation (FDIC), which insures and oversees federally-chartered banks, declared that: 'The financial crisis calls into question the fundamental assumptions regarding financial supervision, credit availability and market discipline that have informed our regulatory efforts for decades.'[67] Mary Schapiro, Chair of the SEC, also cited lax regulation of asset-backed securities, an excessive reliance on credit-rating agencies, executive compensation that encouraged unhealthy risk-taking and a failure to oversee hedge funds and private equity funds.[68]

In the same hearing, the US Attorney General and his assistant both said that they were focusing US Department of Justice fraud investigations on mortgage lenders, underwriters and companies that packaged and sold pooled mortgages to institutional investors. The Illinois State Attorney General accused federal regulators of hampering state regulatory authorities in providing oversight and accused both the US Office of the Comptroller of the Currency and the Office of Thrift Supervision of being 'actively engaged in a campaign to thwart state efforts to avert the coming crisis'.[69]

The Commission received earlier testimony from major bank CEOs, including the Chief Executive Officer and President of Bank of America, who stated, in part, that:

> Over the course of this crisis, we as an industry caused a lot of damage. Never has it been clearer how mistakes made by financial companies can affect Main Street.[70]

Other bank CEOs were not so candid in their prepared written testimony, but under questioning from Commission members admitted mistakes had been made. Some mistakes admitted by CEOs were 'institutional' in nature, over-leveraging or excessive risk-taking. However, Lloyd C. Blankfein, Chairman and CEO of Goldman Sachs, did not admit failures in Goldman's risk model, other than relying too much on historical data which substituted for 'judgment' and perhaps too little risk monitoring by some larger financial institutions. Under questioning, according to CBS News (www.cbsnews.com), following a discussion of negligence, market-making and the norms of behaviour before and after the crisis, Blankfein said that: 'The standards at the time were different.' He never admitted a lack of personal responsibility, fiduciary duty or any sense of morality or need for public ethics on behalf of himself or his banking colleagues.

Phil Angelides, Chairman of the FCIC, spoke passionately about the results of the crisis, the 7 million Americans who had lost their jobs since the economic downturn started, the 25 million Americans (over 16 per cent of the workforce) that were unemployed or under-employed, the 2 million families who had lost their homes to foreclosure, the $13 trillion of wealth that had disappeared with market declines, and the possibility that generations of Americans would avoid the markets in a similar fashion to how Americans responded to the 1929 Depression.[71] What was not mentioned, however, was personal responsibility, morality, public ethics or breaches of fiduciary duty.

Alienation and separation of ownership from control

Contemporary responsible investing, including passive screening and shareholder advocacy, is the result of moral concerns raised by individuals questioning certain business conduct. Avoidance or exclusionary screening of companies considered to be engaged in immoral or morally questionable operations has been consistent with the Wall Street Rule: 'Vote with management or sell.' For the most part, this was the strategy of stakeholders in urging shareholders to divest themselves of securities in companies operating in South Africa which were economically and politically supporting an immoral apartheid racial system. The divestment approach, which eventually led to a global economic boycott and embargo, was supplemented by shareholder advocacy and selective purchasing laws which restricted public agencies and others from buying products or services from corporations supporting South Africa.

SRI policies adopted by some investing institutions following Campaign GM and guidance provided by *The Ethical Investor* were initially successful in creating a self-regulatory mechanism to deal with shareholder issues violating social injury guidelines. As other large institutional investors adopted similar policies and engaged corporate management through dialogue and shareholder advocacy, it became clear that corporate management would have to adopt a strategy that did not appear defensive, but limited shareholder intrusion into corporate policy-making. Voluntary corporate codes managed to appear responsive and open to shareholder and stakeholder concerns, while limiting direct involvement in company decision-making.

The Rev. Leon Sullivan's South African Principles were the first test of a voluntary corporate code of conduct. Even with its failure, relative to Sullivan's announced objectives, it provided a model for future corporate codes, including Sullivan's 1997 Global Sullivan

Principles of Social Responsibility, which encouraged businesses to work with their respective communities toward common goals of human rights, social justice and economic opportunity. These goals, while laudable, are voluntary, are not monitored by an objective third party, are generally unenforceable and there are no sanctions or penalties if a violation is discovered by stakeholders. In other words, there is no rule of law to enforce and sanction violations.

Other 'principles' and corporate codes proliferated in the late-twentieth and early-twenty-first centuries and have included the Caux Round Table Principles for Business, the American Apparel and Footwear Association (AAFA), Worldwide Responsibility Apparel Production (WRAP), the Principles and Certification Program, the Fair Labor Association (FLA), the Workplace Code of Conduct, the Global Reporting Initiative (GRI), the UN Global Compact, the China Business Principles, the Equator Principles, the Extractive Industries Transparency Initiative (EITI), the Common Code for the Coffee Community (CCCC) and the Social Accountability 8000 (SA8000), a cross-industry standard for workplace conditions, among others.

While these codes are designed by corporate management and stakeholders to create an ongoing relationship between shareholders, stakeholders, civil society and corporate management, it has resulted in little progress in substantially providing access to corporate policy-makers even by shareholders. Corporate management in general and corporate legal counsel in particular have advanced management's interests by incorporating business entities in states providing favourable legal defences to shareholder access, i.e., Delaware, whose statutes generally provide greater liability protection for officers and directors regarding corporate activities by providing extensive insurance and officer and director indemnification.

As discussed above, passive screening by investors coupled with shareholder advocacy usually leads to an annual confrontation between stakeholders and some shareholders and corporate management who control an overwhelming majority of shareholder proxies. This control successfully thwarts shareholder efforts to pass advisory (precatory) resolutions as well as binding bylaw amendment resolutions. A large number of the resolutions submitted annually are challenged by management requesting no-action letters from the SEC, while about one-half of those are eventually presented to the shareholders. Only a small percentage of resolutions (less than 2 per cent) are adopted, all of which are precatory, not requiring action by boards of directors or executive officers.

However, the latest fallout from the financial crisis of 2008 has been the rising success of precatory resolutions relative to executive compensation ('say on pay'). The public anger has translated into more votes against management at annual shareholder meetings, especially considering the lax attitude – perceived or factual – by the public regarding members of corporate boards of directors that have approved overly generous compensation packages for senior executives and pools of employees, including traders, at financial firms. Often these directors attend 8–12 meetings a year and are compensated as much as $640,000 annually. Some that sit on multiple corporate boards, including ten highly-paid directors described in a *Bloomberg Businessweek* article of 22 February 2010 entitled 'The Gold-Plated Boardroom', receive a seven-figure sum, including cash, stock grants and other perks.[72] Frequently, these same directors oversee CEOs that receive excessive compensation based on their less than mediocre performance. At Lehman Brothers, for example, whose Risk Committee met only twice a year, between 2000 and 2007 the full board compensated the CEO with salary, stock, options and bonuses to the tune of $484 million. In a quarterly conference call, after the CEO had announced that the firm had lost $3.9 billion in the quarter, he said that 'the board's been wonderfully supportive'. Four days later Lehman filed for bankruptcy, costing shareholders $45 billion.[73]

Increasingly, according to the *Huffington Post* (www.huffingtonpost. com), CEOs and other executives are being charged with breaches of fiduciary duty. For example, Goldman Sachs and its principal officers are being sued by institutional and individual shareholders for abdicating their shareholder duty by setting aside large bonus pools for themselves and other key employees, charging that higher CEO pay may actually damage long-term shareholder value.

Investors have been alienated from the markets by financial institutions and their hedge funds, trading exotic investment instruments, primarily derivatives, including credit default swaps and collateralised debt obligations, utilising excessive leverage and taking excessive risks. These corporations have also had access to TARP and federal guarantees, including access to cheap money from the Federal Reserve. Coupled with the majority of stock traded daily linked to algorithmic trading models, trading billions of shares a day and hundreds of thousands of shares per second has distorted traditional 'buy and hold' management styles, disputed Modern Portfolio Theory (MPT)[74] and disrupted long-term institutional investment strategies. Smith's 'wealth', thought of in the physical sense and later emerging as stock defined by Berle and Means as a 'bundle of expectations', has now become digitised on a computer screen, totally removing any connection between a corporation and its owners. Investors have not only given up control of corporate enterprises for liquidity, they have become totally disconnected and alienated from capital.

This has worked to the disadvantage of investors, stakeholders and civil society, while working to the advantage of corporate management. While increasingly wealth is constantly being created and re-created by generating money from money through leverage and trading strategies, it is to the advantage of fewer large financial institutions, mostly benefiting a few wealthy individuals within those institutions. These institutions also benefit by having access to cheap money from the Federal Reserve System, as well as benefiting from federal guarantees paid for by the public. Individuals within these institutions are protected by corporate legal counsel from risk or individual responsibility which is paid for by shareholders.

While officers and directors of corporations are required to act as fiduciaries, that is, to have undivided loyalty to shareholders, to provide full disclosure, to have a duty of care and to be required to act in good faith regarding shareholders, they are well protected from personal liability based on current law. For example, it has been suggested that the 'duty of care' has been eliminated as an enforceable duty of corporate law as a result of a combination of:

- the business judgment rule, which precludes personal liability for officers and directors taking responsible care in making business decisions;
- indemnification, which authorises or requires the company to reimburse officers and directors for most forms of personal liability;
- exculpation clauses, which companies adopt in their articles of incorporation to eliminate a cause of action for a breach of the duty of care;
- directors and officers (D&O) insurance, which effectively shifts the financial risk of malfeasance to an insurance company.[75]

Specifically, legal studies have evaluated 'outside directors' actual liability risks for failing to meet their "vigilance duties" arising under a range of statues, and found for actions taken in good faith such are negligible, either under corporate, securities, environmental, pension or other laws. This component of directors' and managers' fiduciary duties is important even though it portends no realistic possibility of personal liability'.[76] In other words, under current law, not to mention existing moral and ethical standards of conduct, it is almost impossible that officers and directors will take personal responsibility or have personal financial liability for policies and actions taken by the corporation. To say the least, this reality has led to greater shareholder and public alienation from capital and those that control such capital.

Fiduciary duty and morality

While legal obligations pursuant to fiduciary duty have been narrowed, it has not stopped shareholders from examining and seeking to expand fiduciary duty to shareholders for environmental and human rights violations, transparency, corporate governance and environmental sustainability.

Shareholders and other stakeholders have asked the SEC to examine these issues specifically in the context of Regulation S-K Item 103, which requires corporate disclosure of material financial issues, including potential monetary sanctions imposed by a governmental authority of greater than $100,000 or legal proceedings where claims may exceed 10 per cent of a company's value. Monetary penalties for corporate violations of the US Alien Tort Claims Act (ATCA) and the US Foreign Corrupt Practices Act (FCPA) have on numerous occasions exceeded such thresholds.

The ATCA is a 1789 federal statute that allows US federal courts to hear cases brought by foreign citizens involving violations of human rights, including torture, arbitrary detention and arrest, crimes against humanity, slavery and extra-judicial killings. Numerous corporations have been involved in ATCA claims, including Chevron, Unocal and Yahoo! While there are numerous outstanding claims, most cases have either been dismissed or settled out of court for undisclosed sums of money.

The FCPA of 1977, amended in 1988, prohibits corporate bribery for both individuals and business enterprises. Literally hundreds of

US corporations have admitted to making illegal or questionable payments to foreign officials, politicians or political parties. The SEC has levelled hundreds of millions of dollars in fines since the 1970s for violations of the FCPA. For example, the German engineering group Siemens was fined a record $800 million in 2008 for bribing government officials in Nigeria, Russia and Libya to win government contracts. Litigation pursuant to the ATCA, including out-of-court financial settlements as well as fines levied by the SEC following violations of fiduciary duty by corporate management, increasingly indicates that morality or ethical conduct is an important and necessary ingredient of fiduciary duty.

In response to shareholder activists, the SEC recently issued 'interpretive guidance' to corporations filing disclosure statements to encourage them to disclose the possible effects of climate change on their businesses. The Commission said that companies could be helped or hurt by climate-related lawsuits, business opportunities or government legislation or regulation and should promptly report or disclose such impacts.[77] Social investors have long sought additional disclosure from corporate management on climate change risk as a necessary ingredient of management's fiduciary duty.

Goldman Sachs created and sold collateralised mortgage obligations that it simultaneously sold short. These investments lost value for investors, but Goldman made money on shorting the CDOs or betting against their own clients or customers. In the process of selling CDOs, Goldman lobbied rating agencies to assign the CDOs high ratings, so customers would continue to buy them, even when the firm was shorting the securities. Goldman made money both selling CDOs and shorting them in the firm's own account and possibly for 'selected' special clients.

Goldman Sachs also recommended investors purchase CDSs on municipal debt in 11 states, debt which was also underwritten by Goldman. So, in essence, the bank-holding company encouraged investor bets against municipalities, leading to an increase in the states' borrowing costs, which were Goldman clients. In addition to the SEC filing a lawsuit against Goldman Sachs for fraud on 16 April 2010, claiming the firm duped investors in a CDO called Abacus 2007-AC1 by failing to disclose that it was created with the help of hedge fund firm Paulson & Co., which made a profit of $1 billion when the investment collapsed in value, Goldman also faces several shareholder lawsuits charging its board of directors with a breach of fiduciary duty.[78]

Goldman Sachs also simply speculated by trading derivatives for their own account. According to the Real Clear Markets website (www.realclearmarkets.com), had the federal government not 'bailed out' American International Group (AIG) with an $85 billion credit facility to meet increased collateral obligations, the company would have defaulted on the CDSs held by Goldman as a counterparty, 'which would mean that when the government paid AIG's claims, Goldman Sachs had something like a $12.9 billion windfall gain on its hedges'. FDIC Chair Sheila Bair testified before the FCIC that the CDS market still poses a systemic threat and that she could not access CDS information to accurately assess the exposure of financial institutions. According to *The Nation* (www.thenation.com), SEC Chair Mary Schapiro testified that credit rating agencies had proved to be worthless given that they are paid 'by the very Wall Street firms who are profiting from AAA-rated securitized assets'.

Corporate directors and officers are fiduciaries. They have a duty of undivided loyalty and a duty of care, full disclosure, and a duty to act in good faith regarding shareholders. That fiduciary duty is a moral as well as a legal obligation.

The existence of individuals acting in their own materialistic self-interest within the corporation is a violation of fiduciary duty, in that they are not acting with undivided loyalty, with a duty of care or acting in good faith, pursuant to full disclosure. Such excessive materialistic self-interest is morally unjustifiable, requiring shareholder action.

Given that there are few, if any, constraints on corporate management's lack of full and transparent disclosure and their ability to continue to manipulate governmental regulatory and legislative oversight through their domination of lobbying and campaign expenditures,[79] significant shareholder advocacy is necessary to restore fiduciary and moral oversight and control of corporate management.

Immanuel Kant (1724–1804), a moral philosopher writing in the eighteenth century, believed that the highest good was to act from goodwill regardless of the consequences and that the highest morality came from one's duty, not one's self-interest. He also believed that individuals should act autonomously or freely, and to act autonomously is to act according to a law that is universalised, that man gives himself and accepts himself, and that is not dictated by nature or social convention.

Kant developed what is known as the categorical imperative, or acting morally out of duty, a duty which is unconditional and applies regardless of the circumstances or consequences. This moral duty or categorical imperative is a formula for humanity, because it treats human beings as ends in themselves, rather than using other human beings as means to an end.

Fiduciary duty is Kantian, in that it is a rational process established as a universal law that is unconditional. Fiduciary duty has been universalised and codified by statute, and directors and officers of corporations are required to abide by it. It is a duty that is categorical, a law man has chosen and one in which he must abide.

Corporate directors and officers are fiduciaries and as such they retain their moral authority and personal responsibility, and are agents of shareholders. According to Stephen B. Young, with the separation of management from ownership came the 'rise of agency as a special linkage between the managers of a business and its owners'.[80] That said, acting as agents for owners, directors are subordinated to owners who elect them and are required to have a fiduciary duty to act in the primary and best interests of shareholders. This has a strong Kantian moral and legal grounding.

Conclusion

Investors need to redefine 'social injury' as well as strengthen and enforce fiduciary duty. Contemporary social injury is more than a recognition of 'activities which violate or frustrate the enforcement of rules of domestic or international law intended to protect individuals against deprivation of health, safety or basic freedoms'.

In redefining social injury, investors need to recognise that fiduciary duty cannot be narrowly defined only in immediate quantifiable monetary terms. While shareholders and stakeholders have been successful in convincing the SEC to encourage corporate management to consider that climate change may be a 'material financial issue' to the corporation's bottom line and therefore requiring of public disclosure, violations of the ATCA and the FCPA, which include significant transgressions of moral obligations such as violations of human rights and bribery, clearly contravene the fiduciary duty.

Violations of the ATCA and the FCPA also equate to violations of fiduciary duty because such acts translate into significant monetary costs, due to regulatory sanctions, legal expenses defending the corporation and/or possible settlement costs. These costs are *all* paid for out of shareholders' pockets. These are also violations of 'social injury' recognisable by shareholders and stakeholders alike. In addition, when corporate management allows traders to engage in high-risk leveraged trading strategies, financially endangering both the corporation and US economic security, then directors should have a personal responsibility, a moral obligation and a fiduciary duty to intervene. Excessive materialistic self-interest has blinded all parties to the categorical imperative.

Certainly shareholders need to demand additional disclosure and regulatory oversight. However, risk-related disclosures are often window dressing that avoids more substantive reform measures. In a recent SEC comment letter on a proposed rule that would enhance corporate disclosures regarding compensation and risk, shareholder activists disputed blaming Wall Street simply for excessive risk:

> We believe that, over the past two decades, the financial services industry has discovered 'risk' to be a convenient scapegoat in instances where financial institutions or their clients suffer staggering losses due to fraud or other forms of abuse.
>
> If a man jumps out of an airplane without a parachute, is he taking risk? If he is certain to die, the answer is 'no.' Risk is not about consequences. It is about *uncertain* consequences. If there is no uncertainty, there is no risk. Similarly, there was no risk in many of the securitizations that crippled our economy in 2008. These were bundles of mortgages underwritten as if home prices would rise forever, creating a giant pyramid scheme. They were guaranteed to fail. Mortgage originators, investment bankers and credit rating analysts knew, or should have known, the instruments were unsound. Yet, the entire industry aggressively pushed the instruments because they had incentive compensation that promoted such abuse. In the midst of the ensuing crisis, Congress and other branches of our government did not wait for hearings before they embraced Wall Street's excuse that 'excessive risk' was to blame. We believe this shifting of blame from abuse, where the blame

correctly belongs, to excessive risk, where it is largely misplaced, is forestalling appropriate legislative and regulatory initiatives that might prevent future market panics. We believe the current administration's proposal to form a systemic-risk regulator, regretfully, falls short of what is needed. What our economy needs is a systemic-abuse regulator.[81]

Regrettably, corporate abuses will continue to be sanctioned by excessive materialistic self-interest which threatens US and global economic security. Last year, President Obama's new intelligence chief, Dennis C. Blair, testified in Congress that the US financial crisis was the single most damaging threat to national security and that the longer it took for the recovery to begin, 'the greater the likelihood of serious damage to US strategic interest'.[82] It is doubtful that meaningful regulatory or legislative remedies will be enacted, not only based upon the past history of the dominance of corporate lobbying and political contributions to election campaigns, but also because of the recent Supreme Court decision, which will surely unleash vast sums of corporate contributions, ensuring that excessive materialistic self-interest will prevail as the dominate secular morality.

On the other hand, the morality of obligation is embedded in the fiduciary duty which transcends selfishness. This duty, which is required of corporate officers and directors, must be audited and enforced by shareholders. *The Ethical Investor* proposed oversight and self-regulatory guidelines for institutional investors to address a moral minimum obligation based upon a negative injunction. Shareholders must continue to submit investment decisions to the most rigorous screens, but also seriously engage in shareholder advocacy to expand the narrow monetary range of traditional fiduciary duty.

Avery Kolers suggested that this is necessary 'to broaden the invest/divest dichotomy, replacing it with the possibility of working for moral goals within a deeply flawed system'. He also went on to say that failing to meet moral demands results in investors acting immorally.[83]

While Congress and the President may enact legislation to respond to the financial crisis of 2008, inevitably, I believe, it will be fraught with loopholes sought by the very financial services industry they publicly seek to regulate. I have little faith in the idea that Congress and federal regulators have the will or the ability to rein in corporate abuse, fraud and/or excessive risk, perpetual violations of fiduciary duty and excessive materialistic self-interest which has resulted in the most recent global financial crisis.[84] Congress, the Administration and federal regulators are beyond redemption and are an intricate part of the problem. Shareholders are the 'last resort' and as such must advocate for civil society. Owners must advocate as shareholders by challenging corporate management through corporate governance resolutions and bylaw amendments. Options for broader fiduciary duties for directors includes amendments to corporate bylaws to: (1) limit corporate indemnification for officers and directors that violate the fiduciary duty related to human or environmental rights as well as corporate abuse, fraud and excessive risk-taking; (2) create board committees on human rights and environmental sustainability; (3) require directors and officers of the corporation to affirm their allegiance to the US Constitution; and, in the case of financial firms, (4) create board ethics oversight committees and board committees on US economic security to ensure that corporate policies are supportive of US economic security.

In the case of bylaw amendments recently filed with Citigroup, the Bank of America and Goldman Sachs, all large financial institutions that have received TARP funding and federal treasury guarantees as bank-holding companies, emphasis by shareholders has been placed on the impact of company policies on the long-term health of the US, specifically the impact of company policies on the economic well-being of US citizens as reflected in indicators such as levels of employment, wages, consumer installment debt and home ownership. It is important that corporations primarily owned by US citizens and institutions, which stock trades on American exchanges, which operate and are chartered in the US, and which have extensive federal, state and local government subsidies, including public contracts and federal government guarantees and reduced borrowing rates, have a fiduciary and moral duty to US civil society. Recently, shareholders of several technology companies have introduced bylaw amendment resolutions to authorise boards of directors to create board standing committees on human rights and sustainability. Intel Corporation, a major Silicon Valley chip manufacturing company, responded to shareholder concerns by amending the company's Charter of the Corporate Governance and Nominating Committee to include 'corporate responsibility and sustainable performance' within the Committee's overall policy responsibility. The company also provided shareholders with an outside legal opinion stating that, pursuant to Delaware law, directors have a fiduciary duty to address corporate responsibility and sustainability performance as specified in the amended Charter.

The introduction of corporate governance resolutions, specifically bylaw amendments concentrating on limiting officer and director compensation and indemnification, while enhancing and strengthening personal responsibility and financial liability regarding the protection of human and environmental rights and sustainability, all serve as a counterforce to excessive materialistic self-interest and support a resurgence of a morality of obligation codified in the fiduciary duty based upon Kantian principles.

We must insert into the DNA of every corporation a fiduciary duty to protect civil society from fraud, abuse and excessive risk, based upon a recognition of contemporary 'social injury'. Without continued momentum in this direction, Wall Street's greed, avarice and domination of our political and economic system will lead to the second major financial crisis of the twenty-first century, from which it may take decades to recover. Unfortunately, it is now all but inevitable.

Notes

1. Mark S. Schwartz, 'The "Ethics" of Ethical Investing' (2003) *Journal of Business Ethics*, 196.
2. John C. Harrington, *Investing With Your Conscience: How to Achieve High Returns Using Socially Responsible Investing*, New York: John Wiley & Sons, 1992, pp. 5–6.
3. Charles W. Powers, *Social Responsibility and Investments*, New York: Abingdon Press, 1971, pp. 100–1.
4. John G. Simon, Charles W. Powers and Jon P. Gunnemann, *The Ethical Investor*, London: Yale University Press, 1972, pp. 54–6.
5. Ibid., p. 21.
6. Ibid., p. 16.
7. 'Environmentally injurious operations' were defined as 'activities of a business organization which seriously degrade or cause irreversible, irrecoverable or irreparable harm to the natural environment': AB 974 (Dunlap), 2.
8. John Harrington, *California State and Local Investments: A Guide for Responsible Ownership*, California State Legislature, January 1975, p. 6.
9. Following 'Campaign GM', Oberlin, Stanford, Harvard, Princeton, Yale, Dartmouth, MIT, Wesleyan and Cornell established student, faculty and

administration advisory committees to recommend to their respective trustees votes on issues before corporate shareholders.

10. Harrington, *Investing With Your Conscience*, pp. 196–200.
11. Exclusionary investment criteria is based on more objective data since such data is often easier to access, i.e., tobacco production, while inclusionary information is more subjectively interpreted, i.e., environmental or human rights information.
12. Robert Kropp, 'Responsible Investing Poised to Become Mainstream', 10 August 2009, www.socialfunds.com/news/article.cgi/2754.html, date accessed 6 October 2010.
13. CDFIs are financial institutions that have specialised lending and economic development programmes targeting less fortunate communities, domestically and internationally, in such areas as fair trade, affordable housing, microlending and specifically employment generation.
14. The Calvert Foundation is a 15-year-old 501(c)(3) tax-exempt foundation that utilises a lending programme instead of grants to fund foreign and domestic social justice and community economic development programmes (see www.calvertfoundation.org).
15. John C. Harrington, *The Challenge to Power: Money, Investing and Democracy*, White River Junction: Chelsea Green, 2005, p. 72.
16. Joe Weisenthal, 'Group of Nuns Attack Goldman Over Large Bonuses', *Business Insider*, 14 October 2009.
17. Jay W. Eisenhofer and Michael J. Barry, *Shareholder Activism Handbook*, New York: Aspen Publishers, 2010 Supplement, pp. 3–71.
18. Stephen Grocer, 'Banks Set for Record Pay', *Wall Street Journal*, 15 January 2010, A1.
19. This section is based upon my Master's thesis at the Dominican University of California entitled: 'The Morality of Materialistic Self-interest, the Corporation and the State', 5 May 2006.
20. Adam Smith, *The Wealth of Nations*, New York: Bantam Dell, 1776, p. 338.
21. Ibid., p. 339.
22. Charles Perrow, *Organizing America*, Princeton University Press, 2005, p. 36.
23. William G. Roy, *Socializing Capital: The Rise of the Large Industrial Corporation in America*, Princeton University Press, 1979, pp. 145–6.
24. Kevin Danaher and Jason Mark, *Insurrection*, New York: Routledge, 2003, p. 44.
25. Theodore Roosevelt, *Theodore Roosevelt: An Autobiography*, New York: Charles Scriber's Sons, 1920, p. 423.
26. Conrad P. Waligorski, *Liberal Economics and Democracy*, Lawrence: University Press of Kansas, 1997, p. 40.
27. John Maynard Keynes, *Essays in Persuasion*, New York: Harcourt, Bruce and Company, 1932, pp. 314–15.
28. Mark Mizruchi, 'Berle and Means Revisited' (2004) *Theory and Society*, 33, 1, 581.

29. Adolf A. Berle and Gardiner C. Means, *The Modern Corporation and Private Property*, New York: MacMillian Company, 1939, pp. 346–7.
30. Ibid., p. 348.
31. The Glass-Steagall Act prohibited banks from being 'principally engaged' in non-banking activities, such as insurance and underwriting or trading securities. This was later extended to bank-holding companies. Financial firms had to choose between lending funds or being engaged in securities transactions.
32. Mathew Sherman. 'A Short History of Financial Deregulation in the United States', Centre for Economic Policy and Research, July 2009, p. 9.
33. Harrington, *The Challenge to Power*, p. 16.
34. http://opensecrets.org/pacs/sector.php?cycle=2008&text=F01, date accessed 6 October 2010.
35. Martin McCaughlin, 'Clinton, Republicans Agree to Deregulate Financial System', World Socialist Website, 1 November 1999, www.wsws.org/articles/1999/nov1999/bank-n01.shtml, date accessed 6 October 2010.
36. Harrington, *The Challenge to Power*, p. 28.
37. Derivatives are securities that may or may not trade on public or in regulated markets that derive their value from their claim to another asset, such as an option to purchase or sell a futures contract on a commodity such as coffee or oil, or an option to buy or sell a stock. A derivative can be used to hedge against risk or to protect against a decline in an underlying asset, such as foreign currency. Derivatives can also be used simply as a speculative security, to make money from money. These securities do not involve a transfer of assets, so a buyer or seller may not own the underlying asset.
38. Sherman, 'A Short History', p. 11.
39. Harrington, *The Challenge to Power*, p. 28.
40. Sherman, 'A Short History', p. 11.
41. Richard Beales and Neil Unmack, 'Credit Derivatives That Distort Markets', *New York Times*, 21 December 2009, B2.
42. Sherman, 'A Short History', p. 12.
43. Individual homeowners often borrowed to pay off credit card debt and many borrowed to buy second and third homes, believing that property values would continue to increase.
44. Currently, consumer debt in the US is $2.5 trillion or about $8,100 for every man, women and child in the country. Credit card debt totals $866 billion. See http://money-zine.com/Financial-Planning/Debt-Consolidation/Consumer-Debt-Statistics, date accessed 6 October 2010.
45. Peter Eavis, 'U.S. Aid Benefits Banks, Not Homeowners', *Wall Street Journal*, 19 January 2010, C10.
46. 'Short-selling' is a financial transaction that includes selling securities that have been borrowed from a third party (normally a brokerage firm) and buying them back at a reduced price. The short-seller normally profits if the security goes down in value before it is bought back and returned to the brokerage firm.

47. Auction-rate securities are long-term securities issued by municipalities, charities and other entities that are sold by banks and brokerage firms and are engineered to have short-term features, with interest rates reset at weekly or monthly auctions. These securities were sold by misleading clients and customers about the securities' safety and liquidity. Many of these securities were sold to replace money market funds and were presented as a safe and higher-yielding liquid alternative.

48. Liz Rappaport, 'Firms Fight Back Over Billions in Frozen Notes', *Wall Street Journal*, 2 January 2010, A1.

49. Sara Murray and Conor Dougherty, 'Personal Bankruptcy Filings Rise Fast', *Wall Street Journal*, 5 January 2010, A3.

50. Mike Spector and Jeffrey McCracken, 'Distressed Takeovers Soar', *Wall Street Journal*, 11 August 2009, A1.

51. Randall Smith and Sarah N. Lynch, 'How Overhauling Derivatives Died', *Wall Street Journal*, 28 December 2009, 24.

52. Jesse Westbrooks, 'Not So Radical Reform', *Bloomberg Businessweek*, 11 January 2010, 26.

53. Ibid.

54. Serna Ng, 'Banks Seek Role in Bid to Overhaul Derivatives', *Wall Street Journal*, 29 May 2009, C1.

55. Peter Eavis, 'Digging Into Derivatives' Capital Hole', *Wall Street Journal*, 14 August 2009, B10.

56. Liz Rappaport, Carrick Mollenkamp and Serna Ng, 'U.S. Tightens its Derivatives Vice', *Wall Street Journal*, 15 July 2009, C1.

57. Tyler Durden, 'Goldman Sachs: Why Aren't Trading Profits Raising Any Red Flags?', 6 May 2009, http://seekingalpha.com/article/135785-goldman-sachs, date accessed 6 October 2010.

58. Ibid., and 'Goldman Sachs (GS) High Frequency Trading Profits', www.webofdebt.com/articles/computerized_front_running.php, date accessed 6 October 2010.

59. Paul Wilmott, 'Hurrying into the Next Panic?', *New York Times*, 29 July 2009, p. 29.

60. Bryant Urstadt, 'Trading Shares in Milliseconds', *Technology Review*, January/February 2010, p. 44.

61. Ibid., p. 47.

62. 'Flash trading' is when exchanges appoint designated traders (or preferred customers) to incoming orders, giving them advance notice of price changes. Many say that it is a variation of 'front running', an illegal practice that involved traders buying and selling in advance of later larger orders, thereby profiting on the 'front-end' of trading.

63. Urstadt, 'Trading Shares in Milliseconds', p. 46.

64. Sarah N. Lynch, 'Gensler Puts Blame on Math', *Wall Street Journal*, 21 May 2010, C2.

65. Scott Patterson, 'SEC Aims to Ban 'Naked Access', *Wall Street Journal*, 14 January 2010, C1.

66. Fawn Johnson, 'SEC Plans Trader ID System', *Wall Street Journal*, 15 April 2010, C3.

67. Sewell Chan, 'Lax Regulation Cited as Major Reason for Financial Crisis', *New York Times*, 15 January 2010, B3.
68. Ibid.
69. Ibid.
70. Brian T. Moynihan, Chief Executive Officer and President, Bank of America, Testimony to Financial Crisis Inquiry Commission (FCIC), Washington DC, 13 January 2010, p. 1.
71. Phil Angelides, Chair, Financial Crisis Inquiry Commission, Opening Remarks, 17 January 2010, pp. 1–2. He also noted that it took 25 years for the stock market, as measured by the DJIA, to regain its 1929 peak.
72. Nanette Byrnes, 'The Gold-Plated Boardroom', *Bloomberg Businessweek*, 22 February 2010, pp. 72–3.
73. Harry Hurt III, 'Taking Away Directors' Rubber Stamps', *New York Times*, 17 January 2010, B15.
74. MPT is a portfolio management theory based on maximising return and minimiaing risk by the prudent diversification of assets. However, during the 2008 financial crisis, all asset classes significantly declined in value regardless of asset diversity.
75. Cynthia A. Williams and John M. Conley, 'Is There an Emerging Fiduciary Duty to Consider Human Rights?' (2005–6) *University of Cincinnati Law Review*, 74, 89.
76. Ibid.
77. John Broder, 'SEC Adds Risk Related to Climate to Disclosure List', *New York Times*, 28 January 2010, B1; and Kara Scannell and Siobhan Hughes, 'Divided SEC Makes Climate Another Risk', *Wall Street Journal*, 28 January 2010, C1.
78. Chad Bray, 'Goldman Sued Over CDOs', *Wall Street Journal*, 4 May 2010, C3.
79. On 21 January 2010, the US Supreme Court in a 5-4 decision ruled against any restrictions on direct political contributions by corporations and labour unions to candidates for federal office. The ruling voided a section of the 1947 Taft-Hartley Act that prohibited corporations and unions from spending money to elect federal candidates. Many observers believe that this will allow increased amounts of campaign contributions by corporations, both foreign and domestic, to dominate national elections.
80. Stephen B. Young, 'Fiduciary Duties as a Helpful Guide to Ethical Decision-making in Business' (2007) *Journal of Business Ethics*, 5.
81. http://isuffrage.org/documents/2009_09_SEC_comment_letter_enhanced_disclosures.pdf, date accessed 6 October 2010.
82. Greg Miller, 'Global Economic Crisis Called Biggest U.S. Security Threat', 13 February 2009, http://articles.latimes.com/2009/feb/13/national/na-security-threat13, date accessed 6 October 2010.
83. Avery Kolers, 'Ethical Investing: The Permissibility of Participation' (2001) *Journal of Political Philosophy*, 9, 4, 451.
84. The New York Attorney General filed a civil case against the former CEO of the Bank of America for defrauding BofA shareholders in the acquisition of Merrill Lynch, which led to $16 billion in pre-tax losses in

the fourth quarter of 2008, resulting in the federal government pumping in $20 billion in TARP funding. This came at the same time that the SEC reached a $150 million settlement of a federal suit alleging that BofA mislead investors. Such SEC settlements have no impact on the future conduct of corporations or corporate executives, since executives are not individually responsible for paying the penalties. For corporations, it is simply the cost of doing business.

6
The Achilles' Heel of Competitive/Adversarial Systems

Thomas Pogge

In the modern world, competitive and adversarial systems are omnipresent. The real economy and our financial markets are based on competition: firms and banks are competing over customers, investors and employees. The exercise of political power is based on competition among political parties for votes and campaign contributions. Internationally, states compete for military and economic power as supported by access to natural resources, advanced technologies and the most talented people. The interpretation and application of rules is settled by courts that function as adversarial systems driven by two parties seeking to make their own proposed application of the rules seem compelling and to discredit their opponent's proposal. There is fierce competition among the media over stories, advertisers and consumers – and similarly dogged competition among non-governmental organisations (NGOs) over donations and success stories. And in the academy, as well, there is competition over teachers and researchers, students, donations and the rewards of success such as grants, prizes and media recognition. Organised competition is pervasive in modern life.

Competition can be a very powerful motivator of performance. In a competitive system, agents tend to receive greater rewards the better they perform. This much is also true of non-competitive systems in which agents are rewarded on the basis of some subjective or algorithmic assessment of their performance. But in such non-competitive systems, agents have incentives to play up the difficulties of their task and to downplay their own capacities in order to influence the judges or the designers of the relevant reward algorithms in their favour. By making others believe that they are working harder than they really are, agents can boost the rate at which they get rewarded. Competition avoids this problem by motivating agents to reveal their full capacities. To reap maximum rewards, agents must here put in a good performance not relative to their own presumed capacities but relative to the actual performance of other agents. It is a great virtue of competitive systems that they incentivise agents to reveal their own capacities and then to give their best.

This virtue enables competitive systems to be highly effective at promoting desired outcomes. However, such effectiveness depends on a competitive or adversarial system being properly framed. This means that the rules of the game must be designed so as to ensure that the self-interested pursuits of the 'players' are closely correlated with their contributions to desired outcomes, and that these rules are administered in a transparent and impartial way so that the competing agents know that they will be rewarded for superior performance and *only* for superior performance.

The Achilles' heel of competitive or adversarial systems is related to this need for proper framing. Competitive/adversarial systems contain the seeds of their own demise by providing powerful incentives to reward-focused players to attempt to manipulate the rules or to interfere with their impartial application. The rules and the regulators – supposedly in charge of organising and constraining the competition – thus come themselves to be potential objects of the competition. In the years leading up to the recent global financial crisis, firms such as Ameriquest Mortgage Company and Countrywide Financial spent millions on lobbying activities to defeat anti-predatory-lending legislation and there is evidence to suggest that the response to the crisis has also been heavily influenced by corporate lobbyists.[1] To the extent that efforts by players to influence the design or application of the rules in their own favour – to *corrupt* the competition – succeed, these efforts diminish the effectiveness of the competitive or adversarial system. This happens in two distinct ways: first, player resources diverted towards corruption are no longer available to boost performance; and, second, the incentives to work hard towards superior performance are weakened insofar as such rewards fail to track superior performance.

Here is an example. Suppose the military needs to replace its ageing fleet of refuelling planes. It puts out for tender a large contract for designing and supplying a new model of refuelling plane. Competing firms can now throw all their best efforts at the task of designing a plane that reaches a high level of performance at a relatively low unit cost. But a firm can make other efforts as well. It can try to influence the formulation of the call – by trying to affect who gets to write the call and/or by trying to affect how it is formulated by its authors – so that this call emphasises features of refuelling planes in regard to which this firm has a relative advantage over its competitors and de-emphasises features in regard to which the firm is at a relative disadvantage. And the firm can also try to influence the judgment made pursuant to the call – again, by trying to influence the composition of the judging panel and/or by trying to influence the appointed judges. Euphemistically referred to as 'lobbying', such efforts to corrupt the rules of the competition or their impartial application are costly. When such efforts have no effect, they merely produce a cost to the firm as well as a social cost in those cases where this firm, had it concentrated its effort on delivering a better bid, would have beaten the actual winner. Insofar as such corruption efforts succeed, they cause additional social costs: the formulation of the call for tenders, and the plane it eventually leads to, may not match the real needs of the military; a plane that is superior according to the terms of the call may be beaten by an inferior one; and, for the future, potential defence contractors may be encouraged to divert more of their resources towards corruption efforts, a practice which will result in the military receiving less suitable equipment for the money it spends.

In cases like our example, the corruption efforts typically take advantage of a principal-agent problem which arises from the fact that the people formulating the call for tenders – and those who decide which firm's design best meets the call – are not focused solely on the country's interest in an effective military, but also have strong private interests, for example, in positioning themselves for a lucrative future consultancy (the 'revolving door' phenomenon). But efforts to corrupt can make sense even in cases where there is no principal-agent duality. For example, take a family choosing among competing architects, car dealers, dentists or investment advisors. Here individual competitors can try to win the contract by invoking their expertise to influence their potential customer's or client's decision procedure. One can try to coax one's potential customer or client into valuing more highly those features of the relevant product or service with regard to which one has a potential advantage over one's competitors. Alternatively, one can try to divert the potential customer or client from performing a sober assessment of his or her options. These skills are omnipresent in the modern world and matter greatly not merely for the success of professional lobbyists, but also for that of salespeople, attorneys, politicians, corporate executives and basically everyone filling a social role with competitive or adversarial aspects.

Corruption problems of the sort I have described can be greatly reduced through protective rules that deter corruption efforts. There are many examples of such secondary rules. There are rules governing the conduct of military contractors vis-à-vis military procurement personnel. There are rules about what evidence attorneys may present and what they may say in front of the judge and jury. There are rules governing what representations architects, car dealers, dentists or investment advisors may make to their prospective customers and clients. And there are rules about what gifts and favours purchasing managers and public officials may be offered and may accept. Such rules can be helpful, but as rules they are vulnerable to these same sorts of corruption efforts as the primary rules they are supposed to protect. The application of such secondary rules will often be corrupted or proposed secondary rules will never be adopted in the first place. Lobbyists and political incumbents benefit from a wide-ranging freedom to lobby, and it is therefore hardly surprising that lobbyists will lobby against proposed restrictions on their activities and legislators will be inclined to vote down such proposed restrictions.

An obvious antidote against the corrosive effects of corruption as defined is a shared morality, involving a shared religion or common social purpose, for example, or common moral values, goals, principles or norms. When there is, for instance, a strong and universally shared sense of patriotism in a country – supported perhaps by a manifest threat from a powerful and expansionist neighbouring state – corruption is likely to be kept at bay. Military procurement officers, who formulate calls for tenders or decide among competing bids, will then be single-mindedly focused on the defensive needs of the country. Considerations of personal gain will not occur to them or, if they do, will evoke shame and be quickly dismissed as constituting a betrayal of one's country and fellow soldiers (who would be placed at greater risk if less than optimal equipment were to be purchased). And likewise for employees of the competing supply companies: they will want to win the contract, of course, but they will want to win on the basis of having the better equipment to offer, and they will not want to win at the expense of lesser combat readiness of their country's armed forces.

Absent special situations like the one just stipulated (a manifest threat from a powerful and expansionist neighbouring state), a strong commitment to a widely shared morality is difficult to sustain in the modern world. There are various important reasons for this. One reason is the global spread of an economic mindset that is closely associated with the omnipresence of adversarial and competitive systems. Pursuant to this mindset, controversies over ends and values, including moral ones, are not subject to rational reflection, discussion and resolution; only controversies over effective means to given ends can be rationally resolved. Accordingly, the theory and design of modern economic systems is guided by two principles: (1) there are no ultimate shared purposes that the system as a whole is meant to serve; and (2) the rules of the system can and should be designed so that the diverse purposes of its participants are optimally served by virtue of the fact that each participant is rationally pursuing – within the system rules (including sanctions) – only his or her own purposes. The second principle cannot adjudicate among the many Pareto-optimal designs of the system, and since disagreement over such alternative designs is also presumed to be irresolvable by appeal to authoritative moral values or principles, such disagreement will then be settled on the basis of bargaining, in which each participant will exert pressure on behalf of its own values and interests.

Here it is possible, of course, that these participants have important values in common and are willing to prioritise these shared values over most of their private interests. But such a fortunate coincidence is unlikely in the modern world, characterised as it is by conditions of globalisation. One aspect of globalisation is that competitions are internationalised and the rules organising many competitive systems are now designed through negotiations involving representatives from diverse countries. Moral values could play a substantial role in intergovernmental negotiations only if they were shared and also *known to be* genuinely shared among most of these representatives. This is generally not the case, because such negotiators have learned that others' appeals to moral contents are not always trustworthy and rarely explore such moral contents in any significant depth. Negotiations are then typically driven by bargaining, in which each negotiator seeks to promote the interests or values of its own country or organisation (or even those of himself or herself). This trend is amplified by what one may call the 'sucker exemption': it is a near-universal feature of human moralities that they regard conduct that would be immoral under conditions of full compliance as less wrong or not wrong at all when compliance by others cannot be counted upon. In other words, moralities do not require their adherents to be 'the sucker', that is, someone who can easily be taken advantage of because he or she continues to comply with his or her morality even while others are not complying with theirs.

The sucker exemption renders the moral solution to the corruption problem fragile. When much is at stake, competing agents will not willingly refrain from efforts to influence the formulation or application of rules in their own favour if they have reason to suspect that at least some of their competitors are making exactly such efforts. When even a small minority of the competing agents shows a disposition to get ahead by influencing the design or application of the rules organising the competition, most of the remaining competitors will also shed their inhibitions, will be frustrated by competing at a disadvantage and will attach much diminished weight to their obligation to protect the integrity of the rules and of their application.

When there is no common morality that supports a shared commitment to respect and preserve the integrity of the rules and their application, moral language may still be prominent. But here it will be used by participants strategically, for the sake of promoting their own interests and values. Participants will invoke a shared moral vocabulary in their efforts to revise some rules and to protect others from revision. Because the rules structuring a competitive system are harder to change when they are widely regarded as moralised, competitors will spend resources on 'moralising' rules they are interested in entrenching and on 'de-moralising' rules they are interested in revising. Such efforts produce a degeneration of moral discourse and undermine its standing in the wider culture.

Let me recapitulate how, according to these explanatory hypotheses, the noted Achilles' heel of competitive systems becomes more dangerous with globalisation, that is, with the emergence of an increasingly dense and influential network of supranational rules. This is so for two reasons. First, as noted, our world is very far from having a strong commitment to a morality that is widely shared across continents. And the agents able to affect the formulation or application of those supranational rules do not understand one another's moral outlooks well enough to be sure that most others are complying at least with their own moralities. Second, the temptations towards corruption are enormous. This is so for the obvious reason that so much is at stake in the formulation and application of supranational rules, and it is also so for the less obvious reason that only an unusually small number of agents – namely those corporations and individuals who can successfully lobby the more powerful governments that are shaping these rules with little democratic oversight – have the incentives, expertise and power to partake in the contest over the formulation and application of supranational rules. A serious lobbying effort by a powerful company or industry can make a huge difference to its fortunes. For a very large profit-oriented multinational firm, such as Microsoft, Citibank or Exxon, there is hardly any more lucrative investment than that of influencing the emerging global rules that structure the space in which it will operate.

One systemic problem 'predicted' by the foregoing analysis is polarisation: increasing inequality involving a small minority gaining ground at the expense of all the rest. In a globalised world in particular, the richest and most powerful agents are best positioned to engage in cost-effective lobbying: they have much to gain from favourable rules and therefore can spend a lot on acquiring the necessary expertise, on forming alliances with one another and on lobbying the relevant political decision-makers. Ordinary citizens, by contrast, each have too little at stake to make it worth their while to acquire the necessary expertise and to form alliances that are large enough to engage in effective lobbying that could rival corporate influence. And so the players that are already the richest and most powerful will typically get their way and will thereby increase their own relative wealth and power within the system.

This in turn further increases their capacity to influence the design and application of the rules in their own favour. In the absence of global democratic institutions or other mechanisms through which ordinary people can influence the formulation and application of supranational rules, we can expect regulatory capture with a spiral of increasing polarisation that benefits a small minority at the top – and, unintentionally but no less inexorably, keeps down the bottom half of humankind.

One important example of global regulatory capture is the TRIPS (trade-related aspects of intellectual property rights) Agreement. This Agreement was achieved by large corporations that stood to make a lot of money from licensing their intellectual property. In the early 1990s these firms – mainly in the pharmaceutical, software, entertainment and agricultural industries – overcame their differences in order to lobby together for a global expansion and strengthening of intellectual property rights which was then incorporated into the World Trade Organization (WTO) Treaty. Thanks to this mighty lobbying effort, any country that wants to participate in the WTO trading regime – and remaining outside this regime is a substantial handicap for any country – must now enact and enforce very strong intellectual property protections and thereby, in effect, collect massive economic rents for well-capitalised innovators in the four named industries.[2] The richest have shaped the new global rules in their own favour and thereby have further polarised the distribution of global household income. In this case, the impact on the world's poor majority was especially detrimental as they essentially lost access to advanced medicines. Before 2005, clever Indian manufacturers typically managed to bypass process patents (which were all that pharmaceutical innovators could obtain in India) by developing a different way of making the relevant molecule. After 2004, Indian law became TRIPS-compliant by entitling pharmaceutical innovators to 20-year product patents which allow them to suppress unlicensed copies regardless of how they were produced.

We can observe the effect of the polarisation spiral in the following table (figures supplied by Branko Milanovic, World Bank), which shows a remarkably rapid shift of income share towards the top five per cent of the human population.

Table 6.1 Evolution of global income distribution

Segment of world population	Share of global household income 1988 (%)	Share of global household income 2005 (%)	Absolute change in income share (%)	Relative change in income share
Richest ventile	42.87	46.36	+3.49	+8.1%
Second ventile	21.80	22.18	+0.38	+1.7%
Next three ventiles	24.83	21.80	−3.03	−12.2%
Second quarter	6.97	6.74	−0.23	−3.3%
Third quarter	2.37	2.14	−0.23	−9.7%
Poorest quarter	1.16	0.78	−0.38	−32.8%

We find a similar polarisation within countries that have been heavily involved in globalisation. One example is the US. In the last US economic expansion (2002–7), average per capita household income grew by 16 per cent. But this growth was very unevenly distributed. The top 1 per cent of US households registered a gain of 62 per cent, while the remaining 99 per cent of households registered a gain of 6.7 per cent. The top percentile captured 65 per cent of the real per capita growth of the US economy during these years. This phenomenon is not confined to the Bush Administration or Republican governments. During the 1993–2000 Clinton expansion, the top percentile did similarly well, capturing 45 per cent of the real per capita growth of the US economy.[3]

In fact, the trend is consistent for the entire 30-year globalisation period. During the period of 1978–2007, the share of the bottom half of US citizens in national household income declined from 26.4 to 12.8 per cent. In the same period, the share of the top 1 per cent rose *2.6-fold*, from 8.95 to 23.50 per cent; the share of the top tenth of a per cent rose *4.6-fold*, from 2.65 to 12.28 per cent; and the share of the top hundredth of a per cent rose *7-fold*, from 0.86 to 6.04 per cent of national household income.[4] The top hundredth of a per cent of US households (30,000 people, 14,400 tax returns) now have nearly half as much income as the bottom half (150 million people) and about two-thirds as much as the bottom half (3.4 billion) of the world's population.[5] This trend is dramatically at odds with the still widely propagated Kuznets curve, which depicts the evolution of inequality as a curve in the shape of an inverted U: rising in the early period of industrialisation and then falling off as a national economy matures.[6]

The same sort of phenomenon can be observed in China, another country heavily influenced by globalisation. Here the available data are more spotty, presenting only deciles and going back only to 1990. But the trend is unmistakable: in the period of 1990–2004, the income share of the bottom half declined from 27 to 18 per cent — while that of the top tenth of the population rose from 25 to 35 per cent.[7]

There is a second systemic problem emerging from the foregoing analysis of collective rule-shaping under conditions of globalisation. Relatively few in number, the organisations capable of influencing supranational rule-making through the lobbying of major governments will strategically adjust their efforts to one another. We have already discussed one such phenomenon: such organisations will seek to overcome their differences in order to form alliances devoted to lobbying for a mutually acceptable outcome (such as the TRIPS Agreement). Another, related phenomenon is that such a powerful player (or coalition of players) will make concessions in areas where it has relatively less at stake in exchange for other such players making reciprocal concessions in other areas where it has relatively more at stake. Such trades are collectively rational insofar as they get each of the powerful players more of what they want. But such trades are also dangerous in the long term, in two ways. First, when an elite coalition buys control of some system rules or their application, it will tend to disregard the needs of the rest of humankind and of future generations because it lacks assurances that other elite players practise analogous self-restraint. Second, insofar as various pieces of supranational regulation are shaped by different sets of players with diverse special interests, the whole international rule system will become incoherent and therefore vulnerable to crises that will continue to become increasingly severe. Both phenomena exemplify the structure of 'collective action problems' (as paradigmatically exemplified by the prisoners' dilemma): the strongest players are impelled, by their self-regarding interests, to seek influence in ways that are detrimental and dangerous even to themselves collectively (and even more so, of course, to weaker players). Even the strongest are worse off in the long run than they would be if they abandoned their competitive efforts to corrupt in their own favour the rules and their application. In the long run, they must expect more *risk and loss* from the incoherence of an institutional order shaped by lobbying than *opportunity and gain* from their own lobbying efforts.

This second systemic problem of competitive and adversarial systems – especially prominent at the supranational level where special interests can lobby under unusually favourable conditions – constitutes a serious danger, as exemplified by the recent global financial crisis. But it also indicates a great opportunity to overcome both systemic problems together. If the strongest corporations can be shown that their opportunities to influence the design of supranational institutional arrangements is collectively detrimental to themselves (each does better with this opportunity than without, but each does worse with several having it than with none having it), they may be willing to support a systemic solution that reduces lobbying opportunities and thereby presumably also the great concentration of wealth and lobbying power at the very top. They may also then be willing to work towards the formulation of a basic moral consensus that could guide supranational institutional design decisions towards greater coherence and act as a constraint on corporate lobbying.

Such a basic moral consensus might well form around an agreement on the great scourges we all have a shared interest in banishing: the risk of major wars involving weapons of mass destruction; the degradation of our natural environment, including resource depletion and catastrophic climate change; and the still very high prevalence of severe poverty and disease among the bottom half of the human population. (The scourge of over-population is closely related to that of poverty, in that over-population aggravates poverty and reductions in poverty entail large reductions in total fertility rates.)

Paradoxical as it sounds, a moralisation of supranational rule-making may be in the interests of the most powerful corporations precisely *because* they now have such unusually great power to shape such rules. Insofar as such corporations are taking an intelligent long-term view of their own interests, many of them will find that they have reason on balance to support such a moralisation (which is not to say that their top executives have such an interest). There is a great task and opportunity here for those trained in moral theorising and reflection: we should specify the first steps of such a moralisation in some detail and seek to show how they help to overcome the second systemic problem especially. I have tried to make a small contribution to this task by helping to develop, specify and propagate the Health Impact Fund proposal.[8]

Notes

1. Glenn Simpson, 'Lender Lobbying Blitiz Abetted Mortgage Crisis', *Wall Street Journal*, 31 December 2007; Atif Mian, Amir Sufi and Francesco Trebbi, 'The Political Economy of the U.S. Mortgage Default Crisis', National Bureau of Economic Research Working Paper No. 14468, November 2008.
2. For some more background, see *Access to Medicines*, special issue edited by Thomas Pogge of (2008) *Public Health Ethics*, 1/2, 73–192.
3. Emmanuel Saez and Thomas Piketty, 'Income Inequality in the United States, 1913–1998' (2003) *Quarterly Journal of Economics*, 118, 1–39, as updated in 'Tables and Figures Updated to 2007 in Excel Format', August 2009, available at http://elsa.berkeley.edu/~saez, Table 1 (based on data from the US Internal Revenue Service), date accessed 6 October 2010.
4. Ibid., Table A3.
5. Ibid.; see also finance.yahoo.com/banking-budgeting/article/107575/rise-of-the-super-rich-hits-a-sobering-wall.html, date accessed 6 October 2010.
6. See for example http://en.wikipedia.org/wiki/Kuznets_curve, date accessed 6 October 2010.
7. Camelia Minoiu and Sanjay G. Reddy, 'Chinese Poverty: Assessing the Impact of Alternative Assumptions' (2008) *Review of Income and Wealth*, 54(4), 572–96; and World Bank, *World Development Indicators 2008*, Washington DC: World Bank Publications 2008, Table 2.8, p. 68.
8. See for example my 'The Health Impact Fund: Better Pharmaceutical Innovations at Much Lower Prices', in Thomas Pogge, Matt Rimmer and Kim Rubenstein (eds), *Incentives for Global Public Health: Patent Law and Access to Essential Medicines*, Cambridge University Press, 2010, pp. 135–54. See also more generally the literature collected at www.healthimpactfund.org.

7

Financial Services Providers: Integrity Systems, Reputation and the Triangle of Virtue

Seumas Miller

Ethics and the global financial crisis

The global financial crisis has put the spotlight on a variety of unethical (including imprudent) practices among financial service providers, such as reckless and predatory lending by bankers, the selling of toxic financial products and massive frauds, e.g., Bernie Madoff's Ponzi scheme.[1]

It has become apparent that these corporate collapses and corruption scandals in the overall context of a massive, global, speculative boom/bust are symptomatic of systematic deficiencies in the provision of financial services in particular.

As noted in Chapter 2, the potential response to this problem or problems can be examined on at least two levels or dimensions. At one level, the concern relates to the fundamental global economic, financial and regulatory architecture and the normative preconceptions that underpin this. At another level, the problem is manifestly unethical, incompetent and/or unlawful behaviour; accordingly, relevant regulatory and integrity systems need to be revisited and renovated. My concern in this chapter is with the latter second level of the problem, or at least with one aspect of it.

There are a range of occupational groups involved in the financial services sector. Investment bankers, financial advisors, lawyers and auditors have gate-keeping roles in relation to the provision of loans and the production and selling of a wide range of financial products. In addition, there are a host of other financial services providers who facilitate the workings of the market in relation to these financial products and processes, including fund managers, broker/dealers, securities analysts, credit rating professionals and asset consultants. Most if not all of these groups are causally, if not morally, implicated (directly or indirectly) in the global financial meltdown. However, let us briefly consider only a few of these groups, albeit the important ones.

Auditors are charged with specific duties including independent attestation of corporate disclosures on financial position and performance. However, in a number of cases, auditors and accounting firms have prioritised the proximate goal of economic self-interest over independent adjudication. Indeed, it has been argued that some accountancy firms have (perhaps unconsciously) sought to mask these market influences on the auditing profession – and limit their exposure to civil litigation – by taking refuge in compliance with technical procedural requirements.[2] There is a risk that privileging technical requirements through creative compliance over a commitment to substantive ethical principles, such as the provision of a true and fair record, weakens the reputation of both the profession and its corporate clients more generally. To this extent, an important element in the integrity system has been weakened. It should also be noted that a good deal of critical reflection has recently taken place within the audit profession in relation to the importance of inculcating the ethical virtues in practitioners in the profession, not least because of the reputational risks of not doing so. It is well understood that if an auditing firm loses its reputation for honesty, accuracy, independence, etc., then all may well be lost; consider the collapse of the large accounting firm Arthur Andersen in the wake of its role in the Enron scandal.

Lawyers are another important professional group in the finance sector and are a group that is currently experiencing a process of institutional change. The advent of incorporated legal practices that are increasingly also multidisciplinary represents the response of both the profession and the legislature to the changing legal services market. These practices offer (potentially) greater profit to those who own them. However, they also generate new and more complex forms of ethical problems for the profession and its regulators.[3] Arguably, a corporation's *primary* duty is to enhance shareholder value (this might be so even on a corporate social responsibility model of the corporation). This is usually interpreted as an obligation to return maximum profit within market regulations and norms. However, it seems that these emerging corporate and multidisciplinary settings are exacerbating existing ethical problems and generating new ones. What counts as legal work for the purposes of holding accountable an incorporated multidisciplinary practice staffed, on the one hand, by solicitors offering 'legal advice on tax laws' (supposedly within the solicitors' framework of strict professional accountability) and, on the other hand, by tax experts offering 'tax advice in the context of current tax laws' (outside the solicitors' framework)? If the lines of accountability have become blurred and/or unenforceable, what are the consequences for ethical responsibility? There are well-defined and very strict requirements imposed on lawyers to maintain client confidentiality. However, non-legal members of the multidisciplinary practice (MDP) may have no such responsibility. More generally, these developments raise questions in relation to the ability of lawyers to perform their duties to the court in organisational settings in which there is enormous pressure to prioritise commercial organisational imperatives. It is self-evident that public trust in the judicial system depends in part on lawyers not only discharging their duties to the court, but being seen to do so. So, the above-mentioned ethical failures constitute a reputational risk that can translate into a lack of public trust not only in the legal practitioners and their corporate employers, but in (relevant parts of) the judicial system itself.

Investment bankers provide a range of services, including securities underwriting, due diligence investigations associated with Initial Public Offerings (IPOs), the provision of analytical reports for affiliated retail brokerage facilities or wider market dissemination, private client money management, private equity financing and proprietary trading. There are a range of ethical concerns in this area, including failure to discharge fiduciary duties (insofar as they apply to investment bankers) and conflicts of interest. In the context of the global failure of investment banks and their partial nationalisation in many jurisdictions, conflicts of interest issues have come to the fore, notably with respect to relationships with rating agencies. Credit rating agencies have a key role to play in relation to the ethical health of the financial system, a role which has recently been compromised in the case of securitisation processes.[4] This role hinges on their capacity to enhance or diminish the reputation of financial actors. The key notion here is deserved reputation. Reputation ought to track actual financial health, and the credit rating agencies are crucial here. Perceived conflicts of interest in particular are obviously a key reputational risk.

Having identified some of the main problems and institutional players in relation to some of the key ethical problems in the global financial services sector, I now turn to the question of integrity systems. In the following section I identify some key features of integrity systems and in the section on the virtuous triangle I focus on one element of such systems that I take to be of particular relevance to financial service provider, namely reputational indices.

Integrity systems

Integrity systems are institutional vehicles whose function is to reduce ethical misconduct, to combat crime and corruption and to promote institutional virtues. Integrity systems include aspects of legal or regulatory systems, but they are not identical to them.[5]

While regulatory frameworks and integrity systems typically overlap – and ought to be mutually reinforcing – they are not identical notions, theoretically speaking, albeit that regulatory systems are often understood as including what I am referring to as integrity systems.[6] A regulatory framework is a structured set of explicit laws, rules or regulations governing behaviour, issued by some institutional authority and backed by sanctions. It often serves to ensure compliance with minimum ethical standards (namely those enshrined in a law, rule or regulation), but this is not its only purpose. There are many laws, rules and regulations that have little or nothing to do with ethics. By contrast, an integrity system – at least in the sense in which I am using the term – is an assemblage of institutional entities, roles, mechanisms and procedures, the purpose of which is to ensure compliance with minimum ethical standards and promote the pursuit of ethical goals. Nevertheless, integrity systems obviously rely heavily on regulations and laws.

Integrity systems include both reactive mechanisms (e.g., police agencies and corporate fraud investigation units) and preventative means (e.g., ethics education and the elimination of perverse incentives).

In practice, integrity 'systems' are a messy assemblage of formal and informal devices, processes and roles, and they operate in often indeterminate and unpredictable ways.

The term 'integrity', as used in the expression 'integrity system', appropriates a moral notion normally used to describe individual human agents and applies it to organisations and other large groups of individuals. Roughly speaking, individual human persons have integrity if: (i) they possess the full array of central moral virtues, such as honesty, loyalty and trustworthiness; and (ii) they exercise rational and morally informed judgment in their adherence to any given virtue, including when the requirements of different virtues might seem to come into conflict. By contrast with the notion of an individual person's integrity, there is the integrity of a profession, organisation or industry sector, i.e., an institutional entity. Accordingly, examples of elements of institutional integrity systems would include agencies such as the representative bodies of professional groups (e.g., the Institute of Chartered Accountants) and industry regulators (e.g., the Australian Securities and Investments Commission and the Securities and Exchange Commission).

The integrity of a profession, organisation or industry is in large part dependent on the individual integrity of its members, and therefore an integrity system is in large part focused on developing and maintaining the individual integrity of these members. Nevertheless, these groups are not simply the sum of its members, and so determining the integrity levels for these groups is not simply a matter of summing the levels of integrity of the individual members. For one thing, the virtues of specific occupational groups can differ from those of ordinary citizens, e.g., the numerical exactitude of good auditors.[7] One important task, then, for any specific profession is to determine what precisely the constitutive virtues of the individual role-occupant are and devise strategies to ensure that these virtues are developed and maintained in the members of that profession.

For another thing, the ethical risks of market actors, for example, of traders in large volumes of shares, are different from those of ordinary citizens. More generally, the causes of ethical failure are often at the institutional – indeed, macro-institutional (e.g., global) – level; it is not simply a matter of targeting a few individual rotten apples by means of increased enforcement. This is the case with the current ethical failures in global financial markets. Accordingly, the solutions are to be found at the institutional and macro-institutional levels.

The integrity of an institution is partly a matter of the structure, function and culture of the institution. Consider structure, both legal and administrative. In an institution possessed of integrity, the administrative processes and procedures in relation to, for example, promotion or complaints and discipline would embody relevant ethical principles of fairness, procedural justice, transparency, etc.

Now consider function or ends. In an institution possessed of integrity, the organisational goals actually being pursued would align closely with the morally legitimate (including ultimate) functions of the institution, such as the promotion of public safety for an engineering firm or of the financial health of audited corporations for an auditing firm, rather than purely commercial and other proximate goals, such as profit.

Moreover, in the case of markets and business corporations more generally, realising the ultimate, as opposed to the proximate, institutional purposes is a fundamental ethical concern. Here there is a need to address an array of questions including the contribution of the business, market or industry to human material well-being; for instance, the 'contribution' to human health of the tobacco industry is self-evident, but so is the international pharmaceutical industry if, as appears to be the case, it is neglecting the development of drugs for poverty-related diseases afflicting millions in favour of drugs for the minor ailments of much smaller numbers of the relatively rich. Again, the real costs (e.g., environmental costs) of specific industries need to be factored into institutional cost-benefit analyses of the extent of the realisation of proximate and ultimate ends.

In the case of the financial services sector in particular, there is a lack of clarity with respect to the fundamental ethical question of the ultimate institutional ends of the sector. Yet, without an answer to this question, an integrity system is quite literally without direction: it does not know what ethical ends it is seeking to embed in the target institution(s). I return to this theme in the next section.

Finally, consider culture. A culture in an institution possessed of integrity would be one that was, for example, intolerant of serious incompetence or misconduct.

Integrity systems exist to promote institutional ethical integrity and combat institutional corruption. In order to succeed, they first need to identify the nature and causes of the ethical failures, including at the levels of structure, function and culture.

Second, it is necessary to devise institutional mechanisms, if they do not already exist, to identify the loci of what will be taken to be individual and collective moral responsibility. This amounts to institutionalising ethical responsibility. Importantly, this process does not necessarily involve identifying a pre-existing source of ethical responsibility; it can, and often does, involving creating a locus of institutional responsibility to deal with an identified ethical problem. Perhaps initially no one was aware of conflicts of interest problems in a corporation (e.g., lawyers in incorporated legal practices). However, once the problem is identified, some institution or institutional role occupant (or occupant), for example, a solicitor-director, needs to be created to deal with this issue. That person or persons can now be held institutionally responsible for this ethical problem. Here it is important to note the possibility of collective moral responsibility, i.e., of a number of persons (the members of the board of directors, the managers, the employees, the shareholders and the members of an external regulatory agency) being held to be jointly ethically (and institutionally) responsible. Notice that the person(s) in question are now not only institutionally but are also ethically responsible.

Third, given that the loci of individual and collective ethical responsibility have thus been identified, if not created, the matter of accountability arises in relation to those with ethical (and institutional) responsibility. Such accountability can take the form of a set of rules, mechanisms of compliance and processes for adjudication of alleged non-compliance and, if necessary, for punishment. However, ethical failure does not necessarily translate into legal or even administrative liability. Whether or not it does so depends on the seriousness of the infraction, the efficacy of such liability, etc. This is one of the reasons that an integrity system does not necessarily mirror a regulatory system, even an internal institutional self-regulatory system.

In looking at options to promote integrity and combat ethico-professional failures, it is very easy to leap to a particular kind of solution (e.g., rule-based or principle-based systems of regulation) or even a single 'magic bullet' solution, such as increasing penalties or giving more intrusive powers to investigative agencies, and doing so without considering the full array of implications, including the demonstrable (as opposed to hoped for) benefits (which of these measures has been tested and, as a consequence, is known to work?) and the costs in terms of resources, damage to ethico-professional ethos, etc. Enforcement mechanisms, for example, are important, especially in relation to ethical offences that are sufficiently serious to also be criminal offences. However, enforcement is only one part of the solution to ethical problems, i.e., one component of an integrity system. Again in relation to enforced requirements, rules need to work hand in hand with principles, yet for some problems in some areas, for example, conflicts of interest, the emphasis might need to be on principles in the context of procedural requirements, such as an internal but independent mechanism for the determination of any putative conflict of interest, while in other areas such as disclosure requirements, principles and rules might both need to be met – for example, an auditor's report must be both a true and fair record and comply with technical rules.[8]

Moreover, 'magic bullet' solutions in particular are sometimes offered in relative ignorance of both the actual nature and causes of the problems they are supposed to address. The truth is sometimes in the detail. For example, in attempting to determine the causes of unethical practices in a given profession, there are a number of preliminary questions that need to be addressed. One set of questions pertains to the precise nature of the unethical practice at issue and the context in which it occurs. Consider legal practitioners operating in the context of incorporated, multidisciplinary legal practices. Are there, for example, some compelling practical facts that explain the unethical practice of conflicts of interest or breaches of confidentiality in this context? What pressures and opportunities might there be for the unethical practice in question? Another set of questions concerns the extent of the corruption or unethical practice: is it sporadic or continuing, restricted to a few 'rotten apples' or widespread within the area? In answering these questions, what is called for is the provision of evidence-based conclusions.

Even when the answers to the above-mentioned questions have been provided, further questions will arise in relation to any remedies proposed. For example, any contemplation of mechanisms to redress ethico-professional misconduct that will require the expenditure of energy and resources needs to be justified in terms of the seriousness and extent of the misconduct to be successfully combated. Consider here the claims that the post-Enron Sarbanes-Oxley regulation in the US has had costs that are greater than the benefits it has provided – and, of course, the counterclaims. More importantly, such remedies need to be efficacious, and efficacious over the longer term. Pious rhetoric accompanied by tough regulation does not necessarily deliver the required long-term results. Nevertheless, if Sarbanes-Oxley is working, then surely the costs that it imposes in terms of reporting and disclosure requirements, audit committees with financial expert and independent directors, etc., are justified. Certainly, the costs of an *effective* regulatory system in relation to corporate malfeasance would have to be enormous if they were to outweigh the benefits.

Understanding the causes of ethico-professional misconduct and failures and the tailoring of remedies to address them will involve considering and distinguishing between three sorts of motivation for compliance with moral principles and ethical ends.

One reason for compliance is the fear of punishment, hence the use, or threatened use, of the so-called 'big stick'. So, for example, person A does not defraud organisation B because A fears he or she will get caught and locked up. A second reason for compliance arises from the benefit to oneself, hence the possible utility of the so-called 'carrot' approach. So, for example, B pays B's workers reasonable wages because by doing so the workers are healthy, work productively and B makes good profits. These two reasons are essentially appeals to self-interest. Taken in combination they constitute the 'stick-carrot' approach much loved by many contemporary economists. However, there is a third reason for compliance. This is a moral belief or desire to do what is right. A refrains from fraud because A believes that it is morally wrong to steal.

There are also important connections to be highlighted and promoted between 'self-interest' and 'moral belief and sentiment' so that these conceptions are more in balance and integrated and are less at odds with each other. First, of course, the appeal to moral sentiment must be balanced by the appeal to self-interest. If, for example, it is at great cost to oneself to be honest or fair, then one may have sufficient reason not to be honest or fair. Indeed, the reason need not be purely self-interested, but may also count as moral. Suppose that, faced with retrenchment, an employee commits fraud in order to provide for his or her family; his or her reasons here include those relating to both prudence and morality.

It is evident that widespread and ongoing compliance typically requires appeals to self-interest (sticks and carrots) but also appeals to moral beliefs. Ideally, integrity systems should have penalties for those who do not comply, should enable benefits to flow to those who do comply and should resonate with the moral beliefs of the people thus regulated, for example, laws and regulations should be widely thought of as fair and reasonable.

Thus, institutional design which proceeds on the assumption that self-interest is the only human motivation worth considering fails. It fails because it overlooks the centrality of moral beliefs in human life and therefore does not mobilise moral sentiment. On the other hand, institutional design that proceeds on the assumption that self-interest can be ignored and that a sense of moral duty on its own will suffice also fails; it fails because self-interest is an ineradicable and pervasive feature of all human groups.

Moreover, deserved reputation has a pivotal role to play in the convergence of self-interest and ethical concerns. Here I am not so much speaking of reputation for performance (including economic performance) as reputation for ethical integrity, albeit that performance and integrity are connected and to some extent overlap. In the next section I outline what I refer to as a virtuous triangle and its potential role in mobilising reputation in the service of promoting integrity.

As noted above, integrity systems can be thought of as being either predominantly reactive or predominantly preventive.[9] Naturally, the distinction is somewhat artificial, since there is a need for both reactive elements, (e.g., criminal investigation units and a complaints and discipline system) as well as preventive elements (e.g., occupation-based ethics training, transparency of organisational processes and independent boards of directors)[10] in any adequate integrity system. At any rate, integrity systems can be considered under the two broad headings of reactive and preventive.

Reactive integrity systems

The reactive way of dealing with ethical misconduct and corruption is the one that first comes to mind. The logic is direct: the activity is defined as one that is not acceptable; an individual engages in that activity and therefore, as a direct result, should be held to account for the misconduct and, if found guilty, disciplined in some way. The rationale for the reactive response to dealing with unethical behaviour, including criminality and corruption, is threefold: offenders are held to account for their actions; offenders get their just deserts; and potential offenders are deterred from future offences.

Reactive mechanisms are fundamentally linear and generally take the following form: setting out a series of offences (usually in legislation or regulations), waiting for an individual to transgress, then investigating, adjudicating and finally taking punitive action. The criminal justice system, the investigative arms of regulatory agencies and internal complaints and discipline systems are basically reactive institutional mechanisms.

Reactive mechanisms are necessary; moreover, a high level of intensity of enforcement is often entirely appropriate. Nevertheless, over-reliance on the reactive approach is problematic. One obvious weakness is the passivity of the approach; by the time the investigators swing into action, the damage has already been done. Consider the current situation in relation to fraudsters such as Bernard Madoff in the current financial crisis. Another problem stems from the fact that corrupt behaviour such as insider trading and bribery is often by its nature secretive and can remain so if corporations and professional associations choose to 'close ranks' to protect the reputation of the offending organisation or group. Yet another problem stems from the inadequacy of the resources to investigate and successfully prosecute: investigation and prosecution is resource-intensive. Many fraudulent schemes, for example, are not adequately investigated due to a lack of police and other resources. Again, heavy-handed over-use of reactive methods can alienate even those who believe in compliance with regulations and ethical standards. Consider the responses to the apparent or threatened over-use of negotiated prosecutions in the US in the aftermath of the Enron scandal.[11] Finally, if the chances of being caught or complained about are relatively slight for whatever reason (e.g., under-resourcing, regulatory negligence, lack of political will and an unwarranted belief in the ability of the market to 'self-regulate'), the deterrent effect is undermined, which in turn means there are an even larger number of offences and offenders for investigators to deal with.

Of course, the effectiveness of a reactive approach requires that significant detection mechanisms are available. If so, then those who engage in corrupt or unethical conduct have at least two good reasons to fear exposure: first, detection may lead to legal, regulatory, organisational or associational sanctions, such as imprisonment, fines, suspension or expulsion from the industry; and, second, it may lead to morally-based reputational loss in the eyes of superiors, subordinates, peers, colleagues, clients, customers, the community, friends and/or relatives.

There are a number of sources of information in relation to most forms of ethical misconduct and corruption. One of the most important is fellow-workers, who may report such conduct or suspicious activity to superiors, confidential helplines and watchdog agencies or who may even blow the whistle by going to the media.

Preventive integrity systems

A preventive integrity system will typically embrace, or act in tandem with, a reactive integrity system. However, we can consider preventive mechanisms for dealing with ethical misconduct independently of any reactive elements. If we do so, we see that they can be divided into three categories:

(i) There are institutional mechanisms for promoting an environment in which integrity is specified and rewarded, and unethical behaviour is specified and discouraged, for example, by developing codes of ethics/conduct and ethics training programmes, by establishing transparent and fair promotions, remuneration and other reward processes and by mobilising reputation in the service of self-interest (see next section). The focus of these mechanisms is on reducing the desire or motivation to act unethically, so that opportunities for unethical behaviour are not pursued or taken, even when they arise.

(ii) There is an array of institutional mechanisms which limit (or eliminate) the opportunity for unethical behaviour. Such mechanisms include corporate governance mechanisms such as establishing genuinely independent boards of directors, segregating commercial from investment banks, separating the roles of receiving accounts and paying accounts to reduce the opportunity for fraud, and eliminating structural conflicts of interest.

(iii) There are those institutional mechanisms which act to expose unethical behaviour, so that the organisation, occupational association or community can deal with them, for example, complaints systems, helplines, mandatory reporting requirements, ombudsmen, financial audits, ethics audits and research instruments such as ethical attitude surveys and quantitative complaints data-gathering and analysis.[12] The term 'transparency' may be used to characterise these mechanisms.

I accept that this threefold distinction is somewhat artificial and that some institutional mechanisms will in fact come under more than one heading, and indeed that some, for example, regulations, codes of conduct, ethics and compliance offices,[13] and organisational fraud units, have both a reactive as well as a preventive role.

Holistic integrity systems

I suggest that holistic integrity systems can be looked at in relation to three axes, namely the reactive-preventive axis, the internal-external axis and the self-interest-ethical attitude axis.

Thus far in this analysis of integrity systems, I have looked at integrity systems and mechanisms under the headings of reactive systems and preventive systems. It is evident that in most societies, jurisdictions and, indeed, organisations, the attempt to combat unethical behaviour involves both of the above. That is, integrity-building strategies involve reactive systems as well as preventive systems, and within preventive systems there are the mechanisms that promote ethical attitudes, the mechanisms that reduce opportunities for criminality, corruption and other forms of unethical behaviour, and various transparency mechanisms.

Moreover, it seems clear that an adequate integrity system cannot afford to do without reactive as well as preventive systems, and that preventive systems need to have all three kinds of elements detailed above. This suggests that there are two important issues. The first is the adequacy of each of the elements of the above systems. How adequate are the complaints and discipline processes, including the investigations? How effective are the mechanisms of transparency? The second issue pertains to the level of integration and congruence between the reactive and the preventive systems, and the elements of these systems. To what extent do they act together to mutually reinforce one another?

In this connection, it is also worth noting the distinction between internal and external integrity mechanisms. Many large corporations have an array of internal integrity mechanisms, both reactive and preventative (e.g., ethics and compliance offices).[14] However, many jurisdictions also have external 'watchdog' agencies, including regulatory authorities. Such bodies are established by statutes that also define a range of offences, have powers to investigate and refer matters to the courts for prosecution. However, it is notable that these watchdog agencies also often involve themselves in prevention programmes involving the development of preventive mechanisms; they do not necessarily see their role as merely that of a reactive agency. The key point for our purposes here is that in a holistic integrity system, these internal and external mechanisms ought to complement and mutually reinforce one another. Both types are necessary and they ought not to be seen as being in competition, hence the sterility of some debates between, for example, advocates of external regulation and proponents of self-regulation.

An additional important axis around which the concept of a holistic integrity system rotates pertains to motivational attitudes, specifically self-interest and ethical attitudes. Here we need first to remind ourselves what is presupposed by an integrity system, namely shared ethical attitudes.

There are at least two aspects to these shared ethical attitudes. On the one hand, and most obviously, there must be some shared moral values in relation to the moral unacceptability of specific forms of behaviour and the moral desirability of other specific forms of behaviour – for example, market actors must actually believe that bribery is wrong. In other words, there needs to be a framework of accepted social norms and a means for inculcating these norms (e.g., ethics training programmes and ethical leadership). On the other hand, there also needs to be a shared ethical conception in relation to what institutional and other measures *ought* to be taken to minimise corruption, criminality and unethical behaviour more generally; very harsh penalties and other draconian measures, for example, may simply alienate reasonable, ethical people.

Holistic integrity systems rely on both self-interest and ethical attitudes. As we have just seen, integrity systems presuppose ethical attitudes. However, they also obviously rely on self-interest. For example, they seek to deter wrongdoing by investigating and punishing offenders. They also seek to promote compliance with laws and regulations by providing incentives and removing disincentives and perverse incentives, for example, forms of remuneration that instil a habit of taking undue risks with other people's money. A further element of self-interest that holistic integrity systems should make use of is the desire for good reputation. It is this element that I now want to focus on. I note that, as was the case with reactive and preventative mechanisms and with internal and external mechanisms, holistic integrity systems seek to utilise both self-interest and ethical attitudes in the design of integrity systems, and do so in a manner such that these different motivations end up mutually reinforcing the integrity systems in question.

The virtuous triangle

Professional and corporate reputation

A key element in the establishment of effective integrity systems for occupational groups, organisations and industries in general and corporations and professional groups in particular is the mobilisation of reputation.[15] Naturally, some groups and organisations are more sensitive to reputational loss (and the possibility of reputational gain) than others. Corporations and professional groups in the financial services sector, including bankers and auditors, are very sensitive to reputational loss. Those entrusted to make prudent decisions with other people's money are inevitably heavily dependent on their good reputation; the same is true of those entrusted to provide independent adjudications in relation to financial health.

When a high professional reputation is much sought after by members of an occupational group or organisation, and a low professional reputation is to be avoided at all costs, there is an opportunity to mobilise this reputational desire in the service of promoting ethical standards. Here the aim is to ensure that reputation aligns with actual ethical practice, i.e., that an organisation's, group's or individual's high or low reputation is deserved. The way to achieve this is by designing appropriate integrity systems. As we have seen above, key elements of an integrity system track compliance with regulations, for example, accountability mechanisms ensure compliance with regulations (or, at least, expose non-compliance). The additional thought here is that key elements of an integrity system should track features of organisations and occupational groups that determine (or should determine) reputation. More explicitly, a reputational index could be constructed whereby an ethics audit awards scores in relation to specific ethical standards. In what remains of this chapter I will sketch the broad outlines of such a reputational index.

Deserved reputation can provide an important nexus between the self-interest of corporations and professional groups on the one hand and appropriate ethical behaviour towards consumers, clients and the public more generally on the other hand. More specifically, the deserved reputation of financial services providers, be they corporations or professional groups, can provide such a nexus. Here there are three elements in play: (i) reputation; (ii) self-interest; and (iii) ethical requirements, such as particular ethical standards like compliance with technical accounting standards and the avoidance of specific conflicts of interest, but also more general desiderata such as client/ consumer protection. The idea is that these three elements need to interlock in what might be called a virtuous triangle.

First, reputation is linked to self-interest; this is obviously already the case – individuals, groups and organisations desire a good reputation and benefit materially and in other ways from it. Second, reputation needs to be linked to ethics in that reputation ought to be deserved; as already mentioned, the integrity systems are the means to achieve this. Third, and as a consequence of the two already-mentioned links, self-interest is linked to ethics; given robust integrity systems that mobilise reputational concerns, it is in the self-interest of individuals, groups and firms to comply with ethical standards (which are also professional standards). Here I reassert that self-interest is not the only or necessarily the ultimate motivation for human action; the desire to do the right thing is also a powerful motivator for many if not most people. Accordingly, the triangle is further strengthened by the motivation to do right.

In recent years the notion of a reputation index has gained currency in a number of contexts, especially in business and academic circles. The term seems to have a number of different senses. Sometimes it is used to describe a way of measuring the reputation that an organisation actually has, since reputation exists, so to speak, in the eye of the beholder. Actual reputation does not always match deserved reputation. Accordingly, sometimes the term is used to describe a way of calculating the performance of an organisation on the basis of which its reputation should be founded.

The first step in the process is to determine a way of accurately measuring the ethical performance of individual or organisational members of occupational and industry groups; this is an ethics audit.

Here I stress the importance of *objective* measures of ethical performance. The latter might include such things as: results of consumer satisfaction surveys; gross numbers of warranted complaints and trends thereof; numbers of disciplinary matters and their outcomes; outcomes of financial and health and safety audits (e.g., regarding electronic crime and corruption vulnerabilities). It would also include the existence of institutional processes established to assure compliance with ethical standards, for example, codes of ethics and conduct, financial and other audit processes, ethics committees, complaints and disciplinary systems, fraud and ethics units, ethical risk assessment processes, ethics and compliance officers, and professional development programmes in ethics.

Here I note that while some of these institutional systems and processes might be legally required – and, indeed, some are under Sarbanes-Oxley S406[16] – this is by no means the case for all of them. In short, while reputational indexes include some indicators of compliance with those ethical standards (and associated processes of assurance) that are enshrined in law, they also include indicators of adherence to ethical standards that are above and beyond what is legally required.

In addition to the ethics audit itself, there is a need for a process that engages with ethical reputation. Since ethical reputation should reflect the findings of the ethics audit, an ethical reputation audit should drive the relationship between *de facto* ethical performance (in effect, the deserved reputation) and actual reputation for ethical performance. The way to achieve this is by the participation of as many occupational members and industry organisations as possible in ethics audits, and by the widespread promulgation of the results of their *de facto* ethical performance (as determined by the ethics audit), including in the media. Naturally, the results promulgated could be more or less detailed; they could, for example, simply consist of an overall rating as opposed to a complete description of the ethics audit results.

Reputational indexes give rise to a number of problems. There is the problem of devising acceptable, objective measures of ethical performance. While ethical performance in a general sense is a somewhat nebulous notion, determining minimum ethical standards – which are nevertheless above and beyond legal requirements – and levels of compliance therewith is doable. Indeed, criminal justice and regulatory systems are devised in large part to prescribe objectively specifiable minimum ethical standards, for example, do not defraud or bribe; reputational indexes of minimum ethical standards simply take this process further by, so to speak, raising the ethical bar. Indeed, many of these objective measures have already been developed in the context of so-called corporate social responsibility (CSR) programmes. CSR areas of focus include combating corruption, health and safety, fair trade practices and environmental ethics. Objective measures can include the implementation of systems, for example, anti-corruption processes in procurement and the adoption of standards and of the relevant quality assurance processes (such as testing of products for safety) and independent audits, for example, of greenhouse gas emission levels.

Doubtless, there are a variety of motivations in play here including, but not restricted to, the desire to avoid reputational loss and to acquire reputational gain. For instance, some organisations might be concerned with the quality of services that they provide just for its own sake, and measuring their performance might indicate areas of weakness to them and thereby cause them to lift their game. Moreover, the concern with reputation can itself stem from different motives; it might be that some organisations are concerned with reputation for its own sake, while others are only concerned with the impact of reputational gains and losses on their market share. In fact, it is plausible that any given organisation will have mixed motives, with some motives stronger in the case of some organisations than in others.

While the efficacy of ethical performance measures might be demonstrable, at least in some areas and with respect to some measures, it is not without pitfalls. Thus, measurement of performance is subject to gaming by those being evaluated, it can produce distortions and it does not obviate the need for unquantifiable judgment. Such 'gaming' has included falsifying data. More generally, if performance is measured in terms of X, then resources may well be reallocated so as to ensure that high measures of performance in terms of X are achieved and, as a consequence, other areas or aspects of performance that are not well measured by X may be under-resourced.

In general, the performance of professionals, especially their 'ethical' performance, cannot be evaluated purely by recourse to quantifiable measures; the complexity and subtlety of the activities in question resist such quantification. Thus, a complaints and discipline system might look highly efficient and effective in purely quantitative terms, in that all complaints are investigated and all appeals are examined, but the actual quality of the investigations and adjudications in relation to very important matters might be quite poor; investigations and adjudications of complex matters do not lend themselves to wholly quantifiable forms of evaluation. This is not to say that there is no place for quantification and measurement, but rather that inevitably there is a need for judgment.

Another problem is participation. What means are available to ensure the participation of occupational groups and organisations in reputational indexes? (Of course, in the case of those indices that simply measure compliance with legal requirements, there is no need to secure 'participation'; the compliance failure is already in the public domain and reputational indexes simply provide additional and more targeted publicity.) In relation to the problem of non-participation, there are a variety of responses ranging from the mandatory use of reputational indexes by members of professional or industry groups (e.g., by recourse to corporate law or on pain of exclusion from the relevant professional or industry association) through to the provision of various kinds of incentive. The Professional Standards Council in Australia provides one kind of example for occupational groups. It offers capped liability as an incentive to occupational groups to participate in its ethico-professional standards schemes.

However, what is called for here is the establishment of ethics rating agencies analogous to auditing firms that provide audits of financial health or of credit rating agencies such as Moody's and Standard and Poor's. Here it is crucial that conflicts of interest are avoided. I note the conflict of interest issues that have beset the large accountancy firms (e.g., doing consultancy work for the very firms that they audit) and credit rating agencies (e.g., being funded in part by the investment banks whose toxic financial products they were rating).

A third and still greater problem is effectiveness. The use of reputational indexes can easily reduce into 'tick-the-box' processes on the part of clever, well-resourced organisations seeking to avoid actual compliance with ethical standards in favour of engaging in elaborate exercises in window dressing. This explains the need for meaningful ethical audits conducted by independent, adequately resourced and professionally trained ethics auditors.

Having a good reputation can be made to depend primarily on the possession of an effective integrity system, because an effective integrity system is one that maintains and promotes compliance with high ethical standards and therefore provides an assurance that a good reputation is *deserved*. Accordingly, it is important to establish and reinforce the dependence between a good reputation and the possession of an effective integrity system. As we have seen, integrity systems consist of codes of ethics, ethics training programmes, complaints and discipline processes, fraud and ethics units, etc.; moreover, holistic integrity systems are the preferred model.

The dependence between good reputation and possession of an effective integrity system can be greatly strengthened by mobilising the desire on the part of occupational groups to gain a good reputation and avoid a poor reputation. For example, an integrity system that includes reputational indices for members of an occupational group and corresponding ethics audits directly connects the desire for a good reputation on the part of a member of an occupational group to the maintenance and promotion of ethical standards. To this extent the integrity system in question is more effective than it would otherwise have been.

Naturally, this whole process is predicated on the reputation of occupational groups and firms actually being *deserved*. Good reputation that is *undeserved* is not an ethical good; it does not benefit consumers or clients and it does not serve the public interest. It is also important to stress that the credibility of the independent ethics rating agencies is also on the line – their ratings must be seen to be warranted.

Integrity systems for different groups may vary in the weight they give to certain considerations over others. So, for instance, anti-competitive concerns or claims to professional autonomy with respect to a body of knowledge may be more relevant to some groups than others. Accordingly, deserved reputation will track such differences. It will, for instance, be more significant to the overall deserved good reputation of, say, a real estate agent to establish that he or she does well in relation to anti-competitive and market norms than it will be for most doctors. That is, such an integrity system provides the reputational indices against which reputation may be assessed and so a 'good' reputation may be shown to be deserved or otherwise.

The integrity system for a large contemporary corporation might include the following elements:

- an effective, streamlined complaints and discipline system, including an anonymous complaints process;
- a comprehensive suite of induction processes reflective of the different levels of ethical risk in different areas of the organisation;
- a basic code of ethics and specialised codes of practice – for example, in relation to professional groups such as auditors housed within the organisation – supported by ethics education in recruitment training and ongoing professional development programmes;
- adequate health and safety support systems;
- risk management systems for high-risk areas, for example, bribery in the procurement area;
- internal fraud and anti-corruption investigations, that is, the organisation takes a high degree of responsibility for its own unethical managers and employees;
- ethical leadership, for example, promoting employees who give priority to the collective ends definitive of the organisation rather than their own career ambitions; and
- an external independent ethics audit.

As the foregoing points suggest, a key element in an integrity system for large organisations is an organisation-wide, intelligence-based, ethics risk-assessment process. This involves good intelligence, an organisation-wide ethics risk-assessment plan and – based on good intelligence and the risk-assessment plan – the identification of corruption, rights violations and ethical misconduct risks in the organisation.

Ethical risks in a large contemporary corporation might include risks in many, if not most, of the following areas:

- data security, notably electronic data, and breaches of confidentiality;
- conflicts of interest;
- fraud;
- bribery (e.g., in procurement);
- the abuse of authority (e.g., in promotion);

- substance abuse;
- gambling;
- bullying;
- theft.

Specific ethical risks for a particular profession, namely accountancy, have been identified in a recent Australian study:[17]

- Fair competition: with only four big accounting firms operating in Australia, there is a lack of genuine competition – which is evident in fee-setting practice.
- Auditors' independence: audits are a small and decreasing percentage of the revenue of large accountancy firms which have moved primarily into providing consultancy services to business, often the same business for which they carry out audits. Thus, there is a good deal of competitive pressure which often results in low-priced audits which may not be well carried out:
  (a) since they are part of a larger package or services; and
  (b) they are used as a hook to lead to more consultancy work.
  It is noteworthy that the very recently introduced new legal requirements relate to auditing and its interconnections with other accounting services, the principal ones being:
  (a) a requirement for the rotation of individual auditors after five years;
  (b) a legal obligation to follow the auditing standards established by the Auditing and Assurance Board (from 1 July 2006); and
  (c) a specification of types of conflict of interest that totally compromise auditor independence and whose violation may now constitute a criminal offence.
- Fraud: this was illustrated by cases of senior people in auditing firms colluding with the auditees and coercion within a firm not to disclose (and/or to fall in with) dubious practices.

More attention could be paid to developing a professional culture where professional reporting is more accepted within professional bodies and is therefore a reasonable alternative for accountants who become aware of fraudulent accounting.

Commercial pressure: creative but 'strictly legal' accounting where financial reporting is significantly misleading for audit users. This is exacerbated by the tendency of professionals to resist the routinisation of their knowledge base, including resistance to specific rules.

Identifying ethical risks, whether at an organisational or occupational level, is in part a matter of data gathering, aggregation and analysis. Such data includes: (i) aggregated complaints data; (ii) data such as compliance with ethics assurance processes (extracted, for example, from self-assessment exercises); (iii) the number of investigations (and percentages of investigated complaints upheld); (iv) data from ethics attitude surveys involving ethical scenarios that elicit the ethical attitudes of practitioners; (v) data from ethics audits (perhaps used in conjunction with reputational indexes); (vi) qualitative data from interviews and focus groups. There are also various other sorts of data sources that can be made use of. The general point here is that there is no substitute for actual evidence when it comes to the designing and redesigning of integrity systems. Accordingly, the business of developing, maintaining and improving ethico-professional standards should be evidence-based.

Here there are a number of key issues that need to be addressed, including the following. First, the identification of specific ethical issues confronting particular occupational groups. It is a mistake to think that auditors' ethical problems are always and everywhere identical with those of lawyers or engineers. Second, a determination needs to be made in relation to the seriousness and frequency of ethical transgressions in a given occupation or professional practice at a given time. Third, specific processes need to be designed and implemented in relation to such problem areas, for example, conflicts of interest disclosure and avoidance. Fourth, audits need to be conducted to determine that processes are in place and are working. Fifth, the different working parts of the overall integrity system for an occupational group or particular professional practice need to be appropriately integrated.

However, my first fundamental point is that in relation to all these questions there is a need to investigate, to collect and aggregate data, and to analyse this data. My second fundamental point is that the results of such evidence-based analysis need to be deployed for the purpose of designing and redesigning integrity systems and the elements thereof. In short, I am recommending evidence-based institutional design and, in particular, the practice of what has elsewhere been referred to as *evidence-based designing-in ethics*.[18]

Ethical reputation indexes

If reputation is to be mobilised in the service of raising ethical standards, then the following steps need to be taken.

First, for each occupation or organisation, it needs to be determined what the appropriate ethical standards are, for example, avoidance of specific kinds of conflicts of interest, compliance with technical accounting standards, compliance with health and safety standards, compliance with market norms of fair competition, etc.

Second, an integrity system for these ethical standards needs to be developed comprised of various elements, for example, a code of conduct, an ethical risk assessment process (in relation to conflicts of interest, breaches of confidentiality, etc.), a complaints and discipline system, an ethics and compliance office, a fraud unit and a self-assessment process.

Third, objective indices need to be worked out in relation to what counts as compliance with ethical standards and in respect of such integrity systems and their workings, for example, the number and type of complaints, the success rate of investigations and the responses to identified ethical risks.

Fourth, an applicable reputational index (comprised in part of a set of appropriate indices) needs to be developed and accepted by the occupational group or industry organisations in question.

Fifth, there is a need for the actual participation of a reasonably large cross-section of the occupational group or industry organisations in question. Thus, there is a need to provide some kind of incentive to participate (or disincentive to prevent non-participation). It is likely that at a certain threshold of participation, non-participants will suffer reputational loss simply by failing to participate.

Sixth, an independent entity needs to be established to conduct the actual process of assessing members of the occupational group or industry organisations in question (i.e., applying the reputational index).

Seventh, the results need to be suitably presented in a suitable form for public promulgation and then promulgated.

Reputational indexes can be developed and used to measure a variety of different kinds of entity. Thus, members of an occupational group can be rated as a whole or against one another, as can firms in a given industry. Here I note that what is made publicly available is not necessarily a ranking of members of an occupational group or set of organisations. Rather, there could simply be the statement that the minimum threshold of ethical standards had been met, for example, by way of a 'certificate of ethical health' or perhaps a 'badge of excellence'. Alternatively, there might be, say, a five-star rating system, in which more than one practitioner or firm could get a five-star rating. And there are other possible systems.

Notes

1. An earlier version of some of the material in this section appeared in Seumas Miller, 'Institutions, Integrity Systems and Market Actors', in J. O'Brien (ed.), *Private Equity, Corporate Governance and the Dynamics of Capital Market Regulation*, London: Imperial College Press, 2007.
2. F. Clarke, G. Dean and K. Oliver, *Corporate Collapse: Accounting, Regulatory and Ethical Failure*, Cambridge University Press, 2003, p. 31.
3. Steve Marks and Georgina Cowdroy, 'Incorporated Legal Practices – A New Era in the Provision of Legal Services in the State of New South Wales' (2004) *Penn State International Law Review*, 22, 4, 1–30; S. Miller and M. Ward, *Complaints and Self-Assessment Data Analysis in Relation to Incorporated Legal Practices*, Report for the Office of the Legal Services Commissioner, July 2006.
4. IOSCO, *Report on Credit Ratings Agencies*, 12 March 2009, www.iosco.org.
5. Earlier versions of some of the material in this section appeared in Seumas Miller, 'Social Institutions', *Stanford Encyclopaedia of Philosophy* (Online Winter Edition, 2005); Seumas Miller, Peter Roberts and Edward Spence, *Corruption and Anti-corruption*, Saddle River, NJ: Pearson, 2005; and Miller, 'Institutions, Integrity Systems and Market Actors'.
6. Christine Parker, *The Open Corporation*, Cambridge University Press, 2002; A. Alexandra and S. Miller, *Integrity Systems for Occupations*, Aldershot: Ashgate, 2010.
7. Tom Campbell and Keith Houghton (eds), *Ethics and Auditing*, Canberra: ANU Press, 2008.
8. Clarke, Dean and Oliver, *Corporate Collapse*, p. 320.
9. Miller, Roberts and Spence, *Corruption and Anti-corruption*.
10. P. MacAvoy and I. Millstein, *The Recurrent Crisis in Corporate Governance*, Stanford University Press, 2004.
11. J. O'Brien, *Engineering a Financial Bloodbath*, London: Imperial College Press, 2009.
12. Miller and Ward, *Complaints and Self-Assessment Data Analysis in Relation to Incorporated Legal Practices*.
13. ECOAF (Ethics and Compliance Officer Association Foundation), *The Ethics Compliance Handbook: A Practical Guide from Leading Organisations* (ECOAF, 2008).
14. Ibid.

15. Earlier versions of some of the material in this section appeared in A. Alexandra, T. Campbell, D. Cocking and S. Miller, *Professionalisation, Ethics and Integrity Systems: The Promotion of Professional Ethical Standards, and the Protection of Clients and Consumers*, Report for Professional Standards Council, 2006; Alexandra and Miller, *Integrity Systems for Occupations*; Seumas Miller, *The Moral Foundations of Social Institutions*, Cambridge University Press, 2010; 'Financial Service Providers, Reputation and the Virtuous Triangle', in I. MacNeil and J. O'Brien (eds), *The Future of Financial Regulation*, Oxford: Hart, 2010, pp. 387–400.

16. J. O'Brien, *Redesigning Financial Regulation*, Chichester: Wiley, 2007, pp. 27–54.

17. See Alexandra *et al.*, *Professionalisation, Ethics and Integrity Systems*; and Alexandra and Miller, *Integrity Systems for Occupations*, Chapter 6.

18. Alexandra and Miller, *Integrity Systems for Occupations*, Chapter 6.

8

Who Must Pay for the Damage of the Global Financial Crisis?

Matt Peterson and Christian Barry

In 2009 the President of the UN General Assembly organised an ambitious conference to deal with the effects of the global financial crisis on developing countries. The draft document for the conference called for a coordinated $3 trillion 'Global Stimulus for Restructuring and Survival', intended to 'help address the strains posed by economic downturn on the poor' and 'lay the basis for a new economy based on human needs, human rights and human security'.[1] This bold idea did not survive the final vote. The world's collective governments shied away from the notion of a global stimulus in the adopted resolution, which meekly concluded that 'each country has primary responsibility for its own economic and social development'.[2] The commandingly titled 'Global Plan for Recovery and Relief' adopted by the G-20 in April 2009 was similarly non-committal about the allocation of responsibility for the costs borne by developing countries. The G-20 is willing to help, of course, but only because 'emerging markets and developing countries ... are also now facing challenges which are adding to the current downturn in the global economy'.[3]

Domestically, a government would be hard-pressed to say that its citizens individually bear primary responsibility for responding to a major crisis. If, for example, a devastating tsunami struck the coast of a US state, the emergency response would be paid for first by the state at large and then by the general American public, acting through the federal government. By and large we believe that our fellow citizens should be rescued when struck by forces beyond their control, at least when this leads to severe deprivation. We encounter even less resistance when a culprit can be clearly identified as having caused the disaster through his or her recklessness or failure to take adequate care. When a US Congressman insisted that BP ought not to be forced to pay for the costs of cleaning up the Gulf Coast oil spill, the condemnation of his views was immediate and unanimous – of course the responsible party should pay.[4]

We are not alone in likening the global financial crisis to more familiar disasters. The analogies employed include:

- a tsunami (by former US Federal Reserve Chairman Alan Greenspan);[5]
- an ocean tide (by the World Bank);[6]
- an infectious disease (by the International Monetary Fund);[7]
- a shipwreck, generically (by French President Nicolas Sarkozy);[8]
- the sinking of the Titanic, specifically (by Brazilian President Inacio Lula da Silva);[9] and
- a car wreck (by numerous media commentators).[10]

Thinking about these analogies and their aptness in describing the global financial crisis can be illuminating. The different types of analogies imply different established principles for allocating responsibility to absorb the costs of repairing damage. None of these analogies is perfect, of course, but certainly the first three are the least apt. The financial crisis is entirely man-made and could have been prevented.[11] The notion of a shipwreck is less obviously inappropriate. The negligence and arrogance of the Titanic's crew certainly played a crucial role in its sinking. The difference is that the Titanic combined human failure with the challenges of the natural world (in that case an iceberg), whereas the financial crisis was wrought entirely by human behaviour.

However, the notion of a car crash is a more plausible analogy since it involves human agents employing powerful tools that can cause severe deprivation and other harms.[12] In the aftermath of a car crash, we sensibly ask who, if anyone, is at fault. The costs of recovering from the crash – to the driver, his or her vehicle, whom or what the driver hit, and any third parties involved – are then allocated accordingly. In some cases these costs may be beyond the ability of the relevant parties to pay. The question would be whether these costs should be allowed to lie where they fell or be shifted in part or whole to others.

Our object in this chapter is to draw on the analogy of the car crash to bring out the principles that should guide policy-makers in fairly allocating the costs of responding to the financial crisis and the subsequent global recession. We argue that the approach to the allocation of cost for repairing the damage caused by the crisis adopted by the affluent countries is unacceptable for two reasons. First, it fails to take adequate account of the manner in which the negligent and reckless conduct of affluent countries contributed to it. Second, it fails to recognise that when unpredictable, extraordinary events contribute to severe deprivations, the costs of addressing them should be borne partly by those who can pay for them without much difficulty.

The costs of the financial crisis

Before we discuss principles, we need to know what the costs of the financial crisis are. Just how badly have developing countries been harmed? In the early stages of the crisis, many low- and middle-income countries were expected to be left largely unaffected. The weakness and relative lack of global integration of these countries' financial sectors was seen as a kind of blessing in disguise. Being insulated from the global financial system made them less vulnerable to the rapidly worsening crisis. It wouldn't make much difference to the poor if access to the financial instruments of the affluent were curtailed, since the poor weren't able to access them anyway. Sadly this diagnosis turned out to be incorrect. If nothing else, the crisis has taught us a lesson about the interconnectedness of the global economy.

The crisis has been transmitted to developing countries through a number of channels, including reductions in private capital flows, the increased cost of credit and a reduction in the availability of credit, a sharp fall-off in the volume of trade and decreases in remittances. Estimates of the damage have increased significantly over the past year. Early last year the World Bank expected the economies of developing countries other than India and China to have shrunk by 1.6 per cent in 2009.[13] This proved optimistic. The current estimate is a 2.2 per cent contraction. And the growth of China and India, while still fairly rapid, proceeded at a much slower pace than in recent years.[14] Collectively, the recession implies a loss of $750 billion in income for developing countries, including a $50 billion loss to Sub-Saharan Africa.[15] There is much cause for concern even for developing countries with much healthier economies. As one observer noted, the new global recession 'puts development success stories in danger'.[16]

In discussing the costs of the global financial crisis, we will focus our discussion on severe deprivations – shortfalls that people are likely suffer in their health, civic status or standard of living relative to the ordinary needs and requirements (e.g., food, drink, shelter and minimal health protection) of human beings. Our concern is with the cost of mitigating or alleviating severe deprivations that can plausibly be attributed to the global financial crisis. Much more empirical research and a great deal of counterfactual speculation is required before we can make plausible estimates of the magnitude of severe deprivation that can be attributed to the crisis, but it appears to be quite substantial. The International Labour Organization estimates that 35.7 million people have lost their lobs as a result of the crisis; 19.1 million of those were in developing countries.[17] As a result, the incomes of as many as 84 million people have been pushed below $1.25 per day.[18] As affluent consumers slowed their rampant consumption, the volume of global trade dropped correspondingly, by a staggering 14.4 per cent in 2009.[19] The export-driven growth that has alleviated so much poverty in recent years has fallen correspondingly. In February of last year, China's exports were down by 26 per cent year-on-year, and 20 million migrant workers lost their jobs.[20] Cambodia's critical garment industry dropped in value from $250 million to $100 million per month.[21] In Sub-Saharan Africa, per capita income may have declined by as much as 20 per cent.[22] Education spending per primary school student there has fallen by 10 per cent.[23] Predictably, this loss of income by the world's most vulnerable people will produce very significant hardship: a World Bank study predicts that 1.4 to 2.8 million infants will die over the next six years as a result of the financial crisis.[24]

To make things more concrete, we will focus on just one of the ways in which the financial crisis appears to be contributing to severe deprivations. It is creating a financing gap that makes the debts of many countries unserviceable. The World Bank estimates that the collective financing gap for developing countries in 2009 was $690 billion, and forecasts $315 billion for 2010.[25] Countries will have to either sharply reduce consumption in order to bridge the gap or borrow heavily. High debt levels and financing gaps can limit the capacities of countries' governments to provide social services necessary to ensure even a minimally adequate standard of living for their people, and divert resources and energy from the pursuit of short- and long-term strategies that further the well-being of their people. This effect is particularly acute in the poorest countries and is magnified by exchange rate volatility, since poor countries often borrow in foreign currencies.

The buildup of large debts – so-called debt overhang – creates a climate of permanent financial fragility in a country, leaving that country in a financial and economic slump, without domestic revenue to pay for current expenditures. Because of its financial instability, the country is deemed to be high risk from an investment perspective.[26] Creditors demand a higher interest rate on investment finance – if willing to lend at all – since many of them may have substantial outstanding debt claims on the country.[27] Greece has very visibly found itself in this situation. Fortunately for the Greeks, as a member of the European Economic and Monetary Union, their country's collapse necessitated a rescue by other EU members.

Other countries are not so lucky. For developing countries, the collapse of private finance has left many with nowhere to turn but the International Monetary Fund (IMF), which arguably limits the capabilities of their citizens to exercise meaningful control over their policies and institutions.[28] This threat is very serious for countries like Cape Verde, Cote d'Ivoire, Ghana, Nicaragua and Pakistan, which lack the reserves to implement a fiscal stimulus of their own and are already rated as being at medium to high risk on debt sustainability.[29] As a result of the crisis, one or more of these countries may be forced to choose between expenditures on health, education, and security, or its contractually defined debt obligations.

Principles of assistance and rescue

Who should bear the costs of a country's decision to borrow when that country cannot repay its debts without causing severe deprivations among its people? Should they be borne entirely by the government – and ultimately the people – of that country or should they be pushed in whole or in part on to others? For some human-rights and poverty-relief advocates, the answer is simple. They argue that we cannot demand the fulfilment of contractual obligations that will lead to severe deprivations when these costs could easily be borne by others who would not suffer substantially. The debts of the countries at hand will reliably cause severe deprivations, and these debts are tiny relative to the size of the economies of affluent countries and international financial institutions. The total external debt of all low-income countries is \$156 billion, or about one-fifth of the \$700 billion US stimulus package.[30] (The US stimulus is, in turn, 40 per cent greater than the \$507 billion it would allegedly take to bring all 3.08 billion severely poor people above the World Bank's \$2.50 per day poverty line.)[31]

The Austrian economist Kunibert Raffer asserts that 'one must not be forced to fulfill contracts if that leads to inhumane distress, endangers one's life or health, or violates human dignity. Civilized laws give unconditional preference to human rights and human dignity'.[32] This view is also endorsed by many, including advocates of the Fair and Transparent Arbitration Process (FTAP), developed by Raffer and modelled on Chapter 9 of the US Bankruptcy Code, which governs the bankruptcy of municipalities. The FTAP would ensure that the basic human rights (somehow understood) of citizens of debtor countries are given higher priority than creditors' rights in the management of debt crises.[33]

Those who favour initiatives that ask for certain costs to be shifted from those who are badly off to those who are relatively well off appeal, in effect, to a duty of assistance. The broad version of this claim is that if agents are able to assist the severely deprived at some not excessive cost, those agents have a responsibility to address the need. On this view, those with access to funds ought to spend them in ways that help those at most risk of suffering severe deprivation. The thought is not to deny that market participants should generally bear the risks of their decisions – no market system could function well without risk – but that certain extremely bad outcomes should not be allowed to stand when they can be averted at relatively small cost. In our context, the provision of assistance should depend on how heavily burdened the population of a country would be in absolute and relative terms were that country to pay its debts or absorb the full burden of its financial losses, and how costly it would be for others to offset the costs that it would otherwise face.

Principles of assistance are widely acknowledged, even while their extent is a matter of heated debate. In 'Famine, Affluence, and Morality', Peter Singer famously argues that affluent people have responsibilities to assist the global poor by alluding to an analogy of a person passing a shallow pond where another individual is about to drown.[34] Just as the former bears a responsibility to save the latter, the affluent have a responsibility to assist the global poor. Singer holds that a plausible principle that would explain our reaction to the pond case, and which would also lead us to recognise our responsibility in the global poverty case, states that 'if it is in your power to prevent something bad from happening, without sacrificing anything nearly as important, it is wrong not to do so'.[35] Singer does not specify what it means to claim that something is *nearly* as important as something else – he leaves it up to his readers to decide on the basis of their intuitions.[36]

Though plausible on its surface, the Singer Assistance Principle (SAP) may seem unreasonably demanding.[37] The problem lies in the assessment of relative costs. One way to think about the notion of relative importance is the following: we judge the importance of A's bearing cost X relative to B's bearing cost Y by imagining how some third party, C, ought to act, all other things being equal. C can choose to prevent either A from bearing X or B from bearing Y, but not both. According to the SAP, if we imagine that C ought to prevent A from bearing X, then X is more important than Y. Fleshing this out, if C is faced with the choice of saving A's life or B's hand, then, all other things being equal, he ought to save A's life. And by implication, this reasoning suggests that if faced with the choice of saving someone's life or losing my hand, I ought to sacrifice my hand – quite a demanding conclusion. The natural reply would be to argue that B's hand is *nearly* as important as A's life, but this claim is hard to sustain. All things being equal, if C is faced with the choice of saving A's life or the hands of B, D, E, F, G and H, it still seems clear that he ought to save A's life. A hand is not nearly as important as a life. When we shift from hypothetical hands to actual people struggling to survive extreme poverty, the SAP seems especially demanding. After all, it has no end point: extreme poverty is vast from the perspective of the individual. Fulfilling the obligation of the SAP to alleviate extreme poverty would easily overwhelm the resources of even the wealthiest individuals.[38] The SAP seems extremely – and indeed implausibly – demanding.[39]

However, there are many other *much* less demanding principles of assistance that would favour shifting the costs of alleviating severe deprivation on to others, and even those who believe that the obligations of the affluent to address poverty and inequality are quite limited affirm some of them. In the midst of describing why the affluent do not have extensive duties of justice to the global poor, for example, Thomas Nagel pauses to describe what he sees as the absolute minimum of duties we owe to others:

> I assume there is some minimal concern we owe to fellow human beings threatened with starvation or severe malnutrition and early death from easily preventable diseases, as all these people in dire poverty are. Although there is plenty of room for disagreement about the most effective methods, some form of humane assistance from the well off to those in extremis is clearly called for apart from any demand of justice, if we are not simply ethical egoists.[40]

Minimally demanding as it is, affluent countries clearly fail to live up to Nagel's principle. Provided that there are effective measures that affluent nations could take to alleviate poverty, much more could be done without exceeding a moderate demand on the part of the affluent. First consider the scale of the problem of global poverty: among roughly 6.8 billion human beings alive today, about 1.02 billion are undernourished, 884 million lack access to safe drinking water, 2.5 billion lack adequate sanitation and 1.5 billion have no electricity.[41]

Next, consider the disparity in resources available to affluent countries: the 3.08 billion people – 45 per cent of the world's population – who live below the $2.50 per day poverty line have collectively less than 5 per cent of world income.[42] In contrast, the richest 10 per cent of individuals have 85 per cent of all global wealth; the richest 1 per cent have 40 per cent of wealth.[43] Yet official development assistance (ODA) targeted towards providing basic social services from all affluent countries amounted to just $15.5 billion in 2008.[44] That is, the total amount of ODA disbursed towards meeting basic needs by all affluent countries was only 2.2 per cent of what the US alone spent on its military in that same year. Only five countries exceed the miserly United Nations target of 0.7 per cent of gross national income (GNI) given to aid, agreed to in 1970 at the UN General Assembly.

Given these facts, it appears that affluent countries can indeed prevent something very bad from happening to other people at relatively low cost to themselves and that they are failing to do so.

It is no excuse, of course, that countries are currently facing budget crises that increase the relative cost of giving aid, since they have had these duties for quite some time. A culpable failure to discharge past duties may make duties more, rather than less, stringent. If I see a child fall into a well but decide I'd rather go to the cinema, the cost I must be willing to bear to save him or her is greater once the film has concluded.

That said, we need not endorse even relatively undemanding principles of assistance to argue that the costs of events like the global financial crisis should partly be held in common. What we have in mind is more aptly termed a duty to rescue: when, globally, accidents resulting in severe deprivation occur without negligence on the part of the parties involved, those countries with the greatest capacity to assist without suffering substantially are obliged to rescue the victims. Again, we draw inspiration from the many analogies for the financial crisis. What if, when the earthquake struck Haiti, the nearby and wealthy US had simply opted not to respond? Unlike those duties, a duty to rescue has a clear end point and is therefore not a permanent drain on our resources. Such a duty of rescue expresses a basic minimum standard for international relations – that we ought not to allow others to suffer severe deprivations when unpredictable, extraordinary events contribute to them if we can do so at relatively low cost to ourselves.

The principle of contributory fault

As we have argued, however, the global financial crisis is not entirely like an earthquake. Much of the damage was caused by identifiable agents, and this is relevant when considering how the costs to repair it should be allocated. Outrage over the bonuses received by AIG staff or at the pension demands of the former Royal Bank of Scotland head Sir Fred Goodwin is based on the belief that these individuals were responsible for precipitating the crisis and ought to pay for, or at least not benefit from, recovery measures. To put this in terms of indebted developing countries, what costs they should bear may also depend on how in the first place those countries came to be at risk of suffering severe deprivation as a result of present financial troubles. The principle of *contributory fault* has two sides. On one hand, it can limit the conditions under which those who suffer hardships can shift the costs of alleviating their deprivations on to third parties. They cannot do so when their own negligent or reckless conduct has put them in this situation in the first place. On the other hand, it increases the extent to which these agents can shift the costs of alleviating their deprivation on to *some* third parties, namely those whose reckless or negligent conduct contributed to it. All other things being equal, reasons associated with contributing to harm through negligent or reckless conduct are commonly thought to be important because they are *stringent*. They are stringent in the sense that they *constrain* agents: prospective contributors to deprivation cannot easily justify their conduct by appealing to the costs to themselves of refraining from doing harm or by appealing to the overall good that their conduct will bring about. And they are stringent in the sense that they *demand* much of agents who have ignored constraints against contributing to deprivation, but are now in a position to mitigate or alleviate the deprivation to which they have contributed.

Drawing on the car accident analogy, let us consider how the contributory-fault principle applies to the global financial crisis. Standards of tort liability generally demand that an agent bear the costs of his or her harmful conduct when it can be shown that:

1. the agent has causally contributed to them;
2. the harmful outcome was the agent's fault; and
3. the faulty aspect of the agent's conduct (and not merely the agent's conduct as a whole) was causally relevant to the outcome.[45]

To show that some driver is liable for the injuries of another person, it must not merely be shown that the driver was negligent and that he or she caused the accident, but that the injuries resulted from his or her negligence. Theorists of the law of torts differ over how these conditions should be understood, but there are some elements that are common to nearly all accounts of them. First, the notion of fault operates with some notion of a 'standard of care'. That is, agents are at fault for some harmful outcome, and thus can be held liable for bearing its cost, when they have not lived up to an objectively defined normative standard.[46] When an agent fails to live up to this standard, he or she is deemed to be 'negligent' and is at fault for any harmful outcomes of his or her conduct. Second, the normative standard that is invoked for the purpose of determining negligence depends on some conception of what a 'reasonable person' could be expected to have done in the situation given what was foreseeable in the context in which the agent acted. If the agent acted in the way a reasonable person could have been expected to act in the circumstances, then that agent did not act negligently and is thus not at fault for the costs to others engendered by his or her conduct. Consequently, such an agent should not be made to bear these costs even if his or her conduct is causally relevant to bringing them about. If, when driving at normal speed and obeying all traffic signals, you swerve your car to avoid hitting a child dashing across the street and smash into a parked car, you are not at fault for the damage done to the parked car and are thus not liable in tort for bearing the costs of its repairs.

Of course, that no tort liability is assigned does not mean that the costs vanish, just that they cannot be pushed on to other *specific* parties on the ground of contributory fault. In the case just described, you are responsible for paying the costs of repairing your own car. Similarly, the owner of the parked car is responsible for paying for his or hers, just as he or she would have been if a tornado had picked up the two cars and thrown them together. In some cases, however, the costs may be more than the individuals involved can bear. In these cases, we argue, duties to rescue or to assist apply and some emergency costs will be held in common. Let us stipulate further that the crash occurs in the US and you are a destitute US citizen with no health insurance. If you are terribly injured in the crash, the local hospital must treat you in its emergency room. Since no one is liable for the crash, the costs of your basic treatment will be absorbed by society at large – effectively held in common – through higher insurance premiums and hospital costs. However, the costs that are shared are limited: your car will not be replaced, nor will you be provided with in-home physical therapy. Societies decide collectively how to set limits to which costs are held in common in the absence of liability. The US clearly sets a high minimum threshold and a low maximum payment for medical emergencies, whereas other Western democracies set the levels much lower and higher, respectively.

Contributory fault for countries

The principle of contributory fault can guide our allocation of the costs at the national level as well. Doing so requires spelling out a standard of care for collective agents like countries. Actually establishing what a reasonable country would do is an extremely complex task. Some principle of this kind is, nonetheless, likely to hold quite significant intuitive appeal, not least because failing to hold countries responsible for their irresponsible conduct may provide very poor incentives for the future. And it is difficult to deny that some of the damages of the current crisis have resulted from the failures of developing countries to exercise reasonable care in the management of their financial affairs. Under General Pervez Musharraf, Pakistan borrowed heavily and spent its foreign reserves on imports, only to find itself unable to repay its debts as its currency collapsed in the fall of 2008.[47] And whereas Pakistan's leader was unelected, a number of more democratic developing and emerging economies also behaved in ways that were potentially negligent. In Ukraine, paralysing political infighting has prevented economic reform for years. Latvia chose to direct foreign capital towards now much diminished real estate and mortgage lending.[48] All three – among others – have turned to the IMF for emergency loans to cover their foreign obligations.

By the same token, however, the principle of contributory fault also indicates that many poorer countries should bear lower, if any, costs of the financial crisis. The imprudence or recklessness of poorer countries did not cause most of the damage. To the extent that they were damaged by the actions they took, such as incurring debts that now, post-crisis, are only serviceable (if at all) by cutting social programmes, some of this damage is attributable to the background of the global financial system. The unstable financial environment in which poorer countries operate produces changes to their circumstances that are not only impossible for them to control, but also difficult or impossible to foresee.[49] The present financial crisis is only the most recent and vivid example of such instability.

Domestically, a borrower who makes such claims will face the challenge that these are simply the risks of market activities generally and of borrowing in particular. Economic agents should be aware that there are general risks that accompany activities like borrowing money, which include the risks of financial crises and natural disasters.

It is a common feature of contracts that those who engage in them are usually supposed to assume the risk that fulfilling the conduct will turn out to be more difficult, perhaps much more difficult, than anticipated.[50] But, critically, the law also acknowledges that there are contexts in which this supposition no longer holds. For example, if an unanticipated hurricane of unprecedented ferocity wreaks havoc on a country's economy, this event should not be viewed as part of the 'normal' background risks that agents ought to have considered when entering into contracts or in making other financial decisions. Indeed, contract law and the law of torts has made the distinction between ordinary and extraordinary events that lead to the non-performance of contracts or damages legally relevant. When extraordinary events – including so-called acts of God – lead to the non-performance of contracts, the duty to perform them is excused in many legal systems and the contract is viewed as 'impracticable'.[51] When the performance of a contract becomes impossible for reasons other than the negligence of the contracting parties, it is typically treated as void under the doctrine of frustration.[52]

Even in cases where countries have behaved irresponsibly, we should not conclude that their present and future citizens should pay the full costs. On any plausible reading of the contributory fault principle, it will not follow from the mere fact that an agent's negligence or misconduct has been a contributing factor to some harm that he or she should bear the *entire* cost of that harm. After all, other agents may also have acted negligently or irresponsibly to contribute to these deprivations. Imagine that a pedestrian crosses a busy street against a red light without paying attention to the passing cars and is hit by a driver who does not see the pedestrian because the driver is talking on his cell phone. In this scenario, one might reasonably allocate the liability for the pedestrian's injuries between the driver and the pedestrian to the extent of their fault.

This consideration may be particularly relevant when there is a clear connection between the negligence of one actor and another. For example, the negligence of one agent may have encouraged (and thus significantly raised the risk of) negligent conduct by the other. If an uncle lends a car to his teenage niece, who proceeds to drives it into a tree after drinking several cocktails, she clearly cannot (fully) escape liability for paying her uncle for the repairs to the car. However, her liability may be mitigated by the responsibility of others, if they were in turn responsible for her negligence. If a bartender served her without requesting proper identification, then this bartender (and perhaps also his employer) can also be held partially liable for the costs of the accident. And if the uncle has himself acted negligently by buying alcohol for his niece, it can reasonably be questioned whether he retains any claim whatsoever to compensation for the damages to his car that ensue from her conduct.

Contributory fault in the global financial crisis

The contributory fault principle can help us assess the allocation of costs for responding to the financial crisis. While the negligence of poorer countries may have played some role in creating these costs, the negligent conduct of other countries also seems to have contributed causally to them. In fact, regulators in the US and the UK have admitted as much. In March 2009 Verena Ross, Director of Strategy and Risk at the UK's Financial Services Authority (FSA), laid blame at the feet of the FSA and other major regulators for a 'failure to identify that the whole system was subject to market-wide, systemic risk'.[53] In the US, Christopher Cox, Chairman of the Security and Exchange Commission (SEC) – while resisting broad claims of responsibility – acknowledged that the SEC's programme to regulate Wall Street investment banks was 'fundamentally flawed from the beginning', a failure that in turn contributed to the financial crisis.[54] The SEC seems to have been particularly negligent as a regulator. Under the Bush Administration, the SEC was 'missing in action' and simply failed to regulate according to its mandate, not to mention its failure to act when tipped off regarding Bernard Madoff's Ponzi scheme.[55] The US Federal Reserve has also been a focal point of criticism. Its formerly unimpeachable ex-Chairman Alan Greenspan admitted in a Congressional hearing that his deregulatory ideology was flawed and had contributed to the current crisis.[56] Many critics, such as economist Jeffrey Sachs, go further, arguing that Greenspan's decision to keep US interests rates low after 11 September recklessly encouraged the kind of excessive borrowing that Pakistan, Ukraine and many other countries engaged in.[57]

Furthermore, the widespread official practice of guaranteeing the 'political risk' faced by lenders – the promise to the lender by its government that the latter will bail out the former and take over its claims in case the debtor government declines for whatever reason to honour an obligation – creates a double moral hazard in the international lending system. On the one hand, more capital will flow to reckless governments, which will tend to be willing to borrow more than would be prudent from the standpoint of their population; on the other hand, since creditors will have incentives to lend more, the greater their exposure will be and the greater the likelihood that their government will need to bail them out in order to prevent losses to domestic stockholders will become. This practice shifts a great deal of the risk to the population of the borrower government, which will have to repay or otherwise make other concessions to the government of the lender. In the 1970s, for example, US private banks lent to Indonesia's national oil company Pertamina, even as the US Senate Committee on Foreign Relations declared that the company's debt was uncontrollable and the IMF had put a cap on the loans that should be made available to the country. Nevertheless, banks lent above the IMF ceiling and, when the crisis broke out, the US government stepped in to bail them out and assumed Indonesia's obligations.[58]

It hardly needs mentioning that the same kind of moral hazard is at work in the numerous corporate bailouts enacted by affluent governments.[59] To give one prominent example, the New York Federal Reserve Bank chose to pay out the full face value of the debts that AIG owed to many companies that made risky bets on the housing market when the market value of those debts was clearly considerably lower.[60] The current global financial system is simply not one in which all market participants are expected to bear the risks of their choices.

Moreover, poorer debtor countries are often in so vulnerable a condition that refraining from entering into debt contracts with creditors (even particular creditors) is not a reasonable option for them. Faced with the choice of either taking out a loan that will be difficult to repay or forgoing funds needed to maintain basic services and governmental functions, the decision by a reasonable government to borrow is plausible. In domestic legal contexts of this kind, such contracts are often viewed as non-binding, either because they were entered into under severe duress or because enforcing them would be unconscionable.[61]

Even when, unlike in this case, it seems appropriate to attribute the costs of crises entirely or mainly to the negligent conduct of a country, it may be implausible to hold the vast majority of the country's present and future people solely, mainly and in some cases even partially outcome-responsible for shouldering the costs, especially with respect to severe deprivation. One main reason is that those agents who take out a loan or make financial decisions and those who are obliged to repay it are different. It is the finance ministers and other public officials of a country's government who make borrowing decisions in the name of the country, while it is the present and future citizens and other subjects taxable by the government who are asked to repay. Of course, this is not in itself necessarily problematic. Indeed, when a creditor's claims on individual agents, for example, result from decisions or policies that have been adopted by the agent's political community, and where he or she either played some role in choosing the policy *or* at least had his or her interests given adequate weight by those making the decision, there is at least a prima facie case for taking him or her to be obliged to honour them.[62] The present and/or past governments of many vulnerable countries, however, are not even *minimally* representative of the interests of those they rule, failing to give due consideration to the interests of its people in both the making of decisions and in the decisions themselves.

We have been discussing negligence so far in terms of countries. But the financial crisis has also brought to light the profound effects that corporate negligence can have on the global financial system. It is widely held that firms that transgress fundamental moral rules can be liable to bear the costs of their actions. In his famous denial that corporate social responsibilities extend beyond almost anything other than the maximisation of profit, Milton Friedman nevertheless claims that companies are free to pursue profits only 'while conforming to their basic rules of the society, both those embodied in law and those embodied in ethical custom'.[63] Financial firms in particular have apparently violated both ethical and legal norms and, in the process, have caused tremendous damage to the global poor. While individual agents may pursue civil cases to rectify these kinds of harms, for our purposes, we believe that corporate negligence on this scale also has a bearing on the assessment of national-level policy responses. A country's citizenry is responsible not only for its government officials, but also for the companies that are owned and registered in its territory, at least in countries where they can exercise some collective control over the choice of these policies.

Take the case of the Wall Street hedge fund Magnetar. Magentar exacerbated the financial crisis by betting that the housing market would fail. It sponsored synthetic CDOs – short for collateralised debt obligations, bundles of side bets on mortgages – and then bought low-cost, high pay-off insurance on those CDOs in the form of credit default swaps. Magnetar used its influence as sponsor to encourage the CDO managers to include riskier bonds, thereby making them more likely to fail. And fail they did, wiping out many unsuspecting investors, but earning vast sums for Magnetar and its employees through the credit default swaps (the hedge fund's founder earned $270 million in 2007). Despite its low profile outside of Wall Street, Magnetar became a 'driving force in the market' by entering at a time when CDO sales were expected to decline.[64]

Magnetar was not alone in recklessly inflating the housing bubble for its own gain. In early 2010 the Securities and Exchange Commission charged Goldman Sachs with deceptively selling, and betting against, investments in synthetic CDOs that it knew were designed to fail – essentially the same tactic as Magnetar's trades.[65] It is worth noting that some $13 billion of the US bailout of AIG mentioned above went to Goldman in the form of credit default swap contracts that were cashed in when those CDOs failed.

Goldman is also implicated in additional deprivations. It pioneered a new form of food speculation that engendered the recent food price crisis and pushed the number of malnourished over one billion for the first time in history.[66] In the 1990s Goldman created the Goldman Sachs Commodity Index, which includes wheat, coffee, hogs, cattle, oil and other commodities. They sold this product to investors who agreed to keep buying commodities regardless of their price. Goldman used those investments – minus management fees – to buy futures of the commodities in the index. But since they only had to pay 5 per cent upfront as a 'good faith deposit', they put the rest into Treasury bills and other safe investments, thereby earning money regardless of the performance of the index. Still, the perpetual buying of futures ensured that the price of commodities – that is, food and oil – would rise. As the financial crisis grew worse, the perpetually rising index looked like a safer bet, and more and more investors crowded into the market. The result was enormous profits for Goldman, at the expense of hundreds of millions who could no longer afford food.[67]

Of course, financial recklessness and negligence were not limited to American firms. With £1.7 trillion in assets, the Royal Bank of Scotland is the largest company in the world. The bank aggressively overbid in a 2007 takeover of the Dutch bank ABN Amro, thereby acquiring a substantial amount of sub-prime-based derivatives, and then apparently denied to its board that it had any sub-prime assets. The bank's mismanagement created enormous losses for all those involved in its vast operations and ultimately the British government was forced to spend billions of pounds to bail it out.[68]

How to allocate the costs of the global financial crisis

How should international policy-makers allocate the costs of the financial crisis? Our discussion above recommends the following approach. First, there was considerable negligence on the part of affluent countries, including official failures to adequately regulate financial firms and deliberately risky behaviour on the part of those firms. According to the principle of contributory fault, these countries are liable for the damage they have caused. They ought to pay for the costs of their own recovery, as well as the costs of the recovery of others, to the extent of their fault. Second, some developing countries were also negligent: they took out loans they were unlikely to be able to repay, or engaged in policies that made them likely to need to borrow up to an unsustainable level. In such cases, the contributory fault principle would mitigate the liability of affluent countries for this harm and assign it to an appropriate extent to any negligent developing countries. Third, some countries have contributed negligently to their own downfall but are now so badly off that some of the costs of their recovery should be held in common. Even though they were negligent, the severe deprivation of their citizenry may be such that we ought to rescue them when we can do so at relatively low cost.

Returning to the contributory fault principle, one might object that there is not enough evidence to bring criminal, or even civil, charges against Alan Greenspan, Christopher Cox and other regulators (however, there is enough evidence for the SEC to bring civil charges against Goldman Sachs). But, as we have argued elsewhere, criminal or even civil liability standards are not appropriate for the ethical reflection that should guide international policy-makers in this case.[69] In a criminal case we generally prefer that the guilty go free rather than that the innocent be falsely convicted, and we construct the rules accordingly. But ethical reflection on policy orientation does not call for such a high standard. Rather, for the task at hand, the burden of proof, the standard of proof and the constraints on admissible evidence ought to be designed in order to express a presumption in favour of the severely deprived. In other words, when the lives and livelihoods of the world's poorest people are at stake, our standards for ethical reflection should err in their favour. However these standards are precisely specified, they must hold the world's financial giants, especially the US, the UK and their financial firms, morally liable for harming the developing world.

Even a cursory review of the evidence indicates that affluent countries have not yet made a significant effort to pick up the tab for the financial crisis. As we mentioned in the introduction, requests to share the costs of fiscal stimulus have been largely rebuffed. The President of the General Assembly's call for a $3 trillion stimulus was echoed by the IMF, which urged governments to implement a stimulus of 2 per cent of world GDP.[70] So far, however, the combined global fiscal stimulus amounts to $1.98 trillion, only 1.4 per cent of global GDP.[71] These figures are unlikely to increase much further, as the talk at the G-20 has now shifted to cutting deficits.

Nor has there been a great outpouring of direct aid, despite the promising words at the April 2009 G-20 summit. A UK House of Commons report noted that affluent countries generally intended to uphold their levels of aid as a percentage of GDP, but that since incomes are declining, this actually implies a decrease in aid.[72] Indeed, total ODA fell by about $3 billion from 2008 to 2009.[73] And these aid levels are still well below what affluent countries promised to give at the 2005 G-8 summit. Signs for the future are mixed. Several countries that were themselves badly affected by the crisis have slashed their aid budgets; Ireland, Italy, Greece and Portugal have all cut aid budgets by between 10 and 30 per cent.[74]

To bridge the financing gap, developing countries have had to turn to the international financial institutions, particularly the IMF. IMF lending is expected to increase by up to 40 per cent by 2012.[75] However, these loans have been much criticised over the years for their conditionality. Ukraine, for instance, complained that it would have had to reduce social spending in order to be eligible for additional IMF funding. While a detailed analysis of the human impacts of IMF conditionality is beyond the scope of this chapter, our analysis above gives us some reason to question this method – conditional IMF loans – as a means of responding to the crisis.

Moreover, affluent countries, especially the US, have done little to discharge their responsibility for their corporate actors. Having failed to do so by extending aid to repair the damage from corporate negligence, affluent countries could at least act to ensure that the ability of financial firms to harm developing countries is limited in the future. The US Financial Reform Act does not fundamentally alter the ability of financial giants to inflate another bubble. Nor does it curtail the ability of industry lobbyists to influence the application of rules in their favour.[76] And it is entirely silent on the food speculation that starved millions during the lead-up the crisis.

What would a more appropriate policy response look like? Aside from more equitable stimulus spending and effective financial regulatory reform, governments should give careful consideration to the ramifications of using the IMF as the main vehicle for developing-country assistance. Only three countries, Colombia, Mexico and Poland, are eligible for conditionality-free loans. Others could in principle access conditionality-free financing through special drawing rights (SDRs). The G-20 touted the allocation of $250 billion in SDRs at its April 2009 meeting, but in reality only $82 billion will go to developing countries and only $16 billion to low-income countries.[77] Currently SDRs must be allocated along quota lines, which give the lion's share to affluent countries; governments could consider relaxing this requirement. Similarly, the IMF's move to reduce the interest rate on concessional loans to zero is laudable, but the overall effect will be limited. Countries will only save about $1 million per year over a two-and-a-half-year period.[78] There is clearly room for more aggressive action by those with the greatest capacity.

Moreover, we should question the wisdom of pushing poorer countries even further into debt as a means of rescuing them from a debt-induced crisis. Affluent governments should offer no-strings-attached development aid in the form of grants rather than loans where possible, insofar as it seems likely that doing so would benefit the recipient populations.[79]

Our car crash brings out the absurdity of the current situation. If a driver smashes his car into a victim's home, the driver cannot make good on his actions by offering to let the victim borrow the cost of repairs from him. It makes no difference if the repairs to the car itself will be costly; the driver still bears the burden of repairing the damage to the victim's home. Even if the victim encouraged the damage by building his home close to the busy road, the two then share responsibility to the extent of their individual fault. And if, as in the present case, the driver is fantastically wealthy and the victim is a pauper, and there is no one else to help, then the driver should aid the victim even if neither were at fault.

Notes

1. President of the General Assembly, 'Draft Outcome Document for the United Nations Conference on the World Financial and Economic Crisis and Its Impact on Development', 8 May 2009, pp. 5–6, www.un.org/ga/president/63/interactive/financialcrisis/outcomedoc80509.pdf, date accessed 6 October 2010.
2. United Nations General Assembly, Resolution Adopted by the General Assembly, 'Outcome of the United Nations Conference on the World Financial and Economic Crisis and Its Impact on Development', A/RES/63/303, 13 July 2009, www.un.org/ga/search/view_doc.asp?symbol=A/RES/63/303&Lang=E, para. 10 (date accessed 6 October 2010).
3. G-20, 'The Global Plan for Recovery and Reform', adopted 2 April 2009, London, para. 17, www.g20.org/Documents/final-communique.pdf, date accessed 6 October 2010.
4. Jackie Calmes, 'Republican Backpedals from Apology to BP', *New York Times*, 17 June 2010, www.nytimes.com/2010/06/18/us/politics/18barton.html, date accessed 6 October 2010.
5. *BBC News*, 'Financial Crisis "Like a Tsunami"', 23 October 2008, http://news.bbc.co.uk/2/hi/business/7687101.stm, date accessed 6 October 2010.
6. World Bank, 'Swimming Against the Tide: How Developing Countries are Coping with the Global Crisis', March 2009, http://go.worldbank.org/O9I08DS5B0, date accessed 6 October 2010.
7. International Monetary Fund, 'Global Economic Prospects and Policy Challenges', briefing prepared for the Meeting of Group of 20 Finance Ministers and Central Bank Governors, Busan, Korea, 4–5 June 2010, www.imf.org/external/np/g20/pdf/060410.pdf, date accessed 6 October 2010. The IMF uses the language of 'contagion' repeatedly.
8. Lara Marlowe, 'Sarkozy Calls for Capitalism with a Dose of Morality', *Irish Times*, 26 September 2008, www.irishtimes.com/newspaper/world/2008/0926/1222374595726.html, date accessed 6 October 2010.
9. Diane Francis, 'World Is Titanic without Paddle – Lula', *National Post*, 15 April 2009, http://network.nationalpost.com/np/blogs/francis/archive/2009/04/15/world-is-titanic-without-paddle-lula.aspx, date accessed 6 October 2010.

10. Among many others, see Paul Thomasch, 'Zelnick: Welcome to the Emergency Room', *Reuters*, 4 December 2008, blogs.reuters.com/summits/2008/12/04/zelnick-welcome-to-the-emergency-room, date accessed 6 October 2010; and Emma Simon, 'Financial Crisis: Is It Time to Invest?', *Daily Telegraph* (London), 19 September 2008, www.telegraph.co.uk/finance/newsbysector/banksandfinance/2992018/Financial-crisis-is-it-time-to-invest.html, date accessed 6 October 2010.

11. Prevented, at the very least, by our ancestors not creating a financial system with exceedingly complex financial instruments and high degrees of leverage; no world like ours would lack the movements of the ocean.

12. The manner of contribution in the case of a car crash is of course different, since the driver of the car is linked to the injuries they cause through a complete causal process involving the transfer of energy and momentum – he or she does harm – whereas the damage caused by the global financial crisis resulted from its prevention of economic activity that would have continued to sustain the economies that now suffer – it enabled harm. Tort law also covers cases of enabling harm, such as where a mechanic's failure to exercise due care while repairing a car contributes to an accident that later occurs.

13. World Bank, *Global Development Finance: Charting a Global Recovery: I: Review, Analysis and Outlook*, Washington DC: World Bank, 2009, http://siteresources.worldbank.org/INTGDF2009/Resources/gdf_combined_web.pdf, p. xi (date accessed 6 October 2010).

14. World Bank, *Global Economic Prospects 2010*, Washington DC: World Bank, 2010, Table 1.1. India grew 9.1 per cent in 2007, 6.1 per cent in 2008 and 6.0 per cent in 2009; China's figures were 13.0 per cent, 9.0 per cent and 8.4 per cent, respectively.

15. Dirk Willem te Velde, 'The Global Financial Crisis and Developing Countries: Synthesis of the Findings of 10 Country Case Studies', Overseas Development Institute Working Paper 306, London, June 2009, p. 1.

16. Ibid., p. vii.

17. International Labour Organization, *Global Employment Trends: May 2009 Update*, Geneva: International Labour Office, 2009, www.ilo.org/wcmsp5/groups/public/---dgreports/---dcomm/documents/publication/wcms_106504.pdf, Table B2, p. 27 (date accessed 6 October 2010).

18. In 2005 purchasing power parity dollars. This level, the World Bank's international line for extreme poverty, is equivalent to about $1.40 in current US dollars or $511 per year to cover all human needs. United Nations, *World Economic Prospects and Situation 2010*, New York: United Nations, 2010, p. vi.

19. World Bank, *Global Economic Prospects 2010*, Table 1.1.

20. Chi-Chu Tschang, 'A Tough Year for China's Migrant Workers', *BusinessWeek*, 4 February 2009, www.businessweek.com/globalbiz/content/feb2009/gb2009024_357998.htm, date accessed 6 October 2010.

21. Te Veldte, 'Global Financial Crisis', p. 9.

22. UNESCO, 'Global Crisis Hits Most Vulnerable', press release, 3 March 2009, http://portal.unesco.org/en/ev.php-URL_ID=44687&URL_DO=DO_ TOPIC&URL_SECTION=201.html, date accessed 6 October 2010.
23. UNESCO, *Education for All Global Monitoring Report 2010*, Paris: UNESCO, 2010, p. 3.
24. World Bank, 'Swimming Against the Tide', p. 10.
25. World Bank, *Global Economic Prospects 2010*, pp. 26, 21.
26. Thomas Palley, 'Sovereign Debt Restructuring Proposals: A Comparative Look' (2003) *Ethics & International Affairs*, 17/2, 26–33.
27. Ibid.
28. In 2009 developing countries received only 30 per cent of the net private capital that they did in 2007, a $795 billion reduction; World Bank, *Global Economic Prospects 2010*, p. 22.
29. These and 11 other countries can be classified as medium risk. Peter Chowla, 'The Potential Development Implications of Enhancing the IMF's Resources', Intergovernmental Group of Twenty-Four on International Monetary Affairs and Development, Policy Brief No. 47, 4 August 2009, www.g24.org/pbno47.pdf, pp. 3–4 (date accessed 6 October 2010).
30. World Bank, *World Development Report 2010*, Washington DC: World Bank, 2010, Table 5.
31. Assuming that we could effectively distribute the resources. Thomas Pogge, *Politics as Usual: What Lies Behind the Pro-Poor Rhetoric*, Cambridge: Polity, 2010, p. 70.
32. Kunibert Raffer, 'Risks of Lending and Liability of Lenders' (2006) *Ethics & International Affairs*, 21, 1, 85–106, p. 93.
33. See, for example, Erlassjahr, 'A Fair and Transparent Arbitration Process for Indebted Southern Countries', Updated Submission to Financing for Development, September 2001, www.erlassjahr.de/content/languages/ englisch/dokumente/ftap_englisch_rz.pdf, date accessed 6 October 2010.
34. Peter Singer, 'Famine, Affluence, and Morality' (1973) *Philosophy & Public Affairs*, 1, 3, 229_43, p. 231.
35. Ibid. See also Peter Singer, *The Live You Can Save*, Melbourne: Text Publishing, 2009, arguing that the money spent on luxuries can and should be donated to aid agencies saving children's lives.
36. Singer, *The Live You Can Save*, pp. 11–12.
37. Christian Barry and Gerhard Øverland, 'Responding to Global Poverty' (2009) *Journal of Bioethical Inquiry*, 6, 2, 239–47, pp. 239–40.
38. Which is not to say that *governments* or people collectively cannot easily address global poverty.
39. See, e.g., David Schmidtz, 'Islands in a Sea of Obligation' (2000) *Law and Philosophy*, 19, 683–705.
40. Thomas Nagel, 'The Problem of Global Justice' (2005) *Philosophy & Public Affairs*, 33, 2, 113–47, p. 118. Similar claims are made by others who criticise more demanding principles such as the SAP. See, e.g., Richard Miller, *Globalizing Justice*, Oxford University Press, 2010; and Garrett Cullity, *The Moral Demands of Affluence*, Oxford University Press, 2004.

41. These are the latest available figures. Malnutrition (2009): Food and Agriculture Organization, '1.02 Billion People Hungry', news release, 19 June 2009, www.fao.org/news/story/0/item/20568/icode/en, date accessed 6 October 2010. Water and Sanitation (2008): World Health Organization and UNICEF, *Progress on Sanitation and Drinking Water: 2010 Update*, Geneva: WHO, 2010, www.who.int/water_sanitation_health/ publications/9789241563956/en/index.html, pp. 6–7 (date accessed 6 October 2010). Electricity (2008): International Energy Agency, 'World Energy Outlook: Access to Energy', 2010, www.iea.org/weo/electricity.asp, date accessed 6 October 2010. Thomas Pogge relays this data on poverty in *Politics as Usual*; Matt Peterson compiled the data for that book.

42. In 2005 PPP terms. The authors' calculations are based on Shaohua Chen and Martin Ravallion, 'The Developing World Is Poorer than We Thought, But No Less Successful in the Fight against Poverty', World Bank Policy Research Working Paper WPS 4703, Washington DC, 2008, http://econ.worldbank.org/docsearch, date accessed 6 October 2010; and World Bank, *World Development Indicators Online*, 2010, http://data.worldbank.org/data-catalog, date accessed 6 October 2010.

43. James B. Davies, Susanna Sandström, Anthony Shorrocks and Edward N. Wolff, 'The World Distribution of Household Wealth', UNU-WNU Discussion Paper No. 2008/03, Helsinki, Finland, February 2008, www. wider.unu.edu/publications/working-papers/discussion-papers/2008/en_ GB/dp2008-03, p. 7 (date accessed 6 October 2010).

44. United Nations, 'Millennium Development Goals Indicators', 23 June 2010, http://mdgs.un.org/unsd/mdg/Data.aspx, date accessed 6 October 2010.

45. For discussion, see Richard W. Wright, 'The Grounds and Extent of Legal Responsibility', (2003) *San Diego Law Review*, 41, 1425–531.

46. These notions are well described in Arthur Ripstein, *Equality, Responsibility, and the Law*, Cambridge University Press, 1999, on which the present discussion draws.

47. Shahan Mufti, 'Cash-Strapped Pakistan Finds Few Friends in Time of Economic Need', *Christian Science Monitor*, 23 October 2008, www. csmonitor.com/2008/1023/p04s01-wosc.html, date accessed 6 October 2010.

48. David Stern, 'Economic Crisis Sweeps Eastern Ukraine', 8 April 2009, www. nytimes.com/2009/04/08/world/europe/08ukraine.html, date accessed 6 October 2010; Orla Ryan, 'Latvia's Dramatic Fall from Grace', *BBC News*, 8 June 2009, http://news.bbc.co.uk/go/pr/fr/-/2/hi/business/8085007.stm, date accessed 6 October 2010.

49. For an illuminating discussion by a policy-maker about why so few foresaw the crisis, see David Gruen, 'Reflections on the Global Financial Crisis', Keynote Address at the Sydney Institute, 19 June 2009, www. treasury.gov.au/documents/1564/PDF/Sydney_Institute_Address.pdf, date accessed 6 October 2010.

50. See P.S. Atiyah, *Introduction to the Law of Contract*, 5th edn, Oxford University Press, 1995, esp. pp. 212–15, for discussion.

51. The United States Uniform Commercial Code, §2-615, for example, excuses a party from delivering goods specified in a contract when the reason for their failure to do so results from events such as 'acts of God' whose absence was a 'basic assumption' of the contract, whether or not such exclusion is specifically stated in the contract. For a detailed discussion of the jurisprudence and justification of these measures, see Alan O. Sykes, 'The Doctrine of Commercial Impracticability in a Second-Best World' (1990) *Journal of Legal Studies*, 19, 1, 43–94; and Richard A. Posner and Andrew M. Rosenfield, 'Impossibility and Related Doctrines in Contract Law: An Economic Analysis' (1977) *Journal of Legal Studies*, 6, 1, 83–118.

52. See Atiyah, *Introduction to the Law of Contract*, pp. 229–44 for discussion.

53. Verena Ross, 'Lessons from the Financial Crisis', speech to the Chatham House Conference on Global Financial Regulation, London, 24 March 2009, www.fsa.gov.uk/pages/Library/Communication/Speeches/2009/0324_vr.shtml, date accessed 6 October 2010.

54. Stephen Labaton, 'S.E.C. Concedes Oversight Flaws Fueled Collapse', *New York Times*, 27 September 2009, www.nytimes.com/2008/09/27/business/27sec.html, date accessed 6 October 2010.

55. Jesse Westbrook and Robert Schmidt, 'Cox "Asleep at Switch" as Paulson, Bernanke Encroach', *Bloomberg*, 22 September 2008, www.bloomberg.com/apps/news?pid=20601109&sid=aoM0mju1ARQo&refer=home, date accessed 6 October 2010; Alex Blumberg, 'Now You SEC Me, Now You Don't', *This American Life*, 12 September 2008, www.thisamericanlife.org/Radio_Episode.aspx?sched=1260, date accessed 6 October 2010; and Jesse Westbrook, David Scheer and Mark Pittman, 'Madoff Tipster Markopolos Cites SEC's "Ineptitude"', *Bloomberg*, 4 February 2009, www.bloomberg.com/apps/news?pid=20601103&sid=axvJfch6PDjs&, date accessed 6 October 2010.

56. Kara Scannell and Sudeep Reddy, 'Greenspan Admits Errors to Hostile House Panel', *Wall Street Journal*, 24 October 2008, http://online.wsj.com/article/SB122476545437862295.html?mod=todays_us_page_one, date accessed 6 October 2010.

57. Jeffrey Sachs, 'The Roots of Crisis', *The Guardian*, 21 March 2008, www.guardian.co.uk/commentisfree/2008/mar/21/therootsofcrisis, date accessed 6 October 2010. For an insightful overview of the relationship between low interest rates and the financial crisis, see 'The Giant Pool of Money', *This American Life*, 9 May 2008, www.thislife.org/radio_episode.aspx?episode=355, date accessed 6 October 2010.

58. For a discussion of this example and the (in)operation of risk in international lending, see Raffer, 'Risk of Lending and Liability of Lenders'. For a more extended discussion of the various ways that the international lending system encourages problematic borrowing and lending, see Christian Barry and Lydia Tomitova, 'Fairness in Sovereign Debt' (2006) *Social Research*, 74, 2, 649–69.

59. For details of US bailouts, see 'History of U.S. Bailouts', *ProPublica*, 15 April 2009, www.propublica.org/special/government-bailouts, date

accessed 6 October 2010; and 'Adding Up the Government's Total Bailout Tab', *New York Times*, 4 February 2009, www.nytimes.com/ interactive/2009/02/04/business/20090205-bailout-totals-graphic.html, date accessed 6 October 2010.

60. Office of the Special Inspector General for the Troubled Asset Relief Program, 'Factors Affecting Efforts to Limit Payments to AIG Counterparties', SIGTARP-10-1003, 17 November 2009, www.sigtarp. gov/reports/audit/2009/Factors_Affecting_Efforts_to_Limit_Payments_ to_AIG_Counterparties.pdf, date accessed 6 October 2010.

61. It is worth noting that the domestic law of many countries has traditionally regarded loans to poor persons in distress, such as by payday lenders or check cashers, with great suspicion. For a discussion of this, see John Cartwright, *Unequal Bargaining: A Study of Vitiating Factors in the Formation of Contracts*, Oxford: Clarendon Press, 1991.

62. As argued in David Miller, 'National Responsibility and International Justice', in Deen K. Chatterjee (ed.), *The Ethics of Assistance: Morality and the Distant Needy*, Cambridge University Press, 2004.

63. Milton Friedman, 'The Social Responsibility of Business Is to Increase Its Profits', *New York Times Magazine*, 13 September 1970.

64. Jesse Eisinger and Jake Bernstein, 'The Magnetar Trade: How One Hedge Fund Helped Keep the Bubble Going', *ProPublica*, 9 April 2010, www.propublica.org/article/all-the-magnetar-trade-how-one-hedge-fund-helped-keep-the-housing-bubble, date accessed 6 October 2010.

65. Louise Story and Gretchen Morgenson, 'SEC Accuses Goldman of Fraud in Housing Deal', *New York Times*, 16 April 2010, www.nytimes. com/2010/04/17/business/17goldman.html, date accessed 6 October 2010. See also Matt Taibbi, 'The Great American Bubble Machine', *Rolling Stone*, 9–23 July 2009, www.rollingstone.com/politics/news/12697/64796, date accessed 6 October 2010.

66. Food and Agriculture Organization, '1.02 Billion People Hungry: One Sixth of Humanity Undernourished – More than Ever Before', FAO Media Centre, 19 June 2009, www.fao.org/news/story/0/item/20568/icode/en, date accessed 6 October 2010.

67. Frederick Kaufman, 'The Food Bubble: How Wall Street Starved Millions and Got Away with It', *Harper's*, July 2010, pp. 27–34. Matt Taibbi relates the index to the oil price spikes of the past decade in 'The Great American Bubble Machine'.

68. John Lanchester, 'It's Finished' (2009) *London Review of Books*, 31, 28, available at www.lrb.co.uk/v31/n10/john-lanchester/its-finished, date accessed 6 October 2010. As a curious side-note, RBS was the biggest loser in the particular deal at the heart of the SEC investigation of Goldman: Landon Thomas, Jr., 'A Routine Deal Became an $840 Million Mistake', *New York Times*, 22 April 2010, www.nytimes.com/2010/04/23/business/ 23cdo.html, date accessed 6 October 2010.

69. Christian Barry and Matt Peterson, 'Dealing Fairly with the Costs to the Poor of the Global Financial Crisis', in Ian G. MacNeil and Justin O'Brien (eds), *The Future of Financial Regulation*, Oxford: Hart, 2010. Christian

Barry originally posited this argument in 'Applying the Contribution Principle' (2005) *Metaphilosophy*, 36, 1/2, 210–27.

70. John Lipsky, 'Towards a Post-Crisis World Economy', speech at Johns Hopkins University, 17 November 2008, www.imf.org/external/np/speeches/2008/111708.htm, date accessed 6 October 2010.

71. Sameer Khatiwada, 'Stimulus Packages to Counter Global Economic Crisis: A Review', International Institute for Labour Studies, Discussion Paper DP/196/2009, Geneva, 2009, www.ilo.org/public/english/bureau/inst/publications/discussion/dp19609.pdf, p. 1 (date accessed 6 October 2010).

72. House of Commons International Development Committee, *Aid Under Pressure: Support for Development Assistance in a Global Economic Downturn*, Fourth Report of Session 2008–9, vol. I, 19 May 2009, www.publications.parliament.uk/pa/cm200809/cmselect/cmintdev/179/17902.htm, p. 28 (date accessed 6 October 2010).

73. From $122 to $119 billion. Of this, 11 per cent went to Iraq and Afghanistan. United Nations, 'Millennium Development Goals Indicators'.

74. Organization for Economic Co-operation and Development, 'Development Aid Rose in 2009 and Most Donors Will Meet 2010 Aid Targets', OECD news release, 14 April 2010, www.oecd.org/document/11/0,3343,en_21571361_44315115_44981579_1_1_1_1,00.html, date accessed 6 October 2010.

75. Sylvi Rzepka, 'The Big Post-Crisis Takeover: Trends in IFI Lending to Low Income Countries', Eurodad Briefing, 8 April 2010, www.eurodad.org/whatsnew/articles.aspx?id=4066, date accessed 6 October 2010.

76. See, e.g., Deniz Igan, Prachi Mishra and Thierry Tressel, 'A Fistful of Dollars: Lobbying and the Financial Crisis', IMF Working Paper WP/09/287, December 2009, www.imf.org/external/pubs/ft/wp/2009/wp09287.pdf (date accessed 6 October 2010), which notes that Countrywide Financial and Ameriquest Mortgage, two of the most egregious sub-prime lenders, spent almost $30 million on lobbying and political activities between 2002 and 2008.

77. Chowla, 'Potential Development Implications', p. 3.

78. ActionAid *et al.*, 'IMF Financial Package for Low-Income Countries: Much Ado about Nothing?', 7 August 2009, www.eurodad.org/whatsnew/articles.aspx?id=3803, date accessed 6 October 2010.

79. Injecting more resources into a very poorly governed society or one with a corrupt government would not, obviously, meet this requirement.

Index

-25 Sigma events   12
  see also high-frequency trading
401(k), *see* pension funds

AAA-rated shares   2
  see also rating agencies
Abacus, *see* Goldman Sachs, fraud and
ABN Amro   175
academic research, limits in   58
accounting firms, GFC and   26
Achilles' heel of competitive systems
  description of   121
  see also competitive systems,
    framing and
  globalisation and   125–6
active and passive property   93
adjustable-rate mortgages   5
adjusted liabilities   99
adversarial systems, *see* competitive
    systems
affluent countries   176
  see also moral responsibility,
    affluent countries and
aid, GFC and   177
Aite Group   101
algorithm-based trading strategies,
    see high-frequency trading
Alien Tort Claims Act (ACTA)
    (US)   107, 111
alienation from capital   106
allocation of costs   20, 175–8
Alternative Mortgage Transactions
    Parity Act, 1982 (US)   96
American Apparel and Footwear
    Association (AAFA)   104
American International Group
    (AIG)   9, 55, 109
Angelides, Phil   102
apartheid, ethical investing
    and   84–5

Arthur Andersen   26
  see also accounting firms, GFC
    and
auditing, ethics   147–8, 155
auditor
  independence of   153
  moral purpose of   45–6
  role of   133
auto industry   13, 14, 61
  Ronald Reagan and   65–6
autonomy and risk, *see* risk and
    autonomy

bailout, governments and
    corporations   55, 90–1, 109,
    172
Bank of America   99, 102
Bank of International
    Settlement   16
Bank of the South   60
bankruptcy, personal filings of
    (US)   97
bankruptcy code (US)   163
Basel Accord   7
Bear Stearns   8, 96
behavioural economics   29
Berle, Adolph   92
Bhopal Gas Disaster, India, *see*
    Union Carbide
Blair, Dennis   112
Blair, Sheila   101
Blankfein, Lloyd   102
Boesky, Ivan   26
Bolivia   58, 60
bonuses, *see* CEOs, compensation of
Booz & Company   87–8
BP, Gulf of Mexico oil spill 2010   20,
    40–1, 159
Bradford & Bingley   12
Bretton Woods system   57

bribery, *see* corruption
Buffet, Warren   69

CALPERS, ethical investing and   86
CALSTRS, ethical investing and   86
Calvert Foundation   89
Campaign GM, ethical investing
     and   84, 85
capability, ethical investing and   85
Cape Verde   162
capital, necessary levels of, *see* Basel
     Accord
car crash analogy
   GFC comparisons to   159–60,
     177–8
   moral responsibility and   167–8,
     177–8
car loans, *see* auto industry
causes of GFC   18
   institutional dimensions   27
   unethical practices as   25
central banks, responses to GFC
     14
Centre for Community Capital,
     University of North
     Carolina   6
CEOs, compensation of   26, 38,
     90–1, 101–2, 105, 127–8, 166
charity   69
Chávez, Hugo   57
China   13
   Business Principles   104
   inequality in   129, 160
Citigroup   7, 8, 14, 55, 56, 94, 99
civil litigation, markets and   67
   see also market regulation, moral
     consequences and
climate change
   ethical investment and   90, 108
   GFC and   52, 61
codes of business conduct   104
codes of ethics   2, 7, 8, 32, 49,
     108–9, 142–3, 152
collateralised debt obligations
     (CDOs)   2, 96
collateralised mortgage obligations
     (CMOs)   96

collective action, problems of   19,
     25, 27–28
collective ends   35, 36
collective goods   33–4, 37, 43
   rights to   37–8
collective goods and public goods,
     differences between   33
collective moral responsibility,
   see moral responsibility,
     collective
collusion, inequality and   129
Colombia   177
Commodity Futures Modernization
     Act, 2000 (US)   95
Common Code for the Coffee
     Community (CCCC)   104
Community Development Financial
     Institutions (CDFIs)   88
competing ends, collective goods
     profit maximisation and   35,
     36
   see also market institutions
competition
   comparative performance
     and   121
   incentivisation and   121
competitive systems
   collusion in   129
   corruption and   121–3
   framing and   121
   polarisation and   126
   'suckers' in   125
computer-based statistical
     analysis   3, 99–100
   see also high-frequency trading
conflict of interest   3, 25–6, 28, 155
consent   70, 71, 170
Consumer Protection Act, 2010
     (US)   56
consumers   70
contracts   170
   see also consent
contributory fault   166–75
   developing countries and   169
   GFC and   171
   variable moral responsibility
     and   169, 170

see also principle of contributory fault

coordination problem, *see* collective action, problems of

Corbett, Jack 86–7

corporate financial service providers, moral purpose and 43, 46–7

corporate social responsibility (CSR) 103–4, 113–14, 149

corruption 17, 46, 107–8, 121–3, 152
  costs of 122
  example of 122
  globalisation and 126
  incentivisation and 121–2
  lobbying and 122, 129
  see also lobbying
  private interests and 122
  reduction of 123
  resource diversion and 121–2
  shared morality and 123

costs of GFC 13, 52, 102–3, 160–2
  severe deprivations 161

Cote d'Ivoire 162

Countrywide Financial 4, 15

Cox, Christopher 171

credit default swaps (CDSs) 9–10, 76–7, 95, 98, 99, 108–9
  market values of 95

credit rating agencies, role of 134

Credit Suisse 98

credit-democratisation 5, 15

culture, *see* institutional culture

da Silva, Inacio Lula 159

Davies, Howard 69

debt overhang 162

democratic deficit 58

Dendreon 100

deontic properties 38
  see also moral rights

Department of Defense (US) 87

Department of Housing and Urban Development (US) 5

Depository Institution Deregulation and Monetary Control Act, 1980 (US) 94

designing-in ethics, evidence-based 154

Detroit 65–6
  see also auto industry

Deutsche Bank AG 99

developing countries, effects of GFC on 158, 160–2

Dexia 12

Dodd-Frank Wall Street Reform (US) 56

Dow Jones Industrial Average (DJIA) 100

Dreyfus Third Century Fund 87

'drowning child' example, *see* Singer, Peter

dual consistency of governments 57

duty to rescue, description of 166
  see also principles of assistance, minimum moral duty

East Asia, democracy in 60

Eastman Kodak 84

economic systems, theories of 124

economic theory, individualist models of 29, 44
  see also self-interest

education, effects of GFC on 13

electoral campaigns, contributions to 94–5, 97–8, 177
  see also lobbying

Emergency Economic Stabilisation Act, 2008 (US) 97

End of History, The 64

ends, proximate and ultimate 36
  see also collective ends

enforcement 142–3
  problems in 142

English East India Company 91

Enron 26, 139

environmental concerns 31, 52, 90, 102

epistemic construct of risk, *see* risk as an epistemic construct

Equator Principles 104

ethical investing   19, 82–3
    and apartheid   84–5
    history of   83–91
    moral minimum criteria of   85–6
    South Africa and   84–5, 103
    tobacco and   83, 87
    Vietnam War and   84–5
ethical investment
    climate change and   90
    'green technologies' and   88
    shareholder advocacy and   89
ethical investments
    inclusionary investment
        guidelines and   88–9
    passive exclusionary screening
        and   88
Ethical Investor, The   85–6, 103, 112
ethical leadership   152
ethical performance
    objective measures of   148–50,
        154–5
    quantitative and qualitative
        measures of   149–50, 154–5
ethical risk
    data and   149–50, 152, 154
    examples of   152–3
ethics audit   147–8, 155
    ratings agencies and   150
executive remuneration, *see* CEO
    compensation; injustice
exports, decline in   14
external integrity mechanisms, *see*
    integrity mechanisms
externalities   53
Extractive Industries Transparency
    Initiative (EITI)   104
Exxon Corporation   86

Fair and Transparent Arbitration
    Process (FTAP)   163
    see also bankruptcy code (US)
Fair Labor Association (FLA)   104
'Famine, Affluence and
    Morality'   164
Fannie Mae   3–4, 5, 9, 14, 96
Federal Deposit Insurance
    Corporation (FDIC) (US)   101

Federal Reserve (US)   8
fiduciary duty
    failures of   105, 109
    moral duties and   107, 109–10,
        112
FIGHT, ethical investing and   84
Financial Crisis Inquiry Commission
    (FCIC) (US)   101, 102
Financial Modernization Act, 1999
    (US)   95
Financial Reform Act (US)   177
Financial Regulatory Bill 2010
    (US)   14–15
Financial Services Authority (FSA)
    (UK)   69, 171
financial services sector, professions
    in   132–4
financing gap, estimates of, *see*
    World Bank, estimates of
    financing gap
First Amendment (US), *see* free
    speech, lobbying and
food availability, GFC and   52,
    172
foreclosure, US amounts   6
Foreign Corrupt Practices Act (FCPA)
    (US)   107, 111
framing, competitive systems, *see*
    competitive systems, framing
    and
Freddie Mac   3–4, 5, 9, 14, 96
free speech, lobbying and   94–5,
    98
Friedman, Milton   39–40, 66, 173
Fukuyama, Francis   64

G-20   158, 176, 177
'gaming the system'   149
    see also perverse incentives
Garnaut, Ross   14
General Assembly (UN)   158,
    165–6
General Motors   14, 84
    see also auto industry
Ghana   162
Ginnie Mae   96
Glass-Steagall Act, 1933 (US)   94

Glitnir 12
'Global Plan for Recovery and
    Relief', 2009 (G-20) 158
Global Reporting Initiative
    (GRI) 104
Global Sullivan Principles of Social
    Responsibility 103–4
globalisation 61, 124–6
    corruption lobbying and 125–6,
    129
    polarisation and 126
    rising inequality and 90, 126–8,
    129–30, 160–2
Goldman Sachs 8, 12, 55, 98, 99,
    102, 105, 174
    fraud and 108–9
Goodyear Tire and Rubber 86
government regulation of markets,
    see market regulation
Gramm, Phil 15, 95
Gramm-Leach-Bliley Act, *see*
    Financial Modernization Act,
    1999 (US) 95
Greece 162, 176
    see also sovereign debt crisis
'green technologies', ethical
    investment and 88
Greenspan, Alan 55–6, 67, 94, 159,
    171
gross national income (GNI) 165
Gunneman, Jon 85

HBOS 12
health care, effects of GFC on 13
Health Impact Fund (HIF) 131
hidden hand of markets 64
    see also 'invisible hand', Adam
    Smith's
high-frequency trading 3, 12,
    99–101, 106
    problems of 100–1
holistic integrity systems, *see*
    integrity systems, holistic
Honeywell Corporation 84
House Financial Services
    Committee, lobbying and
    98

Huffington Post 105
human rights 107, 113, 161,
    163
Hungary 24
Hurd, Heidi 72

Iceland 12
impartiality of regulators, lack
    of 28
    see also conflict of interest
incentivisation 27, 30, 35, 47–8,
    68, 121, 143–4, 150
    virtuous triangle and 30
inclusionary investment guidelines,
    ethical investments and
    88–9
Indonesia 172
inequality 90, 126–8, 129–30,
    160–2
    income 16
infant mortality, GFC and 161
information as power 59
informed consent, *see* consent
Initial Public Offerings (IPOs)
    134
injustice 26
insider trading, morality of 46
    see also corruption
institutional culture 137, 153
institutional ends 39, 137
    see also market institutions,
    teleological normative
    account of
institutional integrity, *see* integrity
    of institution
institutional moral rights and
    duties, *see* moral rights and
    duties of institutions
insurance wrapped securities 3
integrity of an institution, structure
    and culture 136–7, 153
integrity mechanisms, internal and
    external 144–5
integrity, moral notion of
    136
integrity of a profession 136
integrity promotion 138

integrity systems   17, 27, 49,
    135–46
  codes of ethics and   143–4
  derivative nature of   28–9
  description of   28, 135
  detection mechanisms in   142
  elements in   152, 154
  function of   135
  holistic   144–6, 151
  justice and desert   141–3
  lawyers and accountants in   45
  participation in   150, 155
    see also incentivisation
  presuppositions of   145
  preventive   143–4
  reputation and   146–56
  rewards in   143–4
  risk management and   152
Intel Corporation   113–14
Interfaith Center for Corporate
    Responsibility (ICCR)   89
internal integrity mechanisms,
    see integrity mechanisms
International Harvester   92
International Monetary Fund
    (IMF)   99, 159, 162, 169
  emergency loans and   169, 176
investment bankers   134
Investment Company Act, 1940
    (US)   11
'invisible hand', Adam Smith's   30,
    35, 36–7, 43–4, 46, 64
Ireland   176
  see also sovereign debt crisis
Italy   176

joint action   37
  and collective good   37
JP Morgan Chase   8, 12, 97, 98, 99
justified self-defence and risk, *see*
    risk and justified self-defence

Kant, Immanuel   34, 109–10
Kantian duty, *see* moral duty,
    individual
Kew Gardens Principle   86
Keynes, John Maynard   57, 92

Kitty Genovese   86
knowledge as power   59
Kodak   84

labour investment theory, *see* private
    property, moral rights to
Landsbanki   12
last resort, ethical investing and   85
Latin America, democracy in   58,
    60
Latvia   169
lawyers, role of   133–4
leadership, *see* ethical leadership
'leashed' capitalism, advocates
    and   63
Lehman Brothers   9, 24, 97, 105
  bankruptcy of   9
Lewitt, Michael   11
liability, moral responsibility
    and   168
liberty
  business   69–70
    see also market regulation,
      moral rights and
  individual   69
limited liability   41
Lloyds TSB   12
lobbying   19, 94–5, 108–9, 121–3,
    129, 177
  amounts of in the US   97–8
  free speech and   94–5, 98
  WTO and   127
Locke, John   40
London Inter-Bank Offered Rate
    (LIBOR)   16

Madison, James   59
Madoff, Bernie   132, 171
  see also 'Ponzi scheme'
'magic bullet solutions', problems
    of   139–40
  see also perverse incentives
Magnetar   174
market discipline   66–7
market fundamentalism   41, 44
market institutions   34–6
  collective ends and   35

instrumental value of 34–5, 44
  profit maximisation and 35, 36
  teleological normative account
    of 30, 34, 39, 43, 46, 137
market regulation 64–71
  alternatives to 66–7
  ethics and 64–71
  harms of 68
  moral consequences and 65
  moral rights and 69–71
  moral virtues and 68–9
  rights and 72
market systems
  externalities and 53
  state-capitalist economic models
    of 53, 58–9
markets, purpose of 45
Mason, Paul 63
materialistic self-interest
  personal 91
  rise of 91–4
Means, Gardiner 92
media, role in democracy 59
Meltdown: The End of the Age of
  Greed 63
Merrill Lynch 8, 97
Mexico 177
Milanovic, Branko 16, 127
Milken, Michael 26
minimum moral concept and
  ethical investing 85–6
minimum moral duty, *see* principles
  of assistance, minimum moral
  duty
minimum wage laws 65
  see also market regulation, moral
    consequences and
misconduct, *see* professional
  misconduct
Modern Corporation and Private
  Property, The 92
Modern Portfolio Theory 106
moral allocation of GFC costs
  175–8
moral duty, individual 34, 109–10,
  165
moral harm 110

moral hazard, political risk
  and 171–2
moral identity, institutional
  138–9
moral language, strategic use
  of 125
moral obligations 162–6
  see also moral duty, individual
moral psychology 140, 149
moral responsibility 38–9, 40–1,
  167–8, 170
  accountability for 138
  affluent countries and 176
  collective 138
  GFC and 17
  institutional 138
  managerial 40–1
  nations and 169–71
  professional roles and 138
moral rights 37
  and duties of institutions 32–4
  relative nature of 33
  individual and joint 37, 38
Morales, Evo 60
Mortgage Back Securities (MBS) 2,
  3, 7, 8, 96
Mozilo, Angelo 15
multidisciplinary practice
  (MPD) 134
Musharraf, Pervez 169

Nagel, Thomas 165
naked access accounts, *see*
  high-frequency trading,
  problems of
national security, threats to 112
need, ethical investing and 85
negative equity 6
  see also strategic default
negligence 168, 170, 173–4
  corporate 177
  national 175
neoliberalism, end of 63–4
Nicaragua 162
non-recourse mortgage debt, *see*
  strategic default
Northern Rock 8

Oberdiek, John   72
obligations, *see* moral responsibility
official development assistance
    (ODA)   165, 176

Pakistan   162, 169, 171
panic   7–8
Pareto-optimal system design, *see*
    economic systems, theories of
passive exclusionary screening,
    ethical investments and   88
paternalism, markets and   70–1
    see also market regulation, moral
    rights and
Paulson, Hank   8
pension funds   13
personal liability, reduction of
    see also perverse incentives   106
Pertamina   172
perverse incentives   28, 47–8, 53,
    106, 139–40, 149, 150
    see also incentivisation
pharmaceuticals
    Indian reverse engineering
    and   127
    mandatory safety testing of   65, 67
    see also market regulation,
    moral consequences and
phase 1 of GFC   25
phase 2 of GFC   25
Phillips Petroleum   86
political risk   171
    see also moral hazard
'Ponzi scheme'   132, 171
Portugal   24, 176
poverty   71, 163, 165
    effects of GFC on   13, 71
Powers, Charles   85
predatory lending   25
preliminary phases of GFC   26
preventative punishment   70
    see also market regulation, moral
    rights and
preventive integrity systems, *see*
    integrity systems, preventive
principle of contributory
    fault   166–8

moral responsibility and   167–8
    national level   169–71
    two sides of   167
Principles and Certification
    Program   104
principles of assistance
    and rescue   20, 162–4
    description of   163–4
    minimum moral duty   165
private interests   122
private property, moral rights
    to   40, 47–8, 92
professional culture, *see* institutional
    culture
professional integrity, *see* integrity
    of a profession
professional misconduct, identifying
    causes of   140
professional moral responsibility,
    see moral responsibility,
    professional roles and
profit maximisation   35, 36, 134
    see also market institutions
property, active and passive   93
proprietary trading   11
protectionism, trade and   53–4
    see also tariffs
proximity, ethical investing and
    85
public goods   33–4, 137
    see also collective goods

'race to the bottom'   4
RAMS Home Loans   8
rating agencies   2, 3, 101–2
    conflict of interest and   25–6
    see also conflict of interest
reactive integrity systems, *see*
    integrity systems, reactive
Reagan, Ronald   53, 65–6
real economy, effects of GFC on   13
'real world' costs of GFC   13, 52,
    102–3, 160–2
reckless lending, *see* predatory
    lending
regulation   27–8
    need for   36–7

regulators 27–8
  purpose of 45
regulatory arbitrage 45
regulatory capture 127
  see also competitive systems,
    framing and
regulatory gap 27
Reisman, George 5
religion, economic practices
  and 83
reputation 19, 146–56
  and corporate social
    responsibility 149
  contextual nature of 151
  deserved 147, 151
  as incentive 68
    see also incentivisation
  loss of interest in 71
  moral value of 68–9, 133, 141,
    146–56
  practical value of 67, 68, 135,
    146–56
reputation index 147–51
  development of 155
  problems in 148–51
rights, limits of 75–6
rights, *see* moral rights
risk 111
  and autonomy 74
  awareness and 72, 170
  and consumers 70
  credit default swaps and 76–7
  damages and 73
  as an epistemic construct 73–4
  imposition of 72
  and justified self-defence 74–5
  moral rights and 72, 73
  offered and accepted 70
  'Russian roulette' example 73,
    74–5
  socialisation of 55–6
  third parties and 71
risk management systems, *see*
  integrity systems, risk
  management and
Robeco Investment
  Management 87–8

Roberts, Russell 5
role responsibility, *see* moral
  responsibility, professional
  roles and
Roosevelt, Theodore 92
Ross, Verena 171
Roy, William 92
Royal Bank of Scotland 12, 175
Rudd, Kevin 64
rules, 'de-moralisation' of 125
'Russian roulette' and risk, *see* risk,
  'Russian roulette' example

Sachs, Jeffrey 171
Santiso, Javier 57
Sarbanes-Oxley 139
Sarkozy, Nicolas 63, 159
Schapiro, Mary 101
Securities Exchange Commission
  (US), (SEC) 11, 89, 171, 174
  Rule 14a-8(i) 89
securitisation 2
self-interest 19, 29, 44, 82, 140,
  145
  business and 36, 44
  corruption and 122
  materialistic 91–4, 111
  reputation and 147
self-interest model of institutions,
  failures of 141
severe deprivations, *see* costs of
  GFC, severe deprivations
shared ethical attitudes 145
  see also integrity systems,
    presuppositions of, and
    shared morality
shared morality 123, 145
  globalisation and 125–6
  limits of 124
shareholder activism 108, 109
shareholder advocacy
  ethical investment and 89
  importance of 109, 113
  limited 104–5
shareholder view 39–40, 41
short-selling 108–9
Silver State 8

Simon, John   85
Singer Assistance Principle
    (SAP)   164
    overdemandingness and   164
Singer, Peter   164
Smith, Adam   30, 36–7, 56, 91, 93
Social Accountability 8000
    (SA8000)   104
social good   55, 123, 137
    state interventions and   55
    see also public goods
'social injury', *see* moral harm
social institutions   30–4
    culture of   32, 153
    description of   30–1
    function of   32
    meta-instructions in   31
    moral identity and   138–9
    sanctions in   32
    structure of   31–2
Social Investment Forum (SIF)   87
Social Responsibility Act, 1973
    (US)   86
    see also ethical investing, moral
        minimum criteria of
social responsibility and
    investing   103–4
    see also Global Sullivan Principles
        of Social Responsibility
socialisation of loss   18
socially responsible investing
    (SRI)   82
    assets and   87–8
Soros, George   16
Soule, Edward   70
South Africa, ethical investing
    and   84–5
sovereign debt crisis   20, 24–5, 162,
    176–7
    Europe and   24–5, 162
Spain   24
Special Drawing Rights (SDRs)   48,
    177
stakeholder view   39–40, 41
Standard and Poors 500   96, 100
Standard Oil   92
Stanley, Morgan   4

state intervention in market
    systems, history of   53–4
Steinbrück, Peer   63
Stiglitz, Joseph   48
strategic default   6, 97
Structured Investment Vehicles
    (SIVs)   7
Sub-Saharan Africa, GFC and   161
'suckers', *see* competitive systems,
    'suckers' in
Sullivan, Leon   84, 103–4
Sunlight Foundation   98
synthetic CDOs   2–3, 174
    see also collateralised debt
        obligations (CDOs)
systemic risk   8, 53

tariffs   53–4, 65
taxpayer, as victim of GFC   66
Teachers Institute and Annuity
    Association/College
    Retirement Equities Fund
    (TIAA/CREF)   84
third party risk, *see* risk, third parties
    and
Titanic, GFC comparisons to   159
tobacco   83, 87
    see also ethical investing, tobacco
        and
'too big to fail'   55, 109
    see also bailout, governments and
        corporations
tort liability   168, 170–1
toxic debt   25
tragedy of commons   47–8
    see also property rights
tranches   2, 7
triangle of virtue, *see* virtuous
    triangle
TRIPS, regulatory capture and   127
Troubled Asset Relief Program
    (TARP)   14, 90–1, 99, 105,
    113
Tyson, Luther   86–7

UBS   8, 95
Ukraine   169, 171, 176–7

UN Global Compact   104
undercapitalisation, *see* Basel Accord
unemployment, GFC and   13
Union Carbide, Bhopal Gas Disaster
   and   31
   see also environmental concerns
Union of South American
   Republics   60

Venezuela   57
Vietnam War, ethical investing
   and   84–5
virtue ethics, *see* market regulation,
   moral virtues and
virtues in professional practice, *see*
   integrity of a profession
virtuous triangle   19, 30, 49,
   146–56
Volcker rule   56
vulnerability, developing countries
   and   172–3

Wachovia   12
wages (US)   15–16
Wall Street and Main Street, relation
   between   26, 29, 102

'Wall Street Rule'   103
Washington Mutual   12
Wealth of Nations, The   56–7, 91
   see also 'invisible hand', Adam
      Smith's
Wells Fargo   12
West, Andrew   69
White, Harry Dexter   57
Williams, Walter   65–6
Wilmott, Paul   100
Wolf, Martin   63
Workplace Code of Conduct   104
World Bank
   estimates of financing gap
      161–2
   figures of inequality and   127–8
World Economic Forum   61
World Social Forum   61
World Trade Organization
   (WTO)   127
WorldCom   26
world's poor   71
Worldwide Responsibility Apparel
   Production (WRAP)   104

Yunus, Muhammad   15